Praise for *Funny, You Don't Look Funny*

"Unlike most books on Jewish humor, Caplan's innovative work explores the place of Judaism within humor itself, allowing Caplan to stay laser-focused on her topic. The reader will be enlightened and entertained as she tracks the evolution of this poorly understood facet of American comedy across four generations."
> —Jarrod Tanny, author of *City of Rogues and Schnorrers:*
> *Russia's Jews and the Myth of Old Odessa*

"You have undoubtedly heard that Jews are funny and, after all, so many iconic Jewish comedian writers are famous for their biting humor, right? Rather than take that sweeping assertion for granted, Jennifer Caplan writes insightfully about the story behind their stories through several generations of literary and film humor by iconic Jews who 'made it' in America. Her profound revelation is that humor as an intellectual and social frame for paradox offers a critical expression of generational difference in views of the role of Judaism in American culture. Her book is a provocative cultural history and at the same time a clarion call for future generations of a people connected to the joke as well as the book."
> —Simon J. Bronner, author of *Jewish Cultural Studies* (Wayne State
> University Press, 2021), a National Jewish Book Award winner

"*Funny, You Don't Look Funny* is a terrific volume, anchored by Jennifer Caplan's sharp, innovative readings of American Jewish comedic work from the late twentieth century through the turn of the millennium. Training her lens on how these comics took on the Jewish religion, Caplan reveals that the comedic process has long been a vital form of religious interpretation for American Jews."
> —Rachel Kranson, author of *Ambivalent Embrace:*
> *Jewish Upward Mobility in Postwar America*

Funny, You Don't Look Funny

Funny, You Don't LOOK Funny

Judaism and Humor from the Silent Generation to Millennials

Jennifer Caplan

WAYNE STATE UNIVERSITY PRESS
DETROIT

Copyright © 2023 by Wayne State University Press, Detroit, Michigan, 48201.

All rights reserved. No part of this book may be reproduced without formal permission. Manufactured in the United States of America.

Library of Congress Control Number: 2022946776

ISBN 978-0-8143-4731-7 (paperback)
ISBN 978-0-8143-4730-0 (hardcover)
ISBN 978-0-8143-4732-4 (e-book)

Cover design by Brad Norr Design

Wayne State University Press rests on Waawiyaataanong, also referred to as Detroit, the ancestral and contemporary homeland of the Three Fires Confederacy. These sovereign lands were granted by the Ojibwe, Odawa, Potawatomi, and Wyandot Nations, in 1807, through the Treaty of Detroit. Wayne State University Press affirms Indigenous sovereignty and honors all tribes with a connection to Detroit. With our Native neighbors, the press works to advance educational equity and promote a better future for the earth and all people.

Publication of this book was made possible through the generosity of the Bertha M. and Hyman Herman Endowed Memorial Fund.

Wayne State University Press
Leonard N. Simons Building
4809 Woodward Avenue
Detroit, Michigan 48201-1309

Visit us online at wsupress.wayne.edu.

Contents

Acknowledgments		ix
Introduction: Funny, You Don't Look Funny		1
1.	Midrash for Atheists	13
2.	Silent No Longer	42
3.	The Baby Boom, Copycat Generation	71
4.	The Turn of the Century	91
5.	What Will Millennials Kill Next?	124
	Notes	139
	Bibliography	159
	Index	171

Acknowledgments

When a project has spanned as much time and distance as this one has there are more people than there is space to thank, and more people than I can possibly remember. If you are reading this and don't see yourself mentioned, then please know I still had you in mind as I was writing these acknowledgments. And yes, I do mean you, random lady in the HEB grocery store cafeteria who saw me writing and said, "I knew a Jew once. He was my gynecologist. He was not very funny."

First and foremost, I have to thank my family—immediate and extended—for their support and help over the years. From helping me decide who to include in the book to listening to me despair over having made the wrong choices, there would be no book without you. It should go without saying, however, that the final decisions were mine, so it is to me you should direct your complaints about omitting Mel Brooks.

Portions of this project were researched and written in six different states at six different universities, and all of them were important incubators for various elements of the final product you now hold. So I would like to thank (in chronological order) Syracuse University, Rollins College, Western Illinois University, Wesleyan University, Towson University, and the University of Cincinnati. All of my colleagues at these institutions have been invaluable resources in completing this project. Additionally, my colleagues and mentors in the Young Scholars in American Religion program held my hand through so many of the ups and downs that come with publishing a book.

Thank you to Marie Sweetman and everyone at Wayne State University Press for getting this book across the finish line, and to Annie Martin for having seen the initial potential of the project. Thank you to the two anonymous reviewers who read the manuscript so closely and offered me such helpful and generative suggestions. Thank you to whoever invented Interlibrary Loan. You are the real hero of this story. Financial support for the

x Acknowledgments

publication phase of this project has come from both the American Humor Studies Association and the Taft Research Center, and I am grateful to both for helping this book come to be.

Of course, I have to thank my friends. I cannot name you all, but I do appreciate you all. My colleagues at all of those universities and my cohort of Young Scholars, you are all obviously also friends, so I thank you on a personal and a professional level. While I cannot mention everyone by name, Angela Tarango, Sara Ronis, and Terry Reeder did extraordinary heavy lifting with me throughout this project, and I would be remiss if I didn't make their personal contributions known.

And finally thank you to all the funny Jews out there who choose to say the quiet parts out loud, to process their pain in public, and who are committed to making all of us laugh. It is to the unsung funny Jews everywhere that I dedicate this book. I bet that lady's gynecologist was a stitch after hours.

Introduction

Funny, You Don't Look Funny

The wise man went to that country. The wise man made up his mind that he had to know the essence of the country. And how could he know the essence of the country? By the country's jokes. Because when one has to know something, one should know the jokes related to it.

—Nachman of Bratslav

Jews and humor seem to go together like peas and carrots, like peanut butter and jelly, like Burns and Allen. Perhaps it has always been that way, though (as I will discuss in the pages to come) I don't think so. Somewhere along the way, along their long and winding road, Jews got funny. Not just in an ontological sense, but in a way that was noticeable from the outside, and was a point of pride from the inside. So while this relationship did not appear suddenly, when *Time* magazine published its now-famous 1978 article "Behavior: Analyzing Jewish Comics," which claimed, among other things, that 80 percent of the working comedians in America were Jewish (despite Jews being then 3 percent of the general population) it both came as a shock and confirmed something people had long suspected.

In the wake of that article "Jewish humor" became something people wanted to study, but that's a tricky thing to do. First, what makes humor Jewish? Sigmund Freud asked this question back in 1905, and nearly a century later Rabbi Joseph Telushkin was still asking the same thing. Does a joke have to be by Jews and for Jews to qualify? This is Freud's view. Telushkin, on the other hand, thought a qualifying joke just needs "Jewish sensibilities." Both of these definitions are so broad, in different directions, that it begs the question as to whether the term "Jewish humor" even means anything anymore. This book is not going to answer that question. I remain unconvinced that any book can answer it with

2   Introduction

finality. What this book is going to do, however, will bear on the question: it will chart the relationship between humor created by Jews, and Judaism. My reasons for approaching the question in this way are many, but primarily I see great value in zeroing in on the ways in which Jewish humorists have engaged Jewish practices and their own Jewishness.[1] It tells us something (or perhaps it tells us many somethings) about the relationship between Jews and humor that goes deeper than the mere coincidence that a certain humorist was born into a certain family.

In order to make sense of this, this book will also focus on change over time. I isolate four sequential generations as classified by sociologists: the Silent Generation (b. 1925–45), the Baby Boom (b. 1946–65), Generation X (b. 1966–79) and Millennials (b. 1980–95). Taking examples of humor from each generation that are about Jewish things, including rituals, texts, and Jewishness itself, I'll track the way each generation's relationship to these Jewish elements changes. I hope that this methodology will illuminate some of the meaning behind the phrase "Jewish humor," while simultaneously showing why it may be impossible to define in a stable way. If something is changing significantly every twenty years or so, no wonder we would have a hard time getting a handle on it. We have to zoom out far enough to recognize those changes are happening.

These generations are, at their core, useful fictions. There is some statistical truth to the increased birth rate after World War II that gave rise to the Baby Boom moniker, but why the Baby Boom is said to end in, say, 1965 when the birthrate had been declining since 1958 is mostly arbitrary. The generational conceit of the book may seem similarly arbitrary. An account of this kind could be chronological, or separated by media type. But there is an important story happening along the generational lines. Traditionally, sociologists and historians have classified American Jews into generational categories—based on distance from immigration—that cut across those used to describe the population as a whole. The humorists I identify as being part of the Silent Generation were mostly part of what has traditionally been called the second generation within American Jewish history. I do not know if any of these humorists would have called themselves second generation, but I am nearly certain none of them would ever have identified as Silent Generation. That lack of a conscious connection to the generation into which sociologists categorized you started to change, however, with the Baby Boom generation and that change is part of the story. Some Baby Boomers may think of themselves as second or third generation Americans, but they *also* think of themselves as Baby Boomers, and if you ask many of them what generation they're part of, if they have an answer it is likely the Baby Boom.

By the time you get to Generation X American Jews had lost any real sense of particularly Jewish generational difference. American Jewish members of Gen X, if asked their generation, will tell you they are Gen X. And moreover that began to *matter* to American Jews. The book chronicles evidence of a changing relationship between American Jews and their conception of Jewishness, and the move from identifying with internal Jewish generation to strongly identifying with American cultural generations is an important data point. If you mistakenly call an American Jew born in 1979 a Millennial she will likely correct you and in no uncertain terms remind you she is Gen X. This book argues that what we see from the way humorists engage with Jewish things in their humor is a shift from prioritizing Jewish peoplehood to protecting Judaism. In this case, the simultaneous shift from identifying in a communal Jewish way to a cross-cultural American way is not arbitrary at all; it is the heart of the issue.

I am framing much of this priority shift in terms of whether or not the comedy of an era is treating Judaism as a Thing. "Thing," in this context, is more than just a vague identifier. Using Bill Brown's Thing theory, I use the word to mean something broken, abandoned, or no longer useful. In Brown's terms the same object can be simultaneously a Thing and an object. A nonfunctional car, for example, is a Thing to the person who now needs a new car but may be a very useful object to the visual artist responsible for Carhenge. In applying this theory to Judaism I am probing whether humorists present Judaism as something vital and useful or dead and dysfunctional. The relationship of immigrant Jews to their religion has been analyzed extensively (see Hasia Diner, Nathan Glazer, Jonathan Sarna, Jack Wertheimer, for example), but my argument is that the children and grandchildren of the turn-of-the-century immigrants, the members of the Silent Generation, began a process of Thingifying Judaism that their Baby Boomer children continued. That in itself might not be a terribly interesting argument. What was the

4 Introduction

unexpected and therefore much more interesting finding is that Gen X pushed back against this Thingification and began to resacralize certain elements in their humor, while profaning others. The Thingification of Judaism seems to be extremely important in the Silent Generation, and disappears almost entirely by the twenty-first century. The full story of Millennial humor is yet to be written, as many of this generation are still building their careers, but we can nevertheless draw some conclusions as to whether they are continuing the trends begun by Gen X or changing the relationship between humor and Jewishness yet again. The generations must exist in pairs, as well, because the humor with which young people grow up, and the popular media they consume that helps shape their sense of self, is what the previous generation has been producing. So there is always a trickle-down effect from one generation to the next. What this research shows, therefore, is that as these generations became more attached to their secular generational identity they also became more interested in normalizing Jewish ritual practice and individual Jewish identities.

Because I'm focusing on humor that has some social or religious target, most of what will be included in this study could be classified as satire. Not all humor is satiric, and not all satire is humorous, though the latter is closer to being true. My definition of satire aligns with that of Ziva Ben-Porat, who says satire is "a critical representation, always comic and often caricatural."[2] Freud argued that meaningful jokes must have a purpose (though the underlying impetus for joking may well be latent, or subconscious), and satiric humor clearly satisfies that requirement.[3] My operating definition of Jewish satire relies on that notion of purpose. Satire must be anchored in reality because it is the real world, or in this case real Judaism or Jews, that is being satirized. What constitutes "real," however, is not so clear. Many of these satires are approaching a Judaism that is real only by virtue of its existing in the collective imagination, which may or may not be terribly related to the "really real" (to borrow from Laura Levitt) Judaism actually being practiced in America. All stereotypes come from some kernel of truth, but though recognizable they are also frequently to some degree false. Whether really real, or only a simulacrum of reality, the *subject* or *target* of the satire in this book is Jewish (or in many of the cases I am discussing, Judaism). I should note, however, that although Jewish humor is a popular topic, the reality of the signifier is not universally accepted. Many people, including those who would know best, have claimed that Jewish humor is some sort of optical illusion. Mel Brooks, one of the cornerstones of American humor (Jewish or otherwise) once said, "You got it wrong. It's not really Jewish comedy—there are traces of it, but it is really New York comedy, urban comedy, street-corner comedy. It's not Jewish comedy—that's from Vilna, that's Poland."[4] Brooks sees *Jewish* comedy as being something from "over there," while "over here" the humor is not Jewish. In the same vein, American Studies scholar Allen Guttmann claims, "there really is no such thing as 'Jewish humor'" because the Bible, "the greatest of Jewish books . . . is scarcely typified by elements of comedy."[5] Guttmann's argument against the designation is, in part, that

> if the term refers to some form of humor which has been characteristic of Jews from the time of Moses to the day of Moshe Dayan, then clearly the term has no referent at all. There *is*, on the other hand, a kind of humor which is common to the great Yiddish writers of the nineteenth century and to many Jewish-American authors in the twentieth century. This kind of humor is not, however, the result of Judaism as a religion and cannot be traced to the experience of Biblical Jews.[6]

The first part of his argument is clearly hyperbole, because if something must be consistent from Moses to Moshe Dayan in order to be considered Jewish, then there is not, of course, a religion, culture, language, practice, or belief that could properly be called Jewish. More to the point is the end of his argument, in which he claims that this thing we are calling "Jewish humor" is not "the result of Judaism as a religion." Although Guttmann does not define what he means by either "Judaism" or "religion," the context of his larger essay indicates it is some sort of nexus of rituals, practices, life cycle events, and texts. Defining terms is the perpetual rabbit hole down which most academic discussions eventually fall, but Guttmann's definition of religion seems largely practical, and that works for my purposes as well. In this book I define "religion" as something that involves both beliefs and practices, and Judaism will be considered a religion using that definition. I prefer to use a definition of religion that sits somewhere between the classic functional reductionists

(Durkheim, Freud) and the cultural anthropologists (Geertz, Evans-Pritchard). Religion has a role in social and cultural development, but I don't think that is all to which we should properly reduce religion. My intention is not to limit what constitutes either religion or Judaism, but to have a stable understanding of the terms that is true to the way satirists and critics alike are using them.

Although I disagree with the way Guttmann defines Judaism for his purpose of discrediting the concept of Jewish humor, he does highlight the difficulty that arises from the arbitrariness of labels. The separation of "Jewish" and "American" in the identity marker "Jewish-American" is a tenuous thing; both must exist in close to equal measure to make the label work. Ken Koltun-Fromm asks: "In what sense is material Jewish identity in America a specifically Jewish or American expression?"[7] and Shaul Magid asks a similar series of questions: "How much 'America' is in American Judaism? How much 'Jewishness' is in America? How much has 'Jewishness' changed in contemporary America? And how much has America changed?"[8] They are both circling around the same problem, which is trying to sort out what makes American Jewish identity distinct from, say, European Jewish identity or Israeli Jewish identity. That question is significant to a book like this one, as it is *American* Jewish humor under the microscope here, and I argue that in humor studies it is vital not to conflate comedy from different language families, cultural settings, or national identities.[9]

So for us to be able to identify Jewish satire separate from the shared American immigration experience of many cultures we have to isolate the aspects of it that could not exist without Judaism. American and Jewish identities have often battled in the lives of American Jews. Norman Leer once wrote, "America's home-made moral system of rational pragmatism does battle with a weaker, but more ancient and durable adversary, traditional Judaism."[10] American Jews have spent generations trying to bring these two adversaries to a peaceful resolution. The push-pull between the Jewish and the American is, in many ways, what lies at the heart of this project, and while I am presenting things in terms of how different generations of Jews relate to Judaism, it could just as easily be read as a study of the effects of Americanization. What I will not call it, however, is a study in American Jewish assimilation, because I strongly resist the idea that what we are seeing is anything as simple as assimilation. American Jews have not become American Protestants, regardless of how many elements of American Protestantism have worked their way into Jewish life and practice. American Judaism today may not look like American Judaism 150 years ago, but it has not disappeared and I therefore refuse to see this as a story of assimilation. Resistance is not, it turns out, futile.

In the following introductory pages I'll look at how Jewish satire and American Judaism have interacted over the last half a century. Most of the current scholarship on Jewish humor has failed to address this interaction, and much current scholarship on Jewish humor has, in fact, gone in the wrong direction entirely. My argument is this: World War II was the watershed event that drew a generational line in the sand for American Jewish humorists. Clearly, World War II changed many things for many people, perhaps none more so as a group than Jews. Deborah Dash Moore has written extensively about American Jewish identity during and after the war, and she said, "the mobilization of the United States for war catapulted American Jews into a radically different world from the one they had known. As the world of home receded, their identities shifted from 'New Yorker' to 'American.' American Jewishness developed legs."[11] Primarily this shift had to do with the breakdown of the ethnic enclave-type neighborhood, and American Jews buying into the melting pot of the American Dream. This happened in the decades following the war, as culturally and communally it took time for the full impact of the Nazi genocide to settle over American Jews, many of whom had little direct connection with the war or its victims. Zachary Braiterman argued that the post-Holocaust thought of the 1960s formed "a new theological discourse in which the memory of Auschwitz and the State of Israel virtually displace God and Torah."[12] The core touchstones of Jewish identity shifted in the 1960s. This influenced the humor of American Jews.

Judaism in the postwar years was largely in transition. The late 1940s and especially the 1950s witnessed the great Jewish migration to what sociologists call the "area of third settlement"—the suburbs. Some of these previously closed communities were allowing Jews and other minorities to buy in for the first time, but in many cases these were brand new neighborhoods and subdivisions, built to capitalize on the postwar increase in American wealth as well as the baby boom. The impact of this social mobility on American Judaism was that it began to resemble what Will Herberg calls "the original moderate Reform program," even

8 Introduction

though Reform Judaism itself was not driving these changes.[13] Whereas the Jewishly identified second generation had been comfortable with the idea of "ethnicity" uniting Jews, Nazi race science gave unfortunate connotations to the term so in a post-Holocaust, post-Israel world they began to rely more on the idea of "peoplehood." "What resulted," Herberg writes, "was substantially similar to moderate Reform, but since it had not come about through direct Reform influence, but rather through the continuing pressure of the American environment, it was not recognized as having any relation to the older Reform idea."[14] So while Conservative Judaism may have become the dominant congregational choice, American Jews across national and demographic lines began to adopt aspects of the old Reform model, focusing on the idea of communal identity as a unifying force and downplaying the role of organized religion.

The antiestablishment counterculture of the 1960s and 1970s continued to value communal identity over ideology. Religion (including Judaism) was seen as flawed, outdated, or corrupt and therefore needed to be lampooned and shown to be ridiculous whenever possible. Jewish peoplehood (meaning Jews as a corporate concept), however, had survived so much for so long, and was important, valuable, and worth protecting. The movers and shakers of the counterculture were largely members of the Baby Boom generation. America went through an intense political and social upheaval, and Judaism was changing in response to those external forces as well as to corresponding internal shifts. The Silent Generation were the young Jews Mordecai Kaplan profiled in *Judaism as a Civilization*, the ones who felt their Jewish identity was "the real tragedy of their lives."[15] In light of these responses, Kaplan championed the notion that the cultural or national identity of Judaism needed to be protected above the religious forms, an approach that aligns with that taken by Silent Generation and Baby Boom comedians. Nathan Glazer pointed out in *American Judaism* that, "in the years between 1920 and 1940, the areas of second settlement [such as the Upper West Side of New York City] contained the greatest number of American Jews, and it was in this zone of American Jewish life that the pattern of the future was being developed. The future, it then seemed, would see the rapid dissolution of the Jewish religion."[16] The handwriting on the wall seemed to portend the transition from Judaism as a religion to Judaism as a civilization, and the young Jews who grew up in that period very much absorbed that mentality. They produced at least two decades' worth of humor that reduced Judaism to an empty set of rituals or beliefs. In other words, they Thingified it.

Gen X and Millennials therefore inherited an America where, especially for Jews to the left of Orthodoxy, attending the opening of a new Woody Allen movie was an act of communal significance at least as religiously real as a JCC Purim carnival. It was a way to get together with other Jews and celebrate one of your coreligionist heroes.[17] It has become a well-known story in the study of Jewish humor that in 1996 a Manhattan day school affiliated with the Conservative movement asked their students to name their Jewish heroes. The results were, in order: Jerry Seinfeld, Adam Sandler, Howard Stern, God.[18] The line between religion and culture becomes increasingly blurry when religion itself seems to be a cultural object. But all of that is public sentiment, the destruction of which allows comedians, especially satiric ones, to thrive. This becomes a game of follow the leader, where humorists create a vision of Jewishness, but as soon as some portion of the masses accept it the humorists flip the script again, always pushing in whatever direction places them opposite complacency.

This book moves through this shifting landscape generation by generation, paying particular attention to humor that engages with Jewishness in some specific way. That means there are beloved examples of "Jewish humor" I will be overlooking. The entirety of Mel Brooks's career, for example. Most of the great Borscht Belt comedians. Norman Lear. Albert Brooks. All brilliant, and funny, but humorists who rarely if ever speak about Judaism in their comedy. Which is not to say that they are not still speaking a secret language, or that *The Producers* is not funnier if you are Jewish. Maybe they are, and maybe it is. But part of the story I am telling here is about an approach to Jewishness that is recognizable to many (if not most) non-Jews. It is also important to note that generational boundaries are just as fictitious as geographic ones. These generations are defined in hindsight, looking backward at social and cultural shifts that cause certain people to have a similar outlook—but the borders are admittedly porous. The line between the Silent Generation and the Baby Boom is perhaps the sharpest, as whether you were born before or after World War II is a significant cultural divide. But where the Baby Boom ends and Gen X begins, and even more significantly where

10   Introduction

Gen X ends and Millennials begin, is not at all clear. So while I will use a comedian's birthdate as a first order organizational tool, if the details of their career push them into a different group I may go against the sociologists. The Coen brothers are solidly Baby Boomers, but their later films (such as *A Serious Man*) embody Gen X trends. And Moshe Kasher is technically Gen X by a few months, but in terms of his career and outlook he fits much more closely with Millennials. One could argue that I am fudging the data to fit my conclusions, but I see it as looking at the trends first, and then assigning them to the comedians exhibiting them. And it so happens that those assignments align quite closely to these generations as defined. There are always exceptions, and where those occur I use their exceptionality to think through why they resemble one thing and not another.

Chapter 1 is the first of two that focus on the Silent Generation. Despite most of these figures being dead, they are still at the top of the list when people are asked to name Jewish humorists. Philip Roth. Woody Allen. Bernard Malamud. Members of the Silent Generation were mostly too young to fight in World War II (that was left to the fabled Greatest Generation), but they were old enough to be aware of what was happening, as much as anyone outside of Europe was. The members of this generation who were combining humor and Jewishness most clearly were primarily authors, so this chapter will take the form of literary analysis. It looks at Silent Generation humor that parodies traditional Jewish scriptures and texts, specifically works by Woody Allen and Joseph Heller.

Chapter 2 continues the description of the humor, specifically satires, of the Silent Generation. This chapter looks not at formal parodies but at stories that criticize the Jewish community for turning its back on Eastern European refugees. Stories by Philip Roth and Bernard Malamud demonstrate that what the Silent Generation is pushing back against is blind, empty fanaticism, whether it be fanaticism in religion or over "fitting in." Either one is a danger to the ongoing survival of the Jewish people, which the Silent Generation values much more highly than the generations that follow. The novels and short stories of the Silent Generation may seem almost quaint today, but in their time they did represent extremely subversive and often controversial approaches to Jewishness.

Chapter 3 will look at the Baby Boom generation. The Baby Boom generation is perhaps the most recognizable in terms of public awareness of the concept and what it signifies, and the least consistent in its attitudes toward Jewishness. Boomers came of age during the period in which the Jewish community was remarkably homogenous in its social composition.[19] Shaul Magid called this period "post-halakhic pietism," which highlights its unique blend of religious liberties taken alongside a developing identity fundamentalism.[20] The fungibility of the Baby Boom shows that my theory in this book is by no means totalizing, and there will always be exceptions. I am proposing a new way of reading Jewish humor that charts the movement of Judaism-as-Thing through the American Jewish experience, and that new reading can change the narrative about American Jewish religious lives. Early Baby Boom humor (from the 1970s to the mid-1990s) carries a lot of inherited baggage from the Silent Generation. Its treatment of Judaism is similar, and in many cases even amplifies what came before. The Baby Boom pushes the dichotomy between Judaism and Jewishness to its furthest extremes.

Chapter 4 moves on to Generation X. Generation X and the Silent Generation exist in an interesting tension with each other. If we speculate that attitudes around Jewishness are cyclical, or even more evocatively pendular, then the swing went from the Silent Generation to Gen X, which explains why the Baby Boom in the middle resembles first one, then the other. From Gen X it appears to be swinging away in another direction, but time will tell what that new pole looks like. For now, however, we can see that Gen X has a more consistent secular, American generational identity than the Baby Boomers, and the humorists who were children and young adults under Reagan and the "Me Era" treat Judaism and Jewishness in quite the opposite way from the Silent Generation. It is not religious practice that they satirize, it's what they appear to see as an outmoded sense of Jewish peoplehood. Coinciding with a precipitous drop in American Jewish engagement with Israel, Gen X humorists shy away from the types of depictions typical in Silent Generation and early Baby Boom humor.

Finally, chapter 5 will attempt to draw some conclusions about Millennial Jewish comedians. The youngest Millennials are only in their mid-twenties right now, so this generation of comedians are very much still making their names and building their careers. I identify Millennials with embracing new media and different approaches to how to become and remain famous. Whether it is Amy Schumer getting noticed on the

12   Introduction

reality show *Last Comic Standing*, Rachel Bloom launching her career as a YouTuber, or Kate Siegel running a popular comedic Instagram account, Millennial comedians harness the power of social networking in a way that none of the generations that came before them could. Their relationship to their Jewishness is, in some cases, more difficult to divine. Fewer of them are writing full novels à la Philip Roth, or essays à la Nathan Englander, that engage specifically with Judaism or Jewishness. So while parsing Tweets has, by necessity, become a valid form of cultural and literary criticism, these still provide less concrete data than longer-form fiction.

In the end I will synthesize these trends, not only to present a coherent look at where Jewish humor has been but to speculate about where it is going. One of the arguments undergirding this project is that it may soon become necessary to separate "Jewish humor" as a genre from "humor done by Jews," by which I mean "Jewish humor" may become a discrete form, like "slapstick," "dark humor," or "farce." It is possible, even probable, that what defines Jewish humor is less the person making it and more their outlook on and engagement with the world. And if that is the case, then Jews may not be the ones producing Jewish humor anymore, at least not exclusively. If both Judaism and Jewishness have become empty Things in twentieth-century Jewish comedy (and I am not certain they have), does the Jewishness of the comedian actually matter anymore? There are contemporary Jewish comedians who identify as atheist (as have many who came before them), who identify as sort of culturally/half-/semi-Jewish, who are Jews by choice, or who claim some Jewish identity without any actual familial or religious claim to it. If their humor is still "Jewish humor" then, just possibly, we need to consider that Aziz Ansari's, or Negin Farsad's, or Jessica Williams's may be as well.

1
Midrash for Atheists

God seems to be keeping out of things these days. Miracles are past.

—Joseph Heller, *God Knows*

I imagine members of the Silent Generation would be surprised to learn that their generation even has a name. Nestled as it is between two much splashier generations, they get a bit lost in the shuffle, as their name implies. They were not quite old enough to be part of Tom Brokaw's Greatest Generation, and by and large they fought in neither world war. Born in the interwar years between 1925 and 1945, they were the children of the Great Depression, a time of peace but hardly peaceful. While most did not fight in World War II, the majority of them were old enough to be aware of it. They were the generation whose formative years were molded by the stories of Pearl Harbor, Normandy Beach, and Iwo Jima, not to mention the Korean War and the first stirrings of the Cold War. They may not have been fighting the wars the Greatest Generation fought, but they were still deeply influenced by them.

Jewish members of the Silent Generation were growing up as well in a rapidly changing Jewish community. American immigration law changed significantly in the early 1920s, and the 1924 Immigration Act effectively ended a century of significant Jewish immigration to the United States. Statistically, therefore, some Jewish members of the Silent Generation were first-generation Americans, and many were second or even third generation. They were raised in households where Yiddish may still have been spoken, but English was their first language. After 1924 immigrants no longer entered through Ellis Island, and many of the cultural touchstones that united their parents' and grandparents' generations were becoming historical artifacts and memories rather than experiences by the time this generation was born.

14   Chapter 1

Furthermore, the American Jewish community was paying close attention to World War II, long before the United States entered the war. Because the bulk of the most recent Jewish immigrants were from Eastern Europe, many still had family and friends in the areas Hitler was absorbing into the Reich. Jewish members of the Silent Generation took in all the social and economic stressors that the rest of their generation experienced, with additional unease about Hitler, the Holocaust, the creation of the State of Israel and subsequent war, and the general existential dread that suffused much of the American Jewish community throughout the 1930s and 1940s. This is why the humor they produced moves so sharply in the directions of both Thingifying Judaism and becoming fiercely protective of Jewish identity.

Although no members of the Silent Generation identified that way at the time (it is a generational label applied backward by sociologists, unlike "Baby Boom," "Generation X," and "Millennial," all of which were created while the members were still young) its Jewish members would have been more likely to still identify themselves in these Jewish generational terms, or as members of what Jewish historians dubbed the second generation. The second generation and the Silent Generation are not a perfect overlap, but they are synonymous enough, and because this book is in part about that move from a Jewishly inflected generational identity to a secular, American identity, I will identify these humorists as Silent Generation simply for consistency. These are the people who established the "normal" of American Jewish interaction with popular culture to which subsequent generations would compare themselves and against which they would push.

The Silent Generation did a great deal of their satiric and comedic wrestling with Judaism in the form of literature. There were, and are, of course, great comedic performers of this generation. People like Jerry Stiller, Mike Nichols and Elaine May, Carl Reiner, and Mel Brooks are all members of the Silent Generation. But, like the Marx Brothers or Three Stooges who came before them, they rarely confront Judaism or Jewishness head-on. They're more likely to use an occasional Yiddish word, a slight inflection recognizable to Jews, or a joke that Jews may find slightly funnier than non-Jewish audience members. There are many factors that likely contributed to this. The biggest may be that the Yiddish theater and film industry was active well into the 1930s, so many of the performers opting for "secular" spaces were doing it because they wanted to be performing for a broad audience. Despite *The Jazz Singer* being both very Jewish and extremely important in the development of American cinema, it was a drama, so it contributed to an early model for Jewish film of humor in Yiddish, drama in English. Additionally, the Hays Code (Hollywood's first censorship rules) and self-regulation of the film industry encouraged religious things, among other touchy subjects, to be handled in oblique manners. Literature, however, has always been a medium that could support niche markets and targeted subject matter. Writers of the Silent Generation often directly addressed the relationships between Jews, Judaism, and each other through both novels and short stories.

This chapter will introduce two giants of the Silent Generation, although neither one is best known for the materials I will be examining. Woody Allen is, of course, best known as a filmmaker, but his short stories contain extensive insights into his religious worldviews. Joseph Heller is known exclusively by most people for his debut novel, *Catch-22*, a satire on World War II. As his career progressed, however, he was drawn closer and closer to Judaism and Jewish themes. Heller is a Silent Generation anomaly, as he is on the older end of the generation and enlisted in the military at seventeen to fight in World War II. Perhaps that has something to do with why his career trajectory was slightly different from other members of his generation. By focusing on the ways in which Allen and Heller perform a kind of parodic midrash, one reading of the way in which they revise and manipulate scripture, I will begin to establish the relationship I see between the Silent Generation and Judaism.

There are several different genres of midrash, but broadly speaking *midrashim* are extrabiblical stories and interpretations that fill in gaps or answer questions about the biblical text; they are scriptural spackle. Allen and Heller are doing midrash by taking the form and content of the Bible and reworking it in a parodic fashion. Throughout this chapter and the next I will demonstrate that members of the Silent Generation routinely reject organized religion, but that this is not synonymous with a rejection of all things Jewish. Both Allen and Heller lean on knowledge of Jewish texts and traditions in order to make the case that it may be necessary to sacrifice Judaism to save the Jews.

Allen and Heller: Twisted Torah

Humorous satires by Woody Allen and Joseph Heller help to construct the picture of the Silent Generation, as these examples deal primarily with Jewish texts, including the Bible, Talmud, and Hasidic hagiographies. Their approach to these sacred texts does not offer the same good-vs.-bad morality that we will see in the next chapter, but it does contain the Silent Generation tendency to Thingify Judaism without wanting to dispense with Jews. Their writing sees religion, especially the idea of a sacred text, as a ridiculous notion, and they each do their best to disabuse their readers of any reverence for texts deemed holy.

The backgrounds of these two representatives of the Silent Generation are so different that it ensures that the trends their writing demonstrates are not simply features of having been raised a certain way or in a certain place. Heller's most famous work, *Catch-22*, is darkly comic, but is not in any identifiable way Jewish. Like many young Jews of his generation, his parents were socialists and atheists, yet he still grew up in an almost entirely Jewish neighborhood. His Jewish upbringing was, therefore, both nonexistent and totalized. When he turned toward Jewish themes and characters later in his career he was not taking Judaism for granted; it was something he sought out and studied in order to best use it in his fiction. Woody Allen had a nearly opposite experience. Both sets of his grandparents were immigrants, spoke Yiddish, and leaned toward Orthodoxy in their Judaism, which rubbed off on his parents.[1] Allen was raised in an observantly Jewish household, but as a young man rejected the religious indoctrination of his childhood. Because of his negative feelings about all things religious, however, he did not take Judaism for granted either. For Allen it was a monster running rampant through society and he was the solitary figure standing between it and an unsuspecting populace. He came armed with a keen satiric eye, and he turned it on religion repeatedly throughout the course of his career.

Both men must have seen scripture as one of the core aspects of Judaism, because that is one of the first places they turned their attention.[2] The meaning of the presence of the Bible as the core of Judaism is very different, however, because Allen and Heller think about religion and Judaism differently. Allen conflates all religion (including Judaism) with "organized religion" which he sees as the great evil of our modern world. The Bible, therefore, has a certain amount of complicity in all of religion's crimes, because (at least in Allen's estimation) Western religion would not exist without the Bible. Heller on the other hand, sees the Bible more positively; it was to the Bible he turned when he decided to explore Judaism, and so the Bible became the de facto center of his Jewish world.

In some ways, scripture is an easy target because it is largely unchanging. Different translations and interpretations come along, certainly, but mostly it seems to be a closed canon and a stable set of references from which to draw. Certainly, with the Bible the authors can assume a passing familiarity on the part of their readers. Allen edges further toward inside joke territory when he works with less well known talmudic or hagiographic forms. In some ways scripture appears to be the religious white whale they have to conquer before being able to take on other aspects of Jewish life and tradition.

To complicate matters further, the difference between Jewish religion and Jewish culture is a moving target and probably a false dichotomy. Rachel Gross encapsulates this false dichotomy in *Beyond the Synagogue* by saying, "when Jewish communal leaders and sociologists distinguish between Jewish culture and Jewish religion, many of the ways that American Jews create individual and communal meaning in their lives are flattened or even erased."[3] What Gross is pointing to here, and what is also at the core of this project, is the need to redefine what constitutes a "Jewish" activity or behavior. If, as I am arguing, engagement with certain forms of humor is something American Jews see as being a specifically Jewish value, then the narrative that twentieth-century generations become increasingly less Jewishly committed is based on a mistaken definition of Jewish practice.

In light of this, let us return, for a moment, to Allen Guttmann, because his denial that Jewish humor constitutes a form at all (as discussed in the introduction) also highlights the centrality of the Bible in some people's views of Judaism. Guttmann acknowledges the Bible as the greatest Jewish book, so his idea of the religion can be inferred to center around the Law and the practices and rituals directly linked to it. He holds the Bible to be almost sacrosanct and believes that when authors parody or satirize the Bible they are taking "irreverent advantage of this almost humorless book."[4] In two ways Guttmann is evoking older, normative understandings of Judaism, the Bible, and their relationship to each other. First, he is assuming the Bible to be humorless, which feminist scholars in particular have shown to be patently untrue.[5] Second, he is assuming that the only purpose in satirizing or even mocking the Bible is irreverence, the disputation of which is a core principle of this chapter.

So, what if satirists are not taking advantage just for sport? What if what is happening is more than just irreverence? A closer analysis of these texts shows that beyond being simply a cultural artifact, beyond being "the product of the social situation of East-European Jews and a minority which maintained a precarious existence within the larger culture of Christendom," they rely on their knowledge of sacred texts to make their satiric points.[6] They demonstrate a deep knowledge and understanding of the holy texts of Judaism, and the humorists use that knowledge to sharpen their cultural critiques. The text is the thing, but the text is also the Thing. And as the Thing, it is what is holding contemporary Jews back, and keeping them from reaching their full potential.

One of the oldest theories of humor, going back at least to Thomas Hobbes, is "superiority theory" in which there is an in-group and an out-group, and the laughter comes from recognizing yourself as part of the in-group. This can be benign, for example, jokes aimed at adults in a children's movie, which are made all the funnier by the fact that you realize the children do not get it, or it can be quite divisive, in the case of racist or sexist jokes. Allen and Heller lean closer to the benign, with the in-group being Jews or those who are immersed enough in Jewish life and culture to get the jokes. This highlights a fundamental tension in Allen's work in particular, for the majority of Allen's audience is actually not immersed enough in the traditional or Old World aspects of Judaism to fully get many of his jokes. But they nevertheless recognize that a joke is pitched to them, and that is enough to elicit the in-group response.

One reason why the in-group for Allen's humor in particular is difficult to pin down is because religion cannot be reduced to God or scripture. And Judaism, as we have seen repeatedly, is impossible to define in simple terms. Mordecai Kaplan once described Judaism as "that religion that is an affirmation of life's worthwhileness, and which should not be tied up with any particular theology."[7] That notion, that Judaism cannot be limited to a narrow category of theological ideas, continues to inform American Jewish identities. To term something "not religious" solely because the author of a text (like Allen) avows atheism shortchanges the role that religion plays in Jewish culture. Moreover, Allen and Heller's satires lose most of their bite if you view them as being simply cultural. Yes, they are satirizing complacent Jewish bourgeois assimilation, but if you see that as all they are doing you miss some of the most cutting critiques in which they engage with Jewish rituals, communities, and beliefs, not simply with stereotypes or neuroses. Full understanding of these satires requires saturation in the rituals, beliefs, life cycles, and scholarship of Judaism.

Allen's Fiction

It is not a stretch to say that when most people hear the name "Woody Allen" they think "actor," "director," "comedian," "producer," or "screen-writer" before they think "author."[8] Though he has published short stories as recently as 2022, fiction is no longer something for which Allen is well known. During the 1970s and 1980s, however, in the period many consider the heyday of his filmmaking,[9] he was a frequent contributor to magazines such as the *New Yorker* and *Esquire* and published three fiction anthologies between 1970 and 1980. His primary literary alter ego is very similar to the one who appears on film, a fellow described as "that hapless, feckless creature befuddled by gadgets, perplexed by a lack of faith, lusting for sexual encounters but scared to death of any emotional involvement."[10] This lack of faith is a vital part of both the character Allen creates and his own admitted personal make-up. But a lack of faith is not the same thing as a lack of religion, and Allen has shown time and again throughout his work that religion has played an important role in making him the cultural critic he is today.

Literary critics have been generous with their praise of the depth and intelligence lurking below the surface of Allen's fiction. Mark Berkey-Gerard claimed that, "by combining comedy with profound questions of morality, ethics, and religion, Allen is onto something—about us."[11] Gary Commins understands that Allen's rejection of religion comes not out of an ignorance of it, but too much experience of it. He says Allen understands that "clichés, empty words, especially when stamped with a religion's seal of approval, are enemies of the human race."[12] Yet, "again and again, despite being put off by mindless religious and philosophical

20   Chapter 1

trivia, Allen pursues God, or at least the idea of God."[13] John Dart recognizes that Allen "poses basic religious or philosophical questions often ignored by the secularly oriented as 'too deep' and skipped over by religionists engrossed in particular issues."[14] And Todd Speidell writes that Allen "humorously and helpfully explores the uncertainty of faith in an all-loving and all-powerful God in light of the ambiguities of life, [and] he ultimately and ironically tends to resolve the ambiguity of faith living with doubt in favor of doubt alone."[15]

One thing all of these critics share is that they were writing for Christian publications. Christians have recognized and either celebrated or fought against the deeply theological aspects of Allen's work for nearly fifty years. Perhaps it takes a Christian understanding of theology to see that what Allen does absolutely requires an understanding of and fluency in religious Judaism. There has long been a love-hate relationship between Judaism and theology; search for "Jewish theology" and you will usually be redirected to "Jewish philosophy," with the term "theology" being reserved for specific cases such as "Holocaust theology" or "process theology." It is not surprising, then, that arguments about the theological nature of Allen's work would not come from within Judaism. Dart even noted that in 1974 a left-of-center Protestant magazine called *The Wittenburg Door* polled its readers to name the "theologian of the year" and Allen won, over runners-up Karl Barth, Jurgen Moltmann, and Pat Boone.[16] Tongue-in-cheek though the award may have been, it nevertheless shows recognition of the fact that Allen's work can be interpreted theologically. All these assessments combined indicate that when Allen calls himself an atheist, his atheism represents a well-considered, constantly evaluated position that could not exist in isolation from the religious traditions of Judaism.

His atheism is also very different from the New Atheism of modern skeptics (Richard Dawkins, Christopher Hitchens, Daniel Dennett, etc.). Allen no more trusts scientists than he does religion, and appears to be averse to many modern advancements. Recall the description of his standard character as "befuddled" by technology. In addition, he has often expressed a great sadness over the lack of God in the universe. He does not necessarily feel that the world is better off without God; he simply feels that that is the world in which we find ourselves. Were there a God Allen would be quite pleased, it seems, because it would

Midrash for Atheists   21

allow him to pose his questions about justice and suffering directly to someone. Just because it became manifestly true that God existed would not mean Allen would let God off the hook, but his statements on God indicate that he would be fine with being wrong. He is, you could say, a reluctant or even theistic atheist.

Allen is also a mordant social critic. Although in much of his work Judaism is treated like some sort of comedic low-hanging fruit, his use of Jewish themes and subjects is actually part of a sharp critique of the American Jewish community of his day. Allen is concerned about what happened when Jews began moving to the suburbs and out of ethnic or religious enclaves for the first time in centuries. Other writers criticized this community for their rejection of European Jewry. Allen on the other hand created Jews who only believed they were assimilating, passing. These Jews could not pretend to be anything else even if they wanted to. Jewishness inflected every word they said, every interpersonal interaction they had, and while it had ceased to be anything like the religion of Judaism we have been discussing, it nevertheless had become whatever this nonspecific, popular conception of "cultural Judaism" was.

The move to the suburbs was more than geographical. It effectively erased the final identity markers of the Eastern European immigrant community. The ethnically demarcated neighborhoods crumbled, accents were lost or Americanized, and the effectively parochial education of predominantly Jewish public schools gave way to the melting pot model of multicultural schools in which a child or set of siblings might suddenly find themselves to be the token Jews. Much of Allen's work in the 1970s and 1980s reflects these dynamics. Allen's writing indicates that he also sees in contemporary Judaism a flattening of history, especially among Jewish "authorities." The uncritical blending of past and present draws some of Allen's harshest critique. There are points in his work at which Allen shows just how much his religious upbringing stuck with him, and several of his short fiction pieces are midrashic. They are a sort of constructive theology; he makes Judaism into a Thing to save it, in a sense. By using Judaism as a Thing, Allen forces aspects of Judaism back into the public, and especially the Jewish, eye. Allen's Jews are highly assimilated, but he makes them think about scripture, remember Bible stories, and recall what they know of the Hasidim, whereas normally there is every chance they would go days, even weeks, without any of these things crossing their minds. Although they are seeing it through a satiric lens, Allen is nevertheless forcing it back on an assimilated populace generally averse to organized religion.

Although others have argued that Allen's religious parodies require no more than "basic cocktail-party knowledge," I actually believe that a great deal of Allen's fiction requires an understanding of religion, often an understanding of Judaism specifically, to grasp the humor fully.[17] The story "No Kaddish for Weinstein," for example, is "obviously a lampoon of [Allen] as well as the Bellow-Malamud loser," all of whom are "'so sad. . . . They're all New York Jewish intellectuals, Communists, impotent.'"[18] So, on the one hand one must be well read and well versed in a certain New York City, the city of Alfred Kazin, a left-wing, intellectual lifestyle, to understand the characters, while on the other hand you need an understanding of the Kaddish prayer for the dead to which the title of the story refers to understand the frame. Similarly, in short stories like "Mr. Big" and short plays such as *God*, an understanding of Jewish conceptions of God significantly increases an appreciation for the story. "Mr. Big" pays homage to the noir detective stories of the 1940s when a young woman tries to hire a detective to find out who killed God. Allen is most likely drawing on Nietzsche's famous statement that "God is dead," but in his story it is the young woman herself who ends up being killed, so he is also echoing the scholar and rabbi Richard L. Rubenstein's take on the death of God, which argues that it is something that happened to humanity, not to God.[19] Even if Allen had not read Rubenstein (which it is likely he had not), the fact that he instinctively took the death of God in what Rubenstein sees as the Jewish direction is indicative of the ongoing influence of his Jewish upbringing and surroundings.

Two stories in particular demonstrate Allen's knowledge of and facility with Jewish religious texts: "Hassidic Tales,[20] with a Guide to Their Interpretation by the Noted Scholar" and "The Scrolls." They are both parodies of religiously important textual forms in Judaism. In each Allen is not simply copying the form of the original; he is demonstrating that he also understands the importance of the original and the role it plays for the religious community that embraces it. In both pieces, Allen is manipulating the boundary between real knowledge and the appearance of real knowledge, which is largely why these pieces work as satire and are not simply funny. The idea of intellectual "authority" bothers Allen nearly as much as religious authority does, and while he is not seen as being anti-intellectual in the same way he is seen as being antireligion, academics are nonetheless a frequent target of his most cutting barbs.[21] Though these stories are prime examples of the "surreal quality bordering on chaos" that typified Allen's early written work, they nonetheless show that behind Allen's absurdism is a high level of cultural facility, which allows him to write characters pretending, at least, to have significant religious knowledge.[22]

"Hassidic Tales" and "The Scrolls"

"Hassidic Tales, with a Guide to Their Interpretation by the Noted Scholar" was published early in Allen's career, in 1970, appearing first in the *New Yorker* and anthologized in *Getting Even*. It demonstrates, clearly and concisely, the role religion has played in bolstering Allen's satire, and the way he is showing it to have outlived its usefulness. The story is a play on the classic genre of the Hasidic wonder story and hagiography. Although certain aspects of Hasidism have made their way into the zeitgeist, neither non-Jews nor the majority of Jews themselves are commonly familiar with these stories. Martin Buber's *Tales of the Hasidim* (1947) experienced a surge of recognition in the 1960s and '70s as the mysticism and spirituality of the stories offered a sort of Jewish alternative to the exploding popularity of Zen Buddhism, but it is still only within the most observant circles that the tales are regularly read and given real weight. Nevertheless, some of the great Hasidic rebbes of the eighteenth and nineteenth century are known today primarily through them. Folktales had been one of the most popular literary forms in Eastern Europe prior to the appearance of Hasidism, and the rebbes continued to use them as a way to present complicated theological or mystical ideas to their functionally illiterate communities.[23]

Hasidic rebbes used this homiletical form, and the great ones had followers who recorded their words and preserved them for future generations. Allen is parodying the reverence and near worship that followers of a rebbe feel for the rebbe's stories.[24] Allen's story consists of six vignettes, each one made up of a fictitious Hasidic tale and a corresponding analysis by the modern-day "Noted Scholar," who is never named. Allen's pseudostories take on not just American Jews but also European

24   Chapter 1

traditions, yet it would nevertheless be a mistake to see his stories as "anti-Hasidic" in any way that is more oppositional than his views on all organized religious entities seem to be. One could say that for Allen Jews are victims in the sense that these texts have been forced upon them, generation after generation. Only by denuding and exposing the texts can he liberate the people.

Allen's vignettes each have two parts: the tale and the interpretation. The voice of the unidentified "Noted Scholar" is as critical a response to the secular world of religious scholarship as the tales themselves are to religious literature. Sid Caesar's first television show, *Your Show of Shows*, featured a number of clueless, pompous "experts" on various subjects; if Allen did not borrow the model from Caesar directly, his Noted Scholar is certainly in the same mold.[25] Allen seems to be similarly questioning the role of the expert in modern American Judaism.[26] His Jewish upbringing, along with being "a voracious reader," gave stories such as "Hassidic Tales" a subtle flavor that "can be appreciated especially by those familiar with the pretentiousness of some religious . . . literature."[27] Additionally, throughout the 1960s the ongoing publication of portions of the Dead Sea Scrolls—the inspiration behind "The Scrolls"—added to a culture in which Americans worshiped every pearl of wisdom that dropped from an expert's lip in much the same way Hasids had followed their rebbes. In both his fiction and his films, Allen has repeatedly ridiculed Jewish traditions in order to highlight what he sees as the watering down of Judaism in late twentieth-century America. Jewish texts are not worth the paper they are printed on, any more than any other aspect of religion is anything but a burden to its members. The reverence for the expert is, to Allen, just one more sign of the hypocrisy of organized religion and the complacency of bourgeois society, and he uses his knowledge to mock not just a theological text, but the obsession with studying such texts as well.

The first of Allen's parodic tales drops the name of Chelm into the first sentence. Chelm is a fictionalized version of a real town in Eastern Poland, which is an inside joke to those members of the reading audience who have some familiarity with traditional European Jewish folktales, as the Jews of Chelm are depicted as ignorant and foolish. An example of Chelmish logic looks like this: a man asks a resident of Chelm why the sea is salty. The Chelmite responds immediately, "because of the herring. The herring is salted—and that makes the water salty, too."[28] Allen begins his own story with a reference to Chelm, but in an inverted fashion. He writes that "A man journeyed to Chelm in order to seek the advice of Rabbi Ben Kaddish, the holiest of all ninth-century rabbis and perhaps the greatest *noodge* of the medieval era."[29] The humor in the line is in the inversion of expectations; one does not expect a great or wise rabbi to hail from Chelm, nor to be described as a *noodge*, a Yiddish term for a bore, or someone who asks unceasingly annoying questions. Allen satirizes the followers of the rebbe by taking what is normally the hagiography of a saintly figure and reducing him to a figure of ridicule, thereby putting those who would seek advice from such a figure even lower down the intellectual ladder.

The interpretation by the Noted Scholar follows the tale itself. The Scholar begins by calling the question asked in the story "meaningless," as well as the man who asked it. He continues: "Not that he was so far away from Chelm to begin with, but why shouldn't he stay where he is? Why is he bothering Rabbi Ben Kaddish—the Rabbi doesn't have enough trouble?" The Noted Scholar, we find, writes in stereotypically Yiddish-inflected prose. His use of questions: "why shouldn't he stay where he is?," "the Rabbi doesn't have enough trouble?"[30] call to mind the speech pattern of a New York Jew, recently immigrated or at least still living in areas of first or second settlement. This is the speech pattern that Dan Ben-Amos described as characterizing "dialect jokes," in which "narrators add comic effect by speaking the new language with the intonation and vocal system of the old language."[31] Though the popular *shm-* reduplication ("satire, shmatire") is absent here, the speech pattern of the Noted Scholar is nevertheless immediately recognizable, especially to a Jewish reader. There was a long history of Jewish dialect comedy, so the "Jewish accent" was (and is) an established inflection that many readers would recognize. Comedians like Fanny Brice, who spoke no Yiddish, affected a Yiddish accent early in her career, and comedic singers like Mickey Katz built entire careers around overdone, tongue-in-cheek dialect humor. The Noted Scholar is, underneath it all, no better than a Lower East Side tailor. He goes on to say that the rabbi's response to the questioner—bashing him over the head with a candlestick—"according to the Torah, is one of the most subtle methods of showing concern."[32]

26   Chapter 1

The second tale involves similar inversion techniques. In this one we are introduced to a rabbi "who was said to have inspired many pogroms with his sense of humor."[33] The idea that humor could result in violence against Jews is jet black comedy, especially for someone like Allen who makes his living through popular humor. This rabbi is asked whether God prefers Abraham or Moses. He initially says Abraham, and when questioned further says Moses. This causes his disciple to take away the lesson that it was a stupid question, to which the rabbi responds: "Not only that, but you're stupid, your wife's a *meeskeit*, and if you don't get off my foot you're excommunicated."[34] As with the first story, the satire of the adoration of these Hasidic *tzaddikim* (wise people, usually men) comes through the depiction of them as fairly despicable people. If Hasidism is a stand-in for Judaism in general here, Allen is clearly implying that all Jews have been duped and are following people and traditions that are unworthy of such loyalty. This rebbe insults both the petitioner and his wife (*meeskeit* being a term for an ugly woman) and threatens the man with excommunication. The humor is operating on several levels at once; those who understand the meaning of words such as *meeskeit* get to feel "in," and the inversion of expectations pulls the rug out from under the normative expectation of what a *tzaddik* should be.

The Noted Scholar points out that the rebbe "has never read the Bible and has been faking it."[35] On the one hand, Allen is further ridiculing those who follow this *tzaddik*, for putting so much faith in a man whom the Noted Scholar has revealed to be a charlatan. On the other hand, Allen could be seen as making a self-deprecating comment, although it is clear from this and other writings that he is much more religiously well read than he wishes to let on. For example, when asked in an interview once if he were an agnostic he responded: "I know as little about it as anyone, you know?"[36] The immediate effect of this statement is not precisely what is being said. Though that reads as an acknowledgement of religious illiteracy, if he knows as little as anyone he also knows as much as anyone. He did go to Hebrew School and had a rigorous religious upbringing.[37] He can claim ignorance, but he is not, in fact, the pretender expert who never read the Bible. He is the pretender ignoramus who as a matter of fact knows the Bible fairly well.

Jewish self-importance in the postwar period is also a target of Allen's pen. In the fourth tale he describes the rebbe as "unanimously hailed as the wisest man of the Renaissance by his fellow Hebrews, who totaled a sixteenth of 1 percent of the population."[38] In Allen's day Jews totaled about 2.7 percent of the total American population[39] and .3 percent of the world population. Not, obviously, a sixteenth of 1 percent, but still a very tiny percentage of the population as a whole.[40] Allen's point, however, is clear. The odds of the wisest man of the Renaissance coming from a group that small are, well, 1600:1. Yet the idea that the Jews would believe the wisest man of the Renaissance came from among their tiny numbers is, at least to Allen, to be expected. Jews in America in the twentieth and twenty-first centuries have been disproportionately represented in many fields and within the academy, where the Noted Scholar lives. Jewish American literature and culture has been equally important as its African American, Asian American, and Latin American counterparts.[41]

It is in the final tale that Allen reveals his view on the entire enterprise of the Hasidic miracle story. The Noted Scholar responds to this tale—of a rebbe who has miraculous dreams and magical experiences—by saying that "the above small masterpiece amply illustrates the absurdity of mysticism."[42] Mysticism is the basis of much Hasidic theology, and if even a Noted Scholar in the field finds it absurd, who can argue against that? In four deftly composed sentences Allen explains the Noted Scholar's position: "The Rabbi dreams *three* straight nights. The Five Books of Moses, subtracted from the Ten Commandments leaves five. Minus the brothers Jacob and Esau leaves *three*. It was reasoning like this that led Rabbi Yitzhok Ben Levi, the great Jewish mystic, to hit the double at Aqueduct fifty-two days running and still wind up on relief."[43] This kind of numerological reasoning is familiar to many Jews, as it weaves through central liturgies such as the Passover seder Haggadah.[44] But Allen, through the Noted Scholar, skewers it: not only is it absurd as a technique, but, if rabbis are using it to win at horse racing, its high purpose is doubtful. And even then, it doesn't work: the rabbi in question still ended up destitute. So what, Allen asks, is the point of it all? What does structured religion give you if a great rabbi can't even profit from it? Judaism is a religion, and religion is a Thing, and Things have no value.

"The Scrolls" was originally published in the *New Republic* in August of 1974 and was anthologized in *Without Feathers* in 1975. In this, one of his best known fiction pieces, Allen applies the same model to the Bible,

28   Chapter 1

by way of the Dead Sea Scrolls, that he utilized in "Hassidic Tales." He introduces the archaeological find using a voice similar to the Notable Scholar (though here not named) of the "Hassidic Tales." He then reproduces three fragments of the find, two of which mimic actual biblical passages from Job and Genesis, and a third that seems to be a whole-cloth invention. He concludes with a short series of "Laws and Proverbs," written in the one-liner style of the book of Proverbs. Although he does not append an interpretation to each piece, it is still possible to glean his social and religious critiques, which take aim at the insatiable public appetite for origins, regardless of whether these urtexts have any actual meaning.

"The Scrolls" draws largely upon incongruity to build its humor, which in turn presents the reader with a strong sense of irreverence on the part of the author/narrator. For example, in the first sentence we are told that a shepherd discovered a cave containing "several large clay jars and also two tickets to the ice show."[45] On the surface this is a simple mash-up of something religiously important with something secular and frivolous. There is also a subtle dig at the scholarly community, not unlike those he made in "Hassidic Tales." He begins "The Scrolls" by noting that "scholars will recall" the discovery of these scrolls. Despite the fact that "for a while everyone talked about the Dead Sea Scrolls," Allen is focusing on the response of the scholarly community to the find.[46] In doing so, he is implicating them in an elaborate hoax through the anachronistic pairing of the clay jars and the ice show tickets.

He makes this point again in the second paragraph when he writes that the "authenticity of the scrolls is currently in great doubt, particularly since the word 'Oldsmobile' appears several times in the text, and the few fragments that have finally been translated deal with familiar religious themes in a more than dubious way."[47] The anachronistic incongruity of the Oldsmobile is the obvious humor in the sentence, but the second half of the sentence, the dubious treatment of religious themes, is less clearly designed to elicit a chuckle from the reader. His decision to deal at all with "religious themes" is noteworthy, but the acknowledgment that there are "familiar" treatments of these themes and that Allen and the reader should both know what those familiar treatments are without further explanation indicate the debt a story such as this one owes to a traditional religious upbringing and scriptural literacy. Although even the casual reader can notice hints such as "ice show" or "Oldsmobile," only someone with actual experience with scripture, and specifically Jewish hermeneutics thereof, can fully appreciate the satire of such a story.

Allen concludes the introduction to the fragments themselves by saying "excavationist A. H. Bauer[48] has noted that even though the fragments seem totally fraudulent, this is probably the greatest archaeological find in history with the exception of the recovery of his cuff links from a tomb in Jerusalem."[49] This follows the same structure as the previous examples: the humor is derived from an incongruity—in this case the recovery of a pair of cuff links is put on a par with the discovery of the Dead Sea Scrolls—but the satire is in the critique of an academic view of the world. The narrator's tone in explaining the importance of the find despite it almost certainly being fraudulent is deadpan; that highlights, however, the irony in the authorial voice. The solipsism of academia renders those within it too self-involved to recognize the difference between what has value and what is worthless; here the opportunity for the implied author to flaunt his professional expertise trumps the legitimacy of the actual work.

The first "fragment" is a parody of the biblical book of Job. Job was in fact represented among the Dead Sea Scrolls, albeit in a very marginal manner; only two verses (33:28–30) were identified.[50] Allen, however, in his scrolls puts Job front and center.[51] This would probably mean very little to a casual reader; Job is a popular story, at least on the level of major themes, so it offers a familiar entry into the form of biblical parody being undertaken. A reader more than casually familiar with scripture would recognize quickly where Allen was drawing on the biblical text itself and where he was inserting his own voice. In this instance, Allen uses the actual text of the Bible extremely sparingly; he primarily relies on the fact that almost everyone knows that bad things happened to Job. The details are unimportant. Though marked by the same incongruous humor as has been identified previously, to see this story as simply silly is to miss the dark tones underlying the foolish veneer.

Reviewer Richard Boston, for example, called Allen's whole collection "hopeless," following the logic of Emily Dickinson that hope is a thing (Thing?) with feathers (recall that the story collection is called *Without Feathers*). And within this hopeless book, Boston calls this retelling of Job "deflating."[52] Here there is no prologue; Job is gunning for God

30   Chapter 1

almost right away. Allen says, "Once the Lord, while wreaking havoc upon his faithful servant, came too close and Job grabbed him around the neck and said, 'Aha! Now I got you! Why are thou giving Job a hard time, eh? Eh? Speak up!'"[53] Allen's Job is very different from the long-suffering paragon of virtue in the Christian interpretation of Job, and combines the defiance of the original Job with Jacob's experience of wrestling physically with the divine.[54] It is also noteworthy that Allen does not capitalize his deity-related pronouns. Even in fiction, where Allen is speaking through his constructed characters, he maintains his independence from religious dogma. The contradiction in his simultaneously showing his familiarity with scripture and refusing to use the traditionally honorific capital letters to refer to God shows the complexity in Allen's relationship to religion, and reflects the larger trend of "reluctant atheism" throughout post-Holocaust literature.

God asks Job to release him but Job "showed no mercy" and continues to scream at God about all God has done to Job, while keeping God in a choke hold. Finally, God fights back. In a summary of the final few chapters of Job, which contain one of the Bible's great monologues, God demands of Job: "Must I who created heaven and earth explain my ways to thee? What hath thou created that thou doth dare question me?"[55] In Allen's story, despite Job having manhandled and yelled at God he does not back down in the face of God's wrath. "'That is no answer!'" Job says. "Then Job fell to his knees and cried to the Lord 'Thine is the kingdom and the power and the glory. Thou hast a good job. Don't blow it.'"[56] The idea that God could potentially lose his job is emblematic of Allen's strand of particularly theistic atheism; Allen does not reject the idea of God, he simply regrets that there is not one. If there were one, on the other hand, Allen does not see why God would have any more job security than anyone else would. That's life.

For a man who proclaims not to believe in God Allen spends a great deal of time writing about God. In his film *Love and Death*, for example, he wrote the following line for his own character: "You know, if it turns out that there is a God, I don't think that he's evil. I think that the worst you can say about him is that, basically, he's an underachiever."[57] The relationship between God and Job in his story is one of many examples of Allen wrestling with traditional notions of divinity. Though he has said that "the universe is godless,"[58] he has also said that "it's a damn shame

Midrash for Atheists 31

that the universe doesn't have any God or meaning . . . you can only lead [a moral life] if you . . . shuck off all the fairy tales that lead you to make choices in life that you're not really making for moral reasons but for taking down a big score in the afterlife."[59] Case in point, the second "fragment" in this story deals even more explicitly with the relationship between God and humanity.[60]

Fragment two is a riff on Genesis 22, known as the *Akedah*, or the Binding of Isaac. One of the challenging aspects of the story as written in Genesis is what, if anything, Isaac knew about what was going on and why he was mostly silent throughout the ordeal. Isaac, in fact, never speaks to his father again in the actual biblical narrative. In Allen's version, however, Isaac is very much aware from the beginning what it is God is asking of Abraham and he is, shall we say, skeptical about it. Sarah is similarly aware of the situation in Allen's narrative, whereas the biblical narrative leaves it unclear as to whether she ever knew what transpired. Allen's Sarah asks, practically, "How doth thou know it was the Lord and not, say, thy friend who loveth practical jokes?"[61] Abraham, however, is not to be denied and replies: "because I know it was the Lord. It was a deep, resonant, voice, well modulated, and nobody in the desert can get a rumble in it like that."[62]

In this, Abraham is the opposite of Job. Job fought back against God. Far from being overawed, Job was resistant and stood his ground. Abraham is, of course, the Knight of Faith. While Sarah and Isaac question God's will, Abraham is steadfast in his belief that his orders come from the well-modulated voice that could only belong to God and that he is going to act according to that voice's instructions. Even when Sarah comes out and questions Abraham's actions, he says he must obey, "for to question the Lord's word is one of the worst things a person can do with the economy in the state it's in."[63] Allen's Abraham may have funnier lines, but he is not substantially different than the Abraham found in Genesis. He is unwavering in his devotion to God and will not be deterred from what he believes he has been ordered to do, no matter how dreadful it may seem. It is interesting, in fact, how little Allen has changed the basic character of Abraham, especially coming as it does on the heels of his version of Job.

It is what happens at the denouement of the story that shows the difference in Allen's approach to the *Akedah* situation. Allen's dialogue between God and Abraham bears reproduction in its entirety:

32   Chapter 1

And so [Abraham] took Isaac to a certain place and prepared to sacrifice him but at the last minute the Lord stayed Abraham's hand and said, "How could thou doest such a thing?"

And Abraham said, "But thou said—"

"Never mind what I said," the Lord spoke. "Doth thou listen to every crazy idea that comes thy way?" And Abraham grew ashamed. "Er—not really . . . no."

"I jokingly suggest thou sacrifice Isaac and thou immediately runs out to do it."

And Abraham fell to his knees. "See, I never know when you're kidding."

And the Lord thundered, "No sense of humor. I can't believe it."

"But doth this not prove I love thee, that I was willing to donate mine only son on thy whim?" And the Lord said, "It proves that some men will follow any order no matter how asinine as long as it comes from a resonant, well-modulated voice."

And with that the Lord bid Abraham get some rest and check with Him tomorrow.[64]

Abraham is as true and faithful as ever, but instead of being rewarded for his faith and promised a great nation of descendants he is chastised and ridiculed by God. The fact that God is even present in this scene is noteworthy, as in the Bible it is not God but an angel who speaks to Abraham. The scroll gives credence to the more popular, less accurate notion that it was God who stopped the sacrifice. Allen's God has no patience for blind faith, nor does he want followers without a sense of humor. John Dart argues that for Allen, "the joke takes the place of a maxim, a Bible text, if you will, or 'moral of the story.'"[65] But what if the joke is the Bible text itself? Allen has done little to the character of Abraham outside of modernizing his speech a bit, and yet he has become a joke. The overarching theme is obviously that humanity is gullible and has been taken in by a "well-modulated voice" to the extent that even that voice would say they should be thinking more for themselves. Allen's view seems to be that people, in this case Jewish people, are victims of religion. Religion has long outstayed its welcome, but it is continuing to exert undue and unhelpful influence on people. Throw off the shackles of God and the Bible, Allen says, because religion itself has no more power over you. Even God thinks your blind faith is a little pathetic.

When viewed as a whole "The Scrolls" indicates Allen's continued intellectual involvement with Judaism and simultaneous rejection of it as a viable modern phenomenon. Insofar as scripture is a rich mine for material it may actually be less of a dead object to Allen than to some of those reading his stories. Which is not to say that it indicates Allen is less an atheist than he claims. As earlier quotations indicate, however, it is an atheism that wishes there were a God one could choose to either argue with or deliberately reject. Allen wishes atheism were a choice instead of a fact. His atheism was formed by coming through a traditional Jewish upbringing, as opposed to being raised without religious ideals. Mark Berkey-Gerard said, "Allen's use of biblical characters and religion for his comedy is, without a doubt, irreverent. And questions of human existence are not solved by making fun of possible revelation. But at the same time, comedy reminds us that religious history is filled with people with the same idiosyncrasies, sex drives, and neuroses we have."[66] Yes, part of what Allen does is humanize and therefore mock God and organized religion. But he is also humanizing figures who are all too often seen as perfect, which is a very Jewish thing to do. Allen is, basically, doing midrash. Funny midrash, sure, but midrash nonetheless. If, however, he were to enter a competition for authors giving biblical heroes feet of clay he would finish a distant second (if that) to Joseph Heller.

Heller's Fiction

It is not surprising that Joseph Heller rarely, if ever, makes it onto lists of the top Jewish American authors. He does not fly his Jewish flag the way some other big names of his generation do. Nevertheless, although his corpus as a whole may not be the most Jewishly influenced, the evolution of Judaism in his writing makes him an excellent subject for analysis. Heller was born in 1923 to Russian immigrant parents living in Coney Island, New York. Whereas Allen came from a traditionally religious family, Heller's upbringing was more "socialist and agnostic" and his parents "saw that [he] was not raised in traditional Jewish ways," meaning that "the family did not keep kosher, [he] did not celebrate becoming a bar mitzvah."[67] Any Judaism that was practiced in his youth was strictly for

34   Chapter 1

show: "His mother made him say Kaddish [for his father] at a nearby synagogue but this was, in Heller's words, 'more to keep up traditional good appearances than from a belief that a prayer from me would be of much help to either my father or the Lord.'"[68] Though Jewish practice was perhaps lacking in his upbringing, an immersion in Jewishness was not. "After all, the 'Jewish experience' was all around him, as natural and omnipresent as the air one breathed."[69] The result of this was a childhood in which, according to Heller, "everyone I knew was Jewish. I never realized that I was Jewish until I was practically grown-up."[70]

Heller served as a pilot in the Air Corps in World War II, mainly on the Italian front. His experiences in the war formed the basis of his first novel, *Catch-22*, which was published in 1961. Though *Catch-22* has been hailed as one of the great novels of the twentieth century, there have been those who have criticized its scope, or lack thereof. It is a dark, often absurdist commentary on bureaucracy and the ridiculousness of war that was embraced as prophetic by the Vietnam-era youths who encountered it in the 1960s. But at the same time, it is a novel of World War II, by a Jewish author, that does not deal with or even mention the Nazi death camps and the extermination of European Jewry. One critic, Sanford Pinsker, was disappointed to see that even at the end of Heller's life, when he published the autobiographical *Now and Then* (1998; Heller died in 1999), he still did not own up to the glaring lacuna in *Catch-22*. Pinsker writes that he "had expected more, if not quite 'regret' that *Catch-22* papered over serious matters with high energy and dark comedy, then at least some recognition that the Holocaust is now a part of every sensitive person's moral landscape."[71]

In truth, Heller can hardly be blamed for *Catch-22* not being a "Holocaust story." When the book was written the term "Holocaust" was not even in wide use, and the book takes place mostly in Italy, which, while not a safe place for Jews, was hardly the center of Nazi activity. Pinsker felt that, in retrospect, Heller should have had *something* to say about the Nazi genocide, although in 1961 not every author, even every Jewish author, wrote the Holocaust into their stories. For some critics it was hard to imagine writing a novel about World War II, especially one with a Jewish protagonist (or not, as allegedly Yossarian "is Jewish in the first draft but becomes non-Jewish in the final version"), and not at least address the Holocaust.[72] Heller's writing did, however, become more Jewishly oriented as his career progressed. His third novel, *Good as Gold* (1979), revolves around an explicitly Jewish protagonist. Though his favorite themes of alienation, existentialism, absurdism, and despair run throughout his fiction, his characters and settings at this point took a decidedly Jewish turn. Heller's course is an example of the Silent Generation's relation to religion: not rejecting it, using it at first as a tool for community building, and then ultimately Thingifying it as they came to feel its uselessness to their generation. Some Jews, like Allen, did formally reject the religion of their youth. But some, like Heller, diverged eventually from the agnostic socialism of the 1930s and came to embrace Jewishness—if not Judaism—as time went on.

Nowhere is this truer for Heller than in his fourth novel, *God Knows*. While the writing of *God Knows* was interrupted by an eight-month struggle with Guillain-Barré syndrome, he claims that his brush with death and subsequent weakness did not affect the tone of the book. In fact, he claims that even before he had a hint of his illness he intended its protagonist David to be frail, frightened, and angry as he stared firmly at the end of his life. "This time," he once said, "I was a prophet."[73] *God Knows* is a look at death and decrepitude as told from the death bed of the protagonist. It uses first-person narration and flashbacks to create movement back and forth between the protagonist's present and his past. And what a past it was. A life full of drama and intrigue, death and betrayal, war and plenty of love, it is, in the words of the opening narration, "the best story in the Bible."[74] *God Knows* is the story of King David as the world had never seen him before.

God Knows

Heller's fourth novel is racy, funny, irreverent, and touching. It is more than a fictionalization of the story of King David, a man who is one of the great biblical heroes and yet, as he tells us repeatedly in this first-person narrative, a man after whom no biblical book is named. Arthur Cooper summarized the novel best when he said, "More than a zany, sexy, poignant retelling of David's story, the novel is a modern allegory about what it's like for a Jew trying to survive in a hostile world."[75] Heller's protagonist may be David, but he is also Heller and every other member of Heller's aging generation. They are facing their own decrepitude

36   Chapter 1

and mortality; being a king does not exempt you from suffering. David in the Bible is brash, young, beautiful, and sensitive through most of the narrative. Heller's David acknowledges he was all those things and more, claiming he was also thoughtful, loving, desperate for paternal pride and affection, misunderstood, plagiarized by everyone from Solomon to Shakespeare, and, most of all, lonely. The satire in this case is more similar to Allen's than it might appear on the surface. Heller takes David from a figure of myth and mystery who spoke to God and sealed the eternal, unconditional covenant into a crotchety, cranky, randy old man who hates his sons and cannot get warm. Like Allen, Heller is showing that blind faith gets you nothing, and shackles you to a tradition that long ago lost its vital purpose.

Heller's methods are, in some ways, the opposite of Allen's. Though they are both clearly plumbing traditional Jewish texts for laughs—Jonathan Kirsch called *God Knows* a "comic masterpiece of midrash"—Heller's motivation and process moves in the opposite direction from Allen's.[76] Though many if not most of Allen's films have autobiographical elements, they are fantastical, and his short stories, like the two we looked at (parodies of society's fascination with mysticism and academia), generally target society at large. I have already mentioned that Heller's protagonists aged as he did, but some critics have gone further and seen the central relationship of *God Knows*, that of David and Bathsheba, as allegorically exploring Heller's own marriage.[77] Furthermore, Allen received a traditional Jewish education and, though he has rejected religion, cannot reject the education that formed his intellectual development. Heller was not raised in an especially religious way and he claims he had very little knowledge of scripture before he had the idea for this novel. Heller immersed himself in Jewish texts in order to write this book, but if David is, in fact, Heller in some way then Heller's rapprochement with Jewishness also came with a rejection of both God and scripture. One of the central themes of the novel is David's loss of God, so Heller is potentially showing that the only way forward is through a dismissal of that which is a useless; lose God in order to rebuild something that *does* have purpose in your life.

Heller claims that the "idea for *God Knows* . . . came, like the ideas for all his novels, in the form of a sentence."[78] In this case, the sentence was "I have the best book in the Bible." The sentence that actually made it into the novel is "I have the best *story* in the Bible," because when the sentence came to Heller he did not even realize there was no book of David. As Heller describes it in an interview with Walter Goodman, "I went to the Bible. Where was David? He was in the books of Samuel. God is not a good editor."[79] So Heller read the Bible and "picked up a one volume encyclopedia of the Bible and an exegesis of the Old Testament" and then began writing.[80] He sought out the text as an adult and committed to it as a means to a literary end as much as a religious text. Scripture is to Heller not a useless Thing; it is his way into this story. This brings out an interesting distinction between the material trappings of religion and the ideas behind it, which is a theme that comes out even more strongly in later generations. But that Heller can see great utility in the text while simultaneously showing the futility of traditional reverence for the text is a nuance that ought not be overlooked.

Which is not to say, however, that he did not appreciate the religious status of his source material. As Walter Clemons explains it: "Heller's irreverence masks reverence for the text he reworks. He clearly relishes the grandeur of the Biblical narrative, and he is operating in the homely, honorable tradition of the medieval mystery plays."[81] If, indeed, Heller had limited experience with the Bible before embarking on this project, he quickly gained virtuosic competence with the text. In *God Knows*, "the Biblical original is worked through closely, with impressive stamina and elaboration," according to one reviewer.[82] He moves adeptly through the Bible, jumping between the Pentateuch, Kings, Samuel, Chronicles, Proverbs, Psalms, and books like Job, Ecclesiastes, and Song of Songs in a way that leaves the reader frantically flipping through her own Bible to keep up. As far as Heller's David is concerned he wrote nearly everything in the Bible anyway, and credit was later stolen from him, so it makes sense that his speech should include biblical aphorisms from all over the text.[83] To Heller, or to Heller's David, the Bible is a collection of misquotations and misattributions that throw doubt on its value as a scripture. Here Heller aligns with Allen, because if the Bible is just a plagiarized mess, then what does it say about those for whom it forms the core of their belief? But for Heller to have gained that level of mastery over the text in such a short period of time indicates a commitment to textual study of which any rabbi or yeshiva student would approve.

38   Chapter 1

Heller's midrash comes from a very adult relationship to the text. When he manipulates the Bible there is a feeling that beyond the humor, beyond the social commentary, and beyond the allegory there is a desire "to get beneath the King James obfuscations and the Rabbinic encrustations in order to reveal the living, breathing, human figures underneath."[84] Heller, like many before him, wants to make scripture relate to modern life. Even his "literary technique in creating a David more like a *folkmensch* than a hero is not original."[85] To borrow from Freud, he is taking something *unheimlich*, a David who outstrips normal humanity in his accomplishments and ability to speak with God, and making him more *heimlich*, or humanized and comfortable. While on the surface this may seem to be taking more liberties than traditional rabbinic midrash, they both seek the same goal of making the text (or the characters therein) more comprehensible and useable. So what Heller is doing is both new and not, and although *God Knows* was, at the time, "the most sustained meditation on the Bible in contemporary Jewish fiction," Heller would probably be the first to say that his intent was not to do something new or revolutionary.[86]

If Allen humanizes biblical characters by showing them to have the same idiosyncrasies, sex drives, and neuroses we have, Heller does the same and more. His David is certainly idiosyncratic and driven by libido, and while he may not be neurotic, many of those around him, such as Michal and even Bathsheba, certainly are.[87] Heller goes deeper, however, "showing the similarity of human concerns, aspirations, and foibles over time and across space. Heller actually creates Midrashim of a high/ low order—the simultaneity of high and low being essential for the novel's thematic points as well as its comic effect."[88] Though the novel comes across as ribald and earthy, it also involves a deep investigation of human relationality. Heller is "trying to help us rediscover the Bible by removing the layers of whitewash that have been applied over the centuries by religious commentators and theologians" and in doing so wants to give it more meaning, not less.[89] He does not make the Bible ridiculous or, at least, does not make it any more ridiculous than life already is.

The novel jumps back and forth between David's present and his past. He is old and dying and is struggling with choosing a successor from among his various sons. Bathsheba, his great love, wants her son Solomon to inherit, even though he is not the oldest. David has more or less decided to concede to her, even though he finds Solomon a slow-witted bore, because he loves Bathsheba and wants to please her. His advisors and priests, however, have already effectively crowned his elder son Adijonah. So the novel vacillates between David's present dilemma and his geriatric musings about his past glory, and it is given structure by three primary themes that drive much of the action: David facing his old age and imminent death, the relationships between fathers and sons, and the way lovers lose their way over time. As previously mentioned, Heller wrote this novel later in his life, and though he makes David a bit older than he was at the time, they are both men in their declining years. It is not a great stretch, then, to see David's concern over his life and legacy as familiar to Heller. Early in the novel, David describes his position as follows:

> My children are waiting for me to die. Who can blame them? I've led a full, long life, haven't I? You can look it up. Samuel I and II. Kings. Chronicles also, but that's a prissy whitewash in which the juiciest parts of my life are discarded as unimportant or unworthy. Therefore, I hate Chronicles. In Chronicles I am a pious bore, as dull as dishwater and as preachy and insipid as that self-righteous Joan of Arc, and God knows I was never anything like that. God knows I fucked and fought plenty and had a rousing good time doing both until the time I fell in love and the baby died. Everything took a turn for the worse after that.[90]

David is, in a way, what Allen wants to be. He is a man who consciously and decisively turns his back on God. Only as he is dying does he really take the time to regret that decision, and wish he could repair a relationship that is obviously irreparable.

David has no lack of ego or self-confidence, and yet he is clearly scared of the way history will remember him and defensive over the potential loss of control in shaping his own image. Heller sees the story and character of David as valuable, and therefore the book that contains the story is also valuable and useful. What *is not* useful in Heller's presentation is a reliance on God or thoughtless piety, because God has been forced into silence.

David wants to make very clear what has caused his relationship with God to fracture. "It was," he says "I who stopped talking to God, not

40   Chapter 1

He to me. It was I who broke up that friendship."[91] David and God are depicted as having a close relationship throughout David's early years. David would ask God for advice, and God would respond in a mixture of biblical prose and vaudeville patter:

> "Will Saul come down to Keilah after me as Thy servant believes?"
>   "You bet your ass," said the Lord
>   "And will the men of Keilah deliver us into the hand of Saul?"
>   "Funny you should ask."
>   "They will?"
>   "They will deliver thee up."
>   "Then we'd better get away, right?"
>   "You don't have to go to college," said the Lord, "to figure that one out for yourself."[92]

The two talked, as friends might, until God punished David for his indiscretions with Bathsheba by killing their baby. That, to David, was unforgiveable. Despite admitting "I want my God back" in the very last moments of the book, David values the relationship between a parent and a child over almost everything else, and God's destruction of that relationship was an act David could not forgive. As David faces his own death, he wants to know God again; as Heller wrote toward the end of his life he engaged with religion seriously for the first time. But wanting to know God and succeeding in knowing God are two different things, and that is a vital point in understanding the way Heller is treating Judaism. His Thingification is a bit different from Allen's because it seems more regretful, but it is nevertheless an admission that there is no place for two-way chats with God in modern life.

Why did Heller write about David? To hear him tell it he did not have a choice, since David popped into his head and informed him he has the best story in the Bible. Heller uses David to depict the Bible as we have understood it to be "false"; David shows us that the Bible's enduring value lies not in the idea of the text, but in the actual written characters and stories. The Bible is truly literature to David, because he lived it and he is telling us the version we got is terribly flawed. And why did Heller explore an aging David? Because Heller, also, was well on in years when he wrote this novel and frequently positioned his protagonists at or around the same stage in life in which Heller found himself. These questions are self-evident. The bigger question is why Heller chose to address any of these issues using traditional religious figures, settings, and texts. The quotation above, "the novel is a modern allegory about what it's like for a Jew trying to survive in a hostile world," is perhaps the most incisive interpretation. What it means to be a Jew surviving in a hostile world is, above all else, to lose your relationship with God and to know that scripture is a fraud. That is harsh indeed, but that is nevertheless what comes through. Though Heller is one of the greatest satirists of American life in general, a side of him is drawn to the telling of specifically Jewish stories. In *God Knows* Heller shows that he can think through midrash as well as any rabbinic sage, and that he struggles with God and religious life in very real and practical ways.

Allen and Heller approach scripture in different ways, but there is a level of investment in both cases that belies their atheism. Both men seem to share a belief that, like it or not, God has left the building, and that modern people, including modern Jews, need to move on. Allen tries to highlight the ridiculousness of religious belief and blind faith, while Heller focuses more on the human stories behind the religious texts and traditions. They share with other members of the Silent Generation a desire to preserve, and even protect, the Jewish people. Where they uncover the illogic in treating sacred texts as any more special than any other, other members of the Silent Generation, as we will see in the next chapter, take a much more direct approach, and bring the fight directly to the Jewish community and to what these authors see as its warped priorities.

2
Silent No Longer

In the spring when the winter's snow had melted, the boy, moved by a memory, wandered in the neighborhood, looking for Schwartz. He found a dead black bird in a small lot near the river, his two wings broken, neck twisted, and both bird-eyes plucked clean.

"Who did it to you, Mr. Schwartz?" Maurie wept.

"Anti-Semeets," Edie said later.

—Bernard Malamud, "The Jewbird"

Midrash of the type Woody Allen and Joseph Heller wrote was not the only way the Silent Generation tried to intervene in what they saw as a disastrous path American Judaism was following. In this chapter, I will look at examples from the writings of Philip Roth and Bernard Malamud. Although Malamud was technically born at the very end of the Greatest Generation, he was exempt from military service and did not serve in World War II, which makes his life experience close to those of his slightly younger contemporaries. This chapter will focus on the group's seemingly flippant or dismissive attitude toward things that smack of organized religion, and their inversely fierce protection of Jewish identity and community. Allen and Heller satirized Jewish texts themselves. Roth and Malamud, on the other hand, were not doing anything as playful as these parodies. They both had a great deal to say about how so-called assimilated American Jews were treating their Eastern European counterparts. All four members of the Silent Generation I am featuring, Allen, Heller, Roth, and Malamud see religion as something that is being done *to* the Jews. The Thingification of Judaism is, in their estimation, therefore fine. But for Roth and Malamud the consequent rejection of Jews for whom Judaism was *not* a Thing was a serious problem.

Roth and Malamud—Assigning Blame

Philip Roth was almost twenty years younger than Bernard Malamud, and his admiration for Malamud was clear throughout his career.[1] His published eulogy after Malamud's death in 1986 spoke to the depth of Malamud's influence on Roth's life and career. Although Malamud became a national presence in 1952 with the publication of *The Natural*, that novel was not Jewish in any particularly significant way. It was the conjunction of the publication of Malamud's short story collection, *The Magic Barrel*, in 1958 and Roth's debut collection, *Goodbye, Columbus*, that forever linked their names as leaders in this new wave of Jewish American writers. Both men continued to explore themes of Jewishness and identity throughout their careers, but a particularly good side-by-side comparison can be made by a look at Roth's "Eli, the Fanatic" and Malamud's "The Jewbird."

It is a study in reception that these two have been treated so differently by the Jewish community as a whole. Malamud has, for the most part, been acclaimed and embraced while Roth (especially early in his career) was, from within the Jewish community, frequently excoriated and defamed, even while he was being praised and rewarded by the general literary world. Although it took nearly sixty years, the Jewish community's reaction to Roth finally mellowed toward the end of his life, as is evidenced by his receiving an honorary degree from the Jewish Theological Seminary in 2014. But even as the press presented an image of Roth redeemed, Roth himself felt that, "it's beginning to appear that I, for one, will not live to see these disapproving Jewish readers of mine attain that level of tolerant sophistication, free from knee-jerk prudery."[2] In general, the problem has been that Malamud is considered "good for the Jews" while Roth is not. Rachel Gross identifies the things supposedly "good for the Jews" as ones associated with religious Judaism and things that were "bad for the Jews" as associated with secularism and assimilation; based on that division there is some irony in seeing Malamud preferred over Roth.[3] They both dismissed organized religion and at the same time were fiercely protective of the Jewish people, a combination I am arguing is the hallmark of the Silent Generation. Both Roth and Malamud present Judaism as something that may have been relevant for Jews who had just arrived in the United States, Jews who were still living in ethnic

44   Chapter 2

enclaves, but for Jews who have moved up and out, they suggest, it is no longer meaningful.

Probably no twentieth-century American Jew was labeled "self-loathing" more times than Philip Roth. Lawrence Mintz once claimed, "Philip Roth may just engender more passionate hostility than any writer in America."[4] Judaism, in Roth, is in many ways such a Thing that it has become nonexistent. His Jews often pride themselves on their total excising of Judaism from their lives. One could argue, however, that Roth himself is quite reliant on Judaism, at least in his fiction. Jane Statlander has called Roth a modern composer of what she calls the "Hebraic American historical romance," saying that Roth is following in the footsteps of Nathaniel Hawthorne as an "allegorist, drawing un-dimensionally compressed ideas of emblematic peoplehood with names that represent the condensation of particular qualities, attitudes, and characteristics."[5] This lends credence to the idea that Roth's critique of contemporary Judaism comes from his recognition of Judaism as a Thing and his simultaneous dissatisfaction with the prevalence of that attitude.

Roth was born in Newark, New Jersey, in 1933 and published his first major work, *Goodbye, Columbus* in 1959. *Goodbye, Columbus* was a collection of the titular novella and five short stories. Two of them, "The Conversion of the Jews" and "Defender of the Faith," "made him a controversial figure in the Jewish world."[6] Roth was probably the catalyst for Leon Uris's 1959 comments about his frustration with "a whole school of Jewish American writers, who spend their time damning their fathers, hating their mothers, wringing their hands and wondering why they were born. This isn't art or literature. It's psychiatry. These writers are professional apologists. Every year you find one of their works on the best seller lists. . . . Their work is obnoxious and makes me sick to my stomach."[7]

Uris's critique subtly highlights the absence of Judaism in these texts, which reinforces the idea that Judaism as a Thing is a standard feature of Silent Generation literature. Uris is also a member of the Silent Generation, but he enlisted to fight in World War II at only 17, and then became deeply involved in the wars surrounding the creation of the State of Israel, so his experience and outlook was much more militaristic than most members of his generation. He had difficulty accepting the version of Jewishness presented by other Silent Generation writers. The kinds of Jews Roth was depicting had determined that Jewish practices were something they were happy to sacrifice for their shot at the American Dream. Uris and other Roth critics saw this as obnoxious, and saw his portrayal of Jews as unpleasant, conniving, and lascivious as unacceptable. But since Roth's characters are generally miserable, he can hardly be seen as praising their misanthropy and narcissism or their choice to sacrifice religion on the altar of progress.

After the publication of *Goodbye, Columbus*, it was perhaps not a given that Roth's career would flourish or that he would become one of the major critical voices in Jewish American satire. Response to the collection was mixed. While some, like Uris, vilified Roth from the outset, he also had some early support. Theodore Solotaroff, one of the leading Jewish literary critics of the 1960s and 1970s, claimed, "Roth is so obviously attached to Jewish life that the charge of his being anti-Semitic or a 'self-hater' is the more absurd."[8] Within five years of his arrival on the American literary scene Roth was such a controversial figure that articles like Dan Isaac's "In Defense of Philip Roth" were already appearing. Isaac argued that, "when Roth is properly understood he is not only a good writer, but [he] can also be in fact '*good* for the Jews.'"[9] Some of the criticisms that prompted this defense were entirely out of proportion: "One of them likened Roth to Hitler; another asserted that the Medieval Jew would have known what to do with him. And a rabbi, in a personal letter to Roth, wrote: 'you have earned the gratitude of all who sustain their anti-Semitism on such conceptions of Jews as ultimately led to the murder of six million in our time.'"[10]

Roth was making strong statements about Jewish American identity; to compare him to Hitler or effectively blame him for the Holocaust, however, is a reflection of the climate: Jewish existential fear at the time was still very real. The 1960s is the decade that really began to come to terms with the Holocaust, and this is why the majority of the satirists from that period trod lightly on the topic of "the Jews" while they ran roughshod over Judaism. Thingify Judaism; that is safe. But protect the Jews at all cost. One of the great paradoxes of this time is that Roth was being every bit as protective of the Jewish people as were his critics; they simply had different visions of what a healthy American Judaism looked like. Roth's critics were, perhaps, too close to the reality of the war to see critiques of one particular assimilated Jewish community as not being

46   Chapter 2

representative of all Jews. Roth's Jews were usually highly acculturated to American life, but through these characters Roth demonstrated what Norman Leer called, "a frame of reference . . . based on traditional Jewish values . . . to locate certain themes which seem to occur throughout Biblical, rabbinic, and contemporary Jewish thought."[11] The nuance of his characters' Judaism was often glossed over in the immediate reaction to his overall depiction of Jews. But as Jane Statlander has already argued, Roth needed Judaism. Bill Brown would agree that you cannot properly make something a Thing if you do not fully understand it. For how can you know that something both had a function and has now lost it if you do not have any real knowledge of the subject?

Identity is a central theme in Roth's work. Critics and supporters alike have noted this throughout his career. In 1966 Leer wrote, "it is both a sign of Roth's intense involvement in Judaism's deepest values, and a criticism of both the Jew and the middle-class in terms of a problem that is not so much sociological as it is spiritual and fundamentally human. . . . 'Eli, the Fanatic' shows the failure of a nominal community to confront the problem of religious identity, and the attempt by one man to come by way of this identity to a closer definition of self."[12] The Thingification of Judaism in "Eli" could be blamed for most—if not all—of the conflict in the story. Roth was perhaps the first satirist to shine a spotlight on the relationship between the postwar demotion of Judaism to a Thing and the growing problems within Jewish communities. In 1975 Michael Rockland sharpened the focus further by saying: "I believe the time has arrived when those American Jews who have regarded Philip Roth as tantamount to an enemy of the Jewish people begin to grapple with the serious problems of identity he is grappling with."[13] And Sylvia Fishman, in 1997, added the postmodern layer to the discussion when she wrote: "Roth transforms issues of Jewish identity into a plotting device by playing with the deconstructionist contention that all perceptions of the human personality can be considered works of fiction. . . . Non-Jews, [Roth] indicates, have historically created group stereotypes of the Jews based on religious, economic, psychological, or social trends in the non-Jewish world, rather than on the realities and great diversity of the Jewish community itself . . . but each Jew invents shifting identities for other Jews and for him or herself."[14] Perhaps Roth frequently criticized American

Jewish complacency not because he hated Jews but because Jewish identity mattered to him.

Malamud's critiques were more oblique, which may be why he was not subject to the same level of criticism as Roth. Malamud was born in Brooklyn in 1914 and was therefore more a child of the Great Depression than a child of World War II. In fact, he likely would have been called to serve in World War II had he not been the only financial support his mother had after the death of his father. Malamud did not have Uris's experience of the war, which may explain why his Jews look more like Roth's Eli than Uris's Ari ben Canaan. It is notable that while Malamud was held up as "good for the Jews" in comparison to Roth, Roth's work, across the board, was consistently more concerned with Judaism and Jewish themes.[15]

The consensus on Malamud seemed to be that "when he treats Jewish matters, most often he universalizes Jews, Jewish culture, history and Judaism to such an extent as to render them no more than bases from which to explore the human condition."[16] Allen Guttmann went so far as to say that Malamud's definition of a Jew "turns out to be remarkably like Immanuel Kant's categorical imperative: to want for others what you want for yourself. . . . What Malamud has done is widen the definition of 'Jew' to the point of meaninglessness."[17] Jewish characters in Malamud seemed to be Jewish more to set a certain tone or establish a certain geography than to actually question anything about the contemporary American Jewish experience. In Malamud's early treatments of Jews, Judaism was already a Thing, but that did not seem to be a problem for the Jews in the story. Their problems, and their conflicts, came from external circumstances and not from their relationship to Judaism.

Roth himself was occasionally critical of Malamud's treatment of Judaism, though never to the extent that people were critical of Roth. He once wrote that Malamud's Jews are "Malamud's invention, a metaphor of sorts to stand for certain possibilities and promises, and I am further inclined to believe this when I read the statement attributed to Malamud which goes 'all men are Jews'. In fact, we know this is not so; even the men who are Jews aren't sure they're Jews" in Malamud's work.[18] Shortly after the publication of *Goodbye, Columbus* Norman Leer described Roth's feelings on Malamud by saying that while he "acknowledges the deep humanity and moral concern of his peer . . . Malamud

48   Chapter 2

'does not—or has not yet—found the contemporary scene a proper or sufficient backdrop for his tales of heartlessness and heartache, of suffering and regeneration.'"[19] Indeed, Theodore Solotaroff wrote that, "While Roth is clearly writing about the modern Jew in America, Malamud appears to be writing mainly about Jewishness itself as it survives from age to age and from place to place."[20] Nevertheless, despite Roth's concern being squarely the Jews of his day, mainly in his native New Jersey, and Malamud's concern being more universal, less religiously, geographically, or chronologically bounded, "both Roth and Malamud seem involved in a similar effort to feel and think with their Jewishness and to use the thick concreteness of Jewish moral experience to get at the dilemmas and decisions of the heart generally."[21] The question, in fact, of whether the "Jewish moral experience" has some sort of life force separate from Jewish religious practices may be one of the most vital elements of both Roth and Malamud's satire. If there is some sort of independent Jewish morality that can exist without religious Judaism, then the Thingification of Judaism becomes all the more natural and understandable. But what the two stories we will examine in this chapter indicate is both Roth and Malamud imagine a world in which the conflict between Jewish identity and an absence of Jewish religiosity leads to violent confrontation.

Whereas identity could be seen as the one unifying theme in all of Roth's work, Edward Abramson says that for Malamud the "basic theme of Jewish identity [is] one not stressed."[22] Again, as Roth put it, even Malamud's Jews are not even sure they are Jews. A generous way of interpreting this use of his characters is, in Stanley Chyet's words, that, "writers like Malamud . . . are interested above all else in delineating and exploring their personalities, the characters, of their protagonists, not in exploiting them as vehicles for doctrines or creeds of any sort."[23] Even Malamud's attempt at neutrality could not change the core of his satire; whether he intended to or not, his harshest critique fell on the kind of Jew who turns his back on another Jew and, in some cases, the Thingification of Judaism seems to be a contributing factor of that betrayal. The very idea that Judaism was only relevant to Old World Jews and had no place in a modern Jewish home undermined any relationship between modern American Jews and their European counterparts. In essence, David Brauner writes, "Malamud once wrote that if a Jew ever forgets he is a Jew, a Gentile will remind him, but in Roth's novels, if a Jew ever forgets he is a Jew, it is a fellow Jew who will remind him."[24]

This inability to allow Jews to forget that they are Jews is one of the obvious critical impulses behind Roth's story, "Eli, the Fanatic." Although Roth and Malamud did not overlap often, "Eli" and Malamud's short story "The Jewbird" share remarkably similar satiric purpose. "The Jewbird" is everything most critics, including Roth, have accused Malamud's work of not being: it is contemporary, specific, and most of all, Jewish. In both stories the authors take Judaism-as-Thing for granted. But where Judaism, and specifically Jewish traditions and rituals, are still operant for Eastern European Jews in these stories, American Jews have no time for it. That causes them to act very poorly toward those Jews who *do* have time for it, and that is a crime neither Roth nor Malamud can let stand.

"Eli, the Fanatic"

"Eli, the Fanatic" is the final story in *Goodbye, Columbus*. It is the longest in the collection beside the titular novella itself. "What Roth established in 'Eli,'" Sol Gittleman wrote, "[was] actually the continuity of Jewish life down through the ages."[25] It shows that from the outset of his career Roth was troubled by issues of identity. "The Defender of the Faith," for example, also deals with issues of identity, but in that story it is the superficially shared Jewishness of two soldiers that is at issue, and not the deeper implications of that Jewishness. Private Grossbart expects special treatment from Sergeant Marx simply because they are both "members of the tribe" and throughout the story Marx does, indeed, give Grossbart special treatment, both positive and negative. "Eli" deals with what appears to be a similar situation. One Jew in the story is appealing to another to overlook the rules and allow him to do what he wants to do. But the stakes of Mr. Tzuref's requests to Eli are much higher than those of Grossbart's to Marx. And while both Marx and Eli snap at the end of their respective stories, Marx lashes out in anger and spite while Eli undergoes what can only be called a "religious experience" (or at least a parody of one). In both cases religious practice is at the core of the conflict, which indicates that even as early as 1959 the process of Thingifying

50   Chapter 2

Judaism was already underway, and satirists were already picking up the theme and running with it.

"Eli" takes place in the bucolic Long Island town of Woodenton in the year 1948. In the period immediately following World War II there was what Rachel Kranson calls "the mass migration to the suburbs that Jews participated in during the postwar years."[26] Many American Jews moved into these bedroom communities, which were ethnically and religiously (if not racially) diverse. As early as 1934 Mordecai Kaplan was already encountering young people who were trying to "pass" as gentiles; they were, for the most part, the generation that made this move away from the neighborhoods in which they grew up and into the suburbs to raise their children with a different experience of what it meant to be Jewish than the one they had. "For the Jews of Woodenton," Gittleman argued, "there is no Torah, and, as far as Roth is concerned, no peace of mind."[27] The Jews of Woodenton seem to fear what sociologists call "surplus visibility," what David Zurawik says ends up manifesting as a Jewish critique of other Jews as being "too Jewish." Zurawik says that this fear "can lead to members of a minority group policing each other's visibility and, in some cases, striving for invisibility."[28] Visibility and invisibility, or even light and darkness, seem to be the primary metaphors Roth is employing to show the difference between assimilated Jewish identity (not-a-Thing) and Old World Jewish identity (Thing).

The Jews of Woodenton are newly transplanted suburban Jews who work in the city and then come home to their perfect houses in their perfect town. The attitude of Eli's Jewish neighbors is that they have finally "made it." They have achieved the American dream. And they react, therefore, with a typical show of fear and anger if anything appears to threaten their perfect existence. For the Jews of Woodenton, this threat comes in the form of an Eastern European Jew by the name of Leo Tzuref, who is running a yeshiva for a group of young boys who are war orphans. As if this is not bad enough (and it seems that, in fact, it *would* have been bad enough) Tzuref is also housing an adult war refugee, or Displaced Person (DP), who is helping with the school. For the Jews of Woodenton, Gittleman says, "the Holocaust has come to Long Island and the figure of the Hassid walking down Coach House Road has enraged them."[29] These terrors, then, the Jews of Woodenton cannot bear; they are terrified that their gentile neighbors, if reminded too often that the Jews are Jews, will turn on them and they will have to leave the Promised Land.

By satirizing Jews who are terrified of being recognized as Jews, or perhaps who just do not want to be seen as *real* Jews, Roth argues that American Jewry as a whole has turned its back on its traditions and its people. The Jews of Woodenton want to evict a school full of Holocaust orphans and an adult DP who were lucky to have survived. They will kick orphans and victims into the street if that is what it takes to preserve their own fragile existence. They send Eli to Tzuref to claim that "zoning laws" are the issue, but zoning laws are just a cover; it is clear that, "Roth means to condemn a society that turns zoning laws into subtle instruments of persecution."[30]

The Jews of Woodenton appeal to Eli in a series of increasingly free indirect, Kafkaesque statements, overwhelming him and showing us the first indications of Eli's mental struggles with this issue. In their private conversations with Eli we see the truth of why these assimilated Jews are so scared. It is not, in fact, about zoning laws but is very clearly about their own desire to flee from a communal past in which they were forcibly marked as Jews. In Woodenton their identity is theirs to form, and they are refusing to give that up. The psychology behind their fear is quite clear:

> "Eli, a regular greenhorn," Ted Heller had said. "He didn't say a word. Just handed me the note and stood there, like in the Bronx the old guys who used to come around selling Hebrew trinkets."
>
> "A Yeshivah!" Artie Berg had said. "Eli, in Woodenton, a Yeshivah! If I wanted to live in Brownsville, Eli, I'll live in Brownsville . . ."
>
> "He walked right by my window, the greenie," Ted had said, "and he nodded, Eli. He's my friend now."
>
> "Eli," Artie Berg had said, "he handed the damn thing to a clerk at Stop N' Shop—and in that hat yet!"
>
> "Eli," Harry Shaw again, "it's not funny. Someday, Eli, it's going to be a hundred little kids with little yamalkahs chanting their Hebrew lessons on Coach House Road, and then it's not going to strike you funny."
>
> "Eli, what goes on up there—my kids hear strange sounds."
>
> "Eli, this is a modern community."

52   Chapter 2

"Eli, we pay taxes"
"Eli."
"Eli!"
"Eli!"[31]

Never mind what the DPs have gone through, the struggle of the comfortable Jews of Woodenton must take precedence. It is a reminder of the old guys in the Bronx, of Brownsville—the greenhorn is behaving in public in a way that embarrasses the community. DPs are like termites; if you ignore the presence of a few, then before you know it you will have a full-blown infestation on your hands. And the neighbors' memories of Judaism are so material: the trinkets in the Bronx, the yarmulkes they expect to see appearing in Woodenton. Judaism in Woodenton is a Thing made up of smaller Things. Not only is Old World Judaism a Thing, it is actually a dangerous Thing, and that sets Roth's satire apart. Throughout Silent Generation satire we see Judaism as useless, but basically benign.[32] But in Roth we see Jews who react to Judaism as though it is not simply useless but could actually cause them real harm. It is not a Thing to be ignored; it is a Thing to be thoroughly avoided.

Eventually Eli focuses on the issue of the way the greenhorn is dressed as the root of the problem and says that he and the yeshiva students can stay if they are "attired in clothing usually associated with American life in the twentieth century" when they appear in public.[33] The issue of surplus visibility is most easily tackled through clothing, as that is the most immediately recognizable marker of Jewishness (or Otherness) in Woodenton.[34] Eli offers a compromise, instead of throwing them all out, because he has a conflicted Jewish identity. As we will see below, the relationship between Judaism and "stuff" runs deep, and the critique of Judaism as being more about objects than about beliefs is an old one. In Roth the fact that the greenie's clothing becomes metonymic for the true danger of Judaism-as-Thing focuses the reader's attention on the role of religious objects, which in turn bears on the Thingification of religion itself. It is here that Roth really turns up the pressure on the Woodenton Jews, who are trying to conform and to live in willful ignorance of what was done to the Jews of Europe during the war. When Tzuref tells Eli that the greenie's suit is "all he's got," Eli misunderstands (perhaps purposely) and tries to pretend that they are speaking about only material possessions, only clothes.[35] Eli believes they have things, including the Thing that the Woodenton Jews are avoiding—namely Judaism—and cannot see that a loss of intangibles could be the real problem.

To be a Jew, to the Woodenton Jews, is to have trinkets and skull caps, but Tzuref has to finally force Eli to see the truth of what happened to the greenie and others. This is when Roth drops the hammer on the Woodenton Jews and, by extension, his readers:

> "But I tell you he has nothing. Nothing. You have that word in English? Nicht? Gornisht?"
>
> "Yes, Mr. Tzuref, we have the word."
>
> "A mother and a father?" Tzuref said. "No. A wife? No. A baby? A little ten-month-old baby? No! A village full of friends? A synagogue where you knew the feel of every seat under your pants? Where with your eyes closed you could smell the cloth of the Torah . . . And a medical experiment they performed on him yet! That leaves nothing, Mr. Peck. Absolutely nothing!"[36]

The greenie has not only lost things, he has lost his entire family, and even, it is implied, been castrated. He has no things, and now Eli wants to take his last Thing by forcing assimilation on him. To the greenie Judaism is not a Thing, it is all he has left, and Eli wants to take even that from him.

Neither Eli nor Roth's readers can hide from the truth of Tzuref's admonishment, and yet Eli has nevertheless become fixated on the idea that the clothes make the man. The real juxtaposition here is that physical items, to Eli, are not Things because they can change your life, which means they are objects with use. Roth critiques the materialism of assimilated Jews like Eli by showing the ways in which he cannot imagine an idea (like religion) being as transformative as a physical object. Eli goes home and takes one of his own suits, his nice green one, and boxes it up with a note explaining the clothes are for the "gentleman in the hat" and goes on to claim the he is "not a Nazi who would drive eighteen children, who are probably frightened at the sight of a firefly, into homelessness."[37]

What transpires next forces Eli to abandon his identity as a comfortable, assimilated Jew. Eli finds his box returned to him, but it no longer contains Eli's good, green suit. It now contains the greenie's black

54   Chapter 2

gabardine suit and black hat. Eli offered the greenie a suit and the greenie reciprocated. The surface meaning would seem to be one of cultural miscommunication, the greenie not understanding that a return gift was not required. Eli's reaction to the gift, however, further demonstrates the way that the things in this story are not Things at all, and are in fact the most powerful objects of all. Eli decides to put on the black suit, to see what it feels like. "The shock, at first, was the shock of having daylight turned off all at once. Inside the box was an eclipse . . . For the first time in his life he *smelled* the color of blackness: a little stale, a little sour, a little old."[38] The usual association of blackness with invisibility is inverted, in a sense. In this case the utter blackness of the suit is what makes it so visible, so Other. Eli perceives that blackness in a synesthetic way as he mentally struggles with what it means to be visibly Jewish and with whether that is something a modern Jew can allow himself to be.

Eli starts with the hat, then the man's fringed undergarment—tzitzit, of ritual significance—which Eli does not even recognize; he calls it "a little fringed serape."[39] Allen Cooper thinks Eli's ignorance of some of these items may be a willful defense mechanism because, "Eli, educated professional . . . must know something, however rudimentary, about the forms of his religion, but has joined these suburban Jews in escaping far from their roots."[40] To Cooper's mind Eli has willfully made Judaism so thoroughly a Thing that he cannot even recall that he once knew what these ritual clothes were. He puts on the jacket, trousers, and vest. When it comes time to look for the socks he discovers "a khaki army sock" in each trouser pocket. "As he slipped them over his toes, he invented a genesis: a G.I.'s present in 1945. Plus everything else lost between 1938 and 1945, he has also lost his socks. Not that he had lost the socks, but that he's had to stoop to accepting these, made Eli almost cry."[41] Again we see Eli missing the forest for the trees. The true enormity of what has been taken from the greenie, and the reality of what it means for Eli to be trying to force him to assimilate, do not affect him like a physical object such as a sock does.

Eli, now fully dressed, steps boldly out into public view. When a neighbor sees him Eli immediately flees back into his house. When his phone begins to ring he imagines the conversation with the neighbor: "Eli, there's a Jew at your door."[42] Though Roth has been hinting at this issue of identity throughout the story, here it is finally articulated: you can be a real Jew if you choose, but you cannot do it in Woodenton. Gittleman argued that, "once [Eli] understood the nature of the Jew as survivor, it became a matter of life and death to look like a Jew, *and to make certain he was recognized as a* Jew, particularly by his gentile neighbors."[43]

Only a man wearing that suit is a real Jew. When Eli puts it on, he becomes a Jew at the door. So if the greenie is no longer wearing it, what is he? If Judaism is a Thing, what is the role of the things of Judaism? For Eli Judaism has been a Thing at least as long as he has been in Woodenton; it is not only an object without use, but it is an object it is dangerous to be caught with. The greenie lives in a world in which Judaism is still an object with use, so for him the taking off of one suit and the donning of another does not change his Jewish identity. But for Eli the use of Jewish ritual objects and traditional clothing for the first time causes a quantum rupture in his sense of self. The objects of Judaism clearly have their own transformative power, even in a place like Woodenton where they have been set aside as Things, and dangerous.

Sanford Pinsker, one of the most well known critics of Jewish American literature, sees this clothing swap as a paradigm shift. Pinsker argues, "Eli not only exchanges his contemporary refinements for the mantle of history, but, more importantly, he assumes the psychic identity of his alter ego."[44] The description of the greenie as Eli's "alter ego" belies the separation Eli and the Jews of Woodenton want to imagine. They believe that they have done away with the archaic forms of Judaism, or even that it is possible to abandon the Judaism-Thing. The relationship between Eli and the greenie, however, demonstrates that the entire process of Thing-making may be a lie assimilated Jews tell themselves to hide from the truth that they are all still greenhorns underneath their American costumes.

As with any good superhero, Eli decides that once he has transformed from mild-mannered Eli into Jewish Eli he is meant to present himself to the town dressed in the black (visible) suit. According to Joseph Landis, "Eli and the Jews of Woodenton must accept the heritage of faith and martyrdom that is symbolized by the suit."[45] As he does so, his neighbors immediately assume Eli is having a nervous breakdown. "Shortly, everybody in Coach House Road was aware that Eli Peck . . . was having a breakdown. Everybody except Eli Peck. He knew that what he did was not insane, though he felt every inch of its strangeness."[46] Eli

56   Chapter 2

is, perhaps, accessing some primal, Jungian, forgotten part of himself; some part that has been tamped down so tightly over the generations that the other Jews of Woodenton do not even recognize it as a part of themselves anymore. Gittleman argues that, "only Eli understood what has happened. His transformation into an East European Hassidic survivor of Hitler's slaughter, has given new strength to the cloth which binds Jew to Jew."[47] How far down the rabbit hole of assimilation have the Jews of Woodenton fallen if Eli's decision to be seen as a Jew in public is immediately assumed to be acute mental illness? This is Roth's driving point—is there room for Judaism in the life of American Jews, or can we only see it as some-Thing performed by those from the Old World and the mentally ill?

Eli ultimately finds neither redemption, expiation, nor peace. He goes to the hospital to see his wife and newborn son, and all his community can say is, "Oh, Christ. . . . You don't have this Bible stuff on the brain."[48] Even the phrase "Bible stuff" underscores how Thingish Judaism and Jewish practices are to the rest of the Woodenton Jews. They begin to speak to him like a child, they patronize him, and they mock him. They cannot believe that a previously "normal" young man would suddenly be parading about in religious garb unless he had gone completely round the bend, so despite Eli's screaming protests they subdue and medicate him. The story ends with the ominous statements that, "in a moment they tore off his jacket—it gave so easily, in one yank. Then a needle slid under his skin. The drug calmed his soul, but did not touch it down where the blackness had reached."[49] The blackness of Jewish visibility has altered Eli's very soul and Eli has been changed, but is it for the good? What will happen when he wakes up? Will he admit it was all a mental breakdown and go back to being an assimilated persecutor of DPs, or will he pack his family up and move back to the city? Probably neither, but regardless it is not Roth's way to tie things up with a bow at the end of the story.

One message, however, is clear. In 1948, in the bucolic suburbs, there is no place for "Bible stuff," whether in the person of the more religiously traditional war refugees or of a neighbor they have known and respected for years. A threat is a threat, and the community will close ranks to eliminate the threat like white blood cells surrounding a foreign body. It is interesting to note that at no point in the story do we hear anything from the non-Jews of Woodenton. We are told a bit about them in one of Eli's letters to Tzuref, "Woodenton, as you may not know, has long been the home of well-to-do Protestants. It is only since the war that Jews have been able to buy property here, and for the Jews and Gentiles to live beside each other in amity. For this adjustment to be made, both Jews and Gentiles alike had to give up some of their more extreme practices in order not to threaten or offend the other."[50]

This is another one of Roth's sharper barbs at assimilated American Jews. He is calling them, in effect, paranoid and possibly delusional. It is difficult to imagine what the "extreme practices" of an affluent, suburban community would look like. Perhaps, as Eileen Watts argues, the Protestants "have adjusted by not restricting so many of their country clubs, neighborhoods, and universities, and Jews have adjusted by not dressing or speaking so much like Jews."[51] The Jews of Woodenton were calling on themselves to sacrifice much more than their Protestant neighbors. Will Herberg calls these "defense activities," and argues that Jews, as the most vulnerable of the major American religious communities, have the "most elaborately developed . . . strategy of minority-group defensiveness."[52] Because of their fear of both antisemitism and "intrusion" of the church, many Jews fought hard for a total secularization of community life and a solid wall between personal religious practice and public performance of Americanness. Dan Isaac says that Roth's criticism is that "Judaism has gone through the quiet metamorphosis demanded by American society and emerged as a co-operative, acquisitive member of the new frontier. That [some people] resent this indictment is understandable; but to attack the critic rather than to face the criticism is unforgiveable."[53]

Moreover, this may all be a self-imposed sacrifice. The opinion of these Protestants about the yeshiva is never actually mentioned; if they have even noticed its presence, they do not seem to have worried about it much. The Jews of Woodenton, however, feel the need to take decisive, prophylactic action to ensure that their neighbors are not reminded of the "extreme practices" of the Jews. It seems to answer the question, "Why aren't there pogroms in Woodenton?" with "Because the Jews use 'common sense' and 'moderation' to gauge their public behavior."[54] In essence, the Jews of Woodenton preemptively blame the victims. They feel they must not provoke their gentile neighbors, and if those neighbors

58   Chapter 2

were to respond to a provocation with violence, well, it would be the Jews' own fault for not keeping up their end of the bargain.

Roth is satirizing the complacency and conformism of postwar suburban Jews, and showing them the potentially eruptive repercussions of their willingness to, in essence, sell their souls for a piece of real estate—the ultimate not-a-Thing thing—in a desirable zip code. "The story 'Eli, the Fanatic,'" Michael Rockland argued, "is an attack on suburban Jewry and their values."[55] Roth sees in the lifestyle of the Woodenton Jews a "danger in American affluence for the Jew, and the threat to his identity."[56] Dan Isaac thinks that for Roth, "American Judaism has become the willing servant of an immoral society, corrupted by the very force it should oppose."[57] Roth is not a hippie or antiestablishment militant; he simply despises inauthenticity and has what David Brauner calls a "preoccupation with questions of authentic Jewishness."[58] This insecurity undergirds the entire story. "In a sense," writes Timothy Parrish, "the yeshiva Jews are 'authentic' Jews, and their authenticity terrifies the suburban Jews whose success depends in part on their belief that their fellow Americans no longer perceive them as Jews. In other words, the story . . . highlights both the Woodenton Jews' sense of their own cultural inferiority and their displaced identification with the Christians whom they live near but do not really know."[59]

Roth himself fought back against the critics of his who, he felt, believed only positive portrayals of Jews should be published. He argued that that sort of myopia only compounds the problem, "when a willful blindness to man's condition can only precipitate further anguishes and miseries. . . . I cannot help but believe that there is a higher moral purpose for the Jewish writer, and the Jewish people, than the improvement of public relations."[60] Michael Rockland puts it even more clearly, "The best Jew, Roth feels these critics of his are arguing, is the invisible Jew."[61] Eli, at the end of the story, becomes the exact opposite of the invisible Jew; he becomes so visible he cannot be ignored, which means he has to be attacked. Bernard Malamud also dealt with the psychological and real violence that can arise when assimilated Jews feel "real" or traditional Jews are threatening their place in society. Despite his reputation for depicting Jews in a "better" way than Roth, his exploration of inter-Jewish conflict actually ends even more disturbingly than does "Eli."

"The Jewbird"

Bernard Malamud is both easier and more difficult to contextualize than Roth. Because he has not faced the same accusations of being self-loathing or bad for the Jews, less work is needed to rehabilitate his image. His career and Joseph Heller's are similar in that his first novel, *The Natural*, was not at all Jewish, and it was only as his career progressed that he began to write Jewish characters or engage with themes of Jewish identity. Malamud's work further supports the claim that the Silent Generation wrote their satires with an eye toward protecting Jews even amid a dismissal of Judaism. Like Roth, Malamud also wrote fiction criticizing the relationship between assimilated Jews and DPs.

Malamud's "The Jewbird" first appeared in the *Reporter* in April of 1963, and was anthologized later that year in his second short story collection, *Idiots First*. Although Malamud felt strongly about the story, literary critics, it seems, did not. This may explain why Roth's take on this particular inter-Jewish relationship received so much more attention, even though the ending of Malamud's story seems much more accusatory than Roth's. Almost none of the reviews of "The Jewbird" seemed to recognize the story as having any real satiric weight or being a particularly interesting take on the relationship between assimilated American Jews and the traditional Judaism-as-Thing. The initial publication in the *Reporter* created no real interest at all, and when the reviews of *Idiots First* began to come in, critics only occasionally singled out "The Jewbird." Furthermore, not all of that singling out was positive. One review, for example, said, "because of an occasional inconsistency in time or genre, such stories as 'The Jewbird' . . . fail to achieve their proper impact."[62] Alone, apparently, "The Jewbird" escapes notice and in collection it suffers in proximity to stories such as "Black Is My Favorite Color" or "The German Refugee," which received nearly universal acclaim. Another review called it "too facile a parable about anti-Semitism."[63] The author of perhaps the most scathing response said of *all* the stories in the collection that they are "full of stereotyped characters, and the plots lack dramatic intensity."[64]

Nevertheless, as often happens with art, time and distance can increase appreciation for a work. This seems to have happened with "The Jewbird" as the years passed, and increasingly people have written

60   Chapter 2

about it more positively.[65] As time passed, "The Jewbird" even became, for some respondents, emblematic of Malamud's entire literary project. "The Jewbird" presents, for example, "a striking illustration of the baneful world that Malamud projects."[66] Nevertheless, much like Roth's "Eli," "The Jewbird" does not dominate Malamud scholarship. There are no books about it, and very few articles devoted to it alone. It is considered a bit of a Malamud outlier; in a career not thought to be too strongly associated with issues of identity, in "The Jewbird," "this positive stress upon Jewish identity is a marked exception to Malamud's usual orientation."[67] More often than not it is included in a larger discussion of Malamud's work; the aspects of it most often singled out are its fantastical nature and its strong condemnation of Jewish self-hatred, both of which show Malamud to be presenting the same image of Judaism-as-Thing that Roth did.

The story itself is short; only nine columns in the original *Reporter* publication. It is told in a third-person, limited omniscience style with short sentences more commonly associated with Hemingway than with Malamud. "The Jewbird" is, on the surface, the story of a talking bird who takes refuge in the apartment of the Cohen family near Manhattan's Lower East Side. Both the location of the apartment—the neighborhood most associated with the Eastern European Jewish migration, and the stereotypically Jewish name of the family, Cohen—lead the reader to think about the process of assimilation and how many things must be thrown off in order to fully assimilate. Eileen Watts writes that, "Cohen is a more or less assimilated immigrant, living in a penthouse apartment, but an apartment nonetheless—a modern ghetto—receiving a newly arrived immigrant . . . as shabbily as his immigrant parents were no doubt received in this country."[68] The Jewbird calls himself Schwartz (Yiddish for black) and tells the Cohens he is fleeing the "anti-semeets" who have been pursuing him. He hopes for shelter and respite in the Cohen home, but finds only more persecution. It is, much like "Eli," about what J. Gerald Kennedy calls, "the Jew's complicated and sometimes scornful attitude about his own cultural roots."[69] The name "Schwartz" is reminiscent of Roth's association between blackness and invisibility, but Malamud's interest here is less in public identity than in humanity and inhumanity or, one might say, humanity and animality. Either we recognize the humanity in the Other, or else we are casting them as animals (and animals can easily be Things), which results in a superior-inferior dynamic that can perhaps only end in tragedy.

The difference between Schwartz and the Cohens is quite stark. The Cohens are an assimilated, working-class family living what appears to be only a nominally Jewish lifestyle. Schwartz, on the other hand, is depicted as "hoarse," "bedraggled," "ruffled," and "dull"; he speaks "in Jewish" and uses traditionally Yiddish rhythms and word inversions while the Cohen family all speak colloquial English. He *davens* and prays "with great passion," while Mr. Cohen refers to him as "a foxy bastard [who] thinks he's a Jew" and a "goddamn pest and a freeloader." Harry Cohen objects to Schwartz's smell, his snoring, his diet, and eventually his very presence. Schwartz is clearly an allegorical figure, but it remains vague what, specifically, he stands for.[70] It is obvious that there is, as in "Eli," a moral about inter-Jewish relationships and identity, but there are other aspects of Schwartz that could represent various other groups. His requests for "simple pleasures (a bit of herring, the Jewish paper) are characteristic of old people," for example.[71] Alternatively, "through his sufferance and survival, Malamud's absurd bird becomes a symbol of the strength of the tragic clown."[72] Robert Solotaroff calls Schwartz "just somebody's cranky, sly, Old World Jewish uncle who moves into crowded quarters for a while and who, at his advanced age, likes 'the warm, the windows, the smell of cooking . . . to see once in a while the *Jewish Morning Journal* and have now and then a schnapps because it helps my breathing, thanks God.'"[73] In both Roth and Malamud the "Old World" Jew is very nearly a Thing himself. He is out of place in our modern, assimilated world. He is not wanted, and more than that he is a threat to the hard-won status quo. Schwartz is a Jew-animal-Thing closely related to Roth's greenie-Thing in his out-of-placeness and his ability to cause harm.

From the beginning Malamud, through Schwartz, hints at the potential violence brewing in the interactions between the Cohens and Schwartz. Harry Cohen takes a swipe at Schwartz when he "wearily flapped through the open kitchen window" and landed on their dinner table.[74] The bird then speaks for the first time by exclaiming: "'Gevalt, a pogrom!'"[75] Those three words establish a disproportionate amount of information about how Malamud wants the reader to see Schwartz. First: *gevalt. Gevalt* is a Yiddish word without a direct translation into English. It is an expression of dismay, close to the more familiar *oy vey. Oy vey* translates reasonably closely as "oh woe"; *oy gevalt* is a slightly stronger exclamation. More than sadness or general malaise it expresses a sharp shock, fear, or even disgust. So Schwartz uses not only a Yiddish word, but a second-order Yiddish word, which marks him as fairly versant with the language, certainly more so than the average English-speaking American.[76] Secondly he says "a pogrom!" This narrows his origins down geographically. The anti-Jewish violence of the pogrom was primarily associated with pre-Soviet Russia and the countries under Russian control. So Schwarz is a Yiddish-speaking bird most likely from Russia, Poland, or Lithuania. The greenie in "Eli" has a much more specific backstory; he is a victim of the Nazis, and a Holocaust survivor. Schwartz is more of an Old World everyJew; he is not fleeing a specific time, place, or persecution, and therefore he can stand in for the ways assimilated American Jews have felt about and treated their Old World counterparts for decades before and after the war. "The Jewbird" is not just about post-Holocaust inter-Jewish relations; it is about the disdain American Jews have shown for Eastern European Jews for a very long time.

Literary critic Harold Bloom wrote of Malamud that, "alone among American writers he has fixed on the Jew as representative man—and on the schlemiel as representative Jew. His Jewish Everyman is an isolated, displaced loner, Easterner in the West, German refugee in America, bird among bipeds."[77] Bloom identifies Schwartz as the representative Jew in the story, not the Cohens. But he is representative because he is alone and unwanted. According to Bloom the relationship between the assimilated American Cohen and the displaced Schwartz is what *makes* Schwartz a Jew in Malamudian terms, because if he were accepted he would no longer be a schlemiel. To extend Bloom's argument a step further, the process of Thingification grants a form of legitimacy through the very attempt at delegitimizing. Cohen wants to erase Schwartz just as Woodenton wanted to erase the yeshiva. But in both cases instead of erasing them they actually make them even more of an exemplar of Jewishness than they were before.

Schwartz is seeking food and rest, but Cohen is immediately suspicious of the bird's intentions. When Cohen asks him "what do you want?" Schwartz responds that he would like "a piece of herring with a crust of bread. You can't live on nerve forever."[78] Schwartz is only concerned with the immediate; he is hungry and tired in this moment, and that is as far as his thinking has gone. Cohen, however, is more concerned with Schwartz's long-term plans. He responds "all I'm asking is, what brings you to this address?"[79] Why here? Why now? Why us? Why has Schwartz singled out the Cohen family? To Schwartz there is no reason: "the window was open" he tells them, and the narrator tells us at the outset of the story: "That's how it goes. It's open, you're in. Closed, you're out and that's your fate."[80] Windows, it could be said, are a metaphor for borders. Schwartz thinks he just got lucky; in fleeing from the "anti-Semeets . . . eagles, vultures, and hawks. And once in a while . . . crows" he happened to find an open window.[81] It was not his fate to die, not today. To Cohen, on the other hand, Schwartz's very presence is a kind of persecution or oppression, furthering the idea that traditional Jews themselves are Things when they upset the balance of an assimilated Jew's life. Cohen just wants to go about his routines and not be bothered by the needs of an indigent, Yiddish-speaking, beleaguered houseguest.

Cohen seems to mistrust Schwartz and is suspicious that he even is what he claims to be. Cohen first accuses him of being "'some kind of ghost or dybbuk,'" a malevolent dead spirit from Yiddish folklore, which Schwartz dismisses—although, "in a sense, Schwartz does possess the Cohen family"—but Schwartz acknowledges that he had a relative who had been possessed by a dybbuk.[82] The tone of the conversation indicates that Cohen does not really believe in such things and was only trying to dislodge this unwanted visitor.[83] Schwartz, on the other hand, takes it as a matter of truth that dybbuks do, in fact, exist but simply denies that he is under the control of one. Again, the subtext of the conversation shows the deep cultural differences between Schwartz and Cohen. Mrs. Cohen seems to have slightly more fanciful notions than her husband does; even after Schwartz has denied being a dybbuk, she suggests he could be "'an old Jew changed into a bird by somebody.'"[84] There are layers within layers here; if an old Jew is a Thing and a bird is a Thing, is an old Jew who has been turned into a bird doubly a Thing? Is he reclaimed from being a Thing by the double negative? Schwartz is a bit more sanguine about the potential of his being transformed, responding, "'who knows? Does God tell us everything?'"[85]

There is a piety to his response that is entirely lacking in the Cohens, and his attitude seems to "imply that God bears some of the responsibility for the unfortunate situation into which [he] has been thrust."[86]

64   Chapter 2

Cohen is the primary force within his home; he directs what his wife and son do and (he hopes) think. Schwartz is willing to shrug some things off and chalk them up to a higher power about which he cannot know. That unknowability, however, does not frighten or unsettle Schwartz as it seems to do to Cohen. Here, as in the end of "Eli," we see the discomfort of Americanized Jews with traditional forms of religion; in "Eli" it was the "Bible stuff," here it is a belief in God and spirits, but in both cases the author is focusing on the American rejection of Jewish (Thingish) religiosity.

Cohen continues to try to eject Schwartz from his home. He wants his wife to feed Schwartz outside; however, "after that, take off," he insists.[87] This is where Schwartz's true situation emerges. "I'm tired," he tells Cohen, "and it's a long way." "'Which direction are you headed, north or south?' Schwartz, barely lifting his wings, shrugged. 'You don't know where you're going?' 'Where there's charity, I'll go.'"[88] He is, "an exemplary image of the Malamudian victim . . . constantly pursued by anti-Semites and fate . . . opportunist and saint who tests . . . the humanity and compassion of others."[89] Schwartz has no home and he has no destination; he is truly a wandering Aramean, what Neil Rudin calls "the Wandering Jew who can find no resting place."[90] Like the greenie in Woodenton, Schwartz has nothing and no one, and the American cousins he thought would be welcoming and supporting are turning out to be just as cold and dismissive as those enemies from whom he is fleeing. Cohen decides to allow Schwartz to stay the night, but when he tries to evict him the next morning his son, Maurie, cries, forcing Cohen to relent and allow Schwartz to stay longer term. He makes his disapproval clear, however, and tells his wife, "I'm dead set against it. I warn you he ain't gonna stay here long."[91]

It is at this point that Cohen's self-loathing really becomes manifest. His wife wonders aloud what he has against the "poor bird" to which Cohen responds, "Poor bird, my ass. He's a foxy bastard. He thinks he's a Jew."[92] Whether Malamud intended it or not, the use of the word "foxy" hearkens directly back to medieval European anti-Judaism where Jews were traditionally depicted as sly, cunning, conniving, dishonest, and untrustworthy. It is also apparent that whatever Cohen considers to be a true Jew, it does not include traditional prayer, *davening*, Yiddish, or superstitious belief in dybbuks or God. Being a Jew, to Cohen, means being assimilated, rational, secular, and forward thinking. This is the Thingification of the Old World Jew; all of his beliefs and practices are anachronistic or out of place, and they therefore do not matter. Having an outdated attachment to Jewish religious practices renders you not-a-Jew. In much the same way Eli reduces the greenie to his clothes, Cohen reduces Schwartz to his beliefs. You hold on to a Thing, it makes you into a Thing. Cohen continues his polemic against Schwartz: "A Jew-bird, what a chutzpah. One false move and he's out on his drumsticks."[93] Interesting here in addition to Cohen's continued invective against Schwartz is that he tries to use a Yiddish word for the first time in the story. It is almost as though Schwartz's presence is forcing Cohen to try for some imagined authenticity in his own Jewishness, but he is failing; it is unnatural to him and he uses *chutzpah* incorrectly by giving it an indirect article.[94] Cohen's major blow-up comes when Schwartz refuses the dried corn Cohen has brought home for him: "Cohen was annoyed. 'What's the matter, Cross-eyes, is your life getting too good for you? Are you forgetting what it means to be migratory? I'll bet a helluva lot of crows you happen to be acquainted with, Jews or otherwise, would give their eyeteeth to eat this corn.'"[95] *Migratory* is obviously a euphemism for *Jewish* here. Cohen, the assimilated Jew, is actually using assimilation as a weapon against Schwartz. If Cohen assimilated it is because he is a modern American, but if Schwartz is becoming bourgeois in his tastes it indicates a character flaw. One hallmark of a Thing is that, as it has no purpose, it also does not evolve or change. So because Cohen views Schwartz (and by extension all Old World Jews) as a Thing, he is not allowed the same right to adapt to his surroundings that Cohen takes for granted for himself and his family.

Cohen is expressing a sentiment similar to that of the Jews of Woodenton. As Eileen Watts puts it, "Cohen articulated an unexpressed feeling in this country about immigrants: you're lucky to be here; be happy with what little you have."[96] The established Jews do not understand why these immigrant-types, who seem to have it so good, cannot just adjust and behave the way their American counterparts think they should. Toss your Judaism up on a shelf like everyone else and appreciate your new life. From Cohen's point of view, Schwartz is abusing his hospitality and should remember his place. He is starting to act like "one of us," and it is very important to Cohen that he remain "one of them," which is

66   Chapter 2

hypocritical on Cohen's part and shows that there really is not a way the Old World immigrant can win in this scenario. Schwartz is permanently and physically marked as other; he is, after all, a talking bird before you even get to his alleged religious affiliation. It is, to Cohen, a reflection on all American Jews if one who is so radically other begins to act as though he is one of them. This is the fear in Woodenton as well; if the Protestants of Woodenton see this yeshiva with its Old Country ways and accents accepted by their Jewish neighbors, they may assume that they are the same. There is an impossible push-pull being enacted on the outsider Jew in which he (in these cases) must simultaneously act American so as not to embarrass the assimilated Jews but remain distant so as not to implicate the assimilated Jews.

Schwartz, eventually, makes the mistake of trying to speak realistically about the son Maurie's limitations and tells Cohen, "'he's a good boy—you don't have to worry. He won't be a shicker or a wife beater, God forbid, but a scholar he'll never be, if you know what I mean, although maybe a good mechanic. It's no disgrace in these times.'"[97] This truth-speech is the final crack in the fragile détente Cohen and Schwartz had established. Cohen tells him to keep his "'big snoot out of other people's private business," and returns to calling him "cross-eyes."[98] The "big snoot" comment, obviously, evokes the old canard of Jews having large noses. Schwartz, wisely, tries to avoid Cohen but Cohen, when he can find Schwartz alone, picks fights with him, often about Schwartz's hygiene. "For Christ sake, why don't you wash yourself sometimes? Why must you always stink like a dead fish?" Cohen asks Schwartz.[99] Schwartz prosaically responds, "if someone eats garlic he will smell from garlic. I eat herring three times a day. Feed me flowers and I will smell like flowers."[100] Cohen, of course, points out that he does not have to feed Schwartz at all, to which Schwartz responds: "I'm not complaining . . . you're complaining."[101] Cohen then begins to berate the bird about his snoring, and calls him "a goddamn pest and free-loader" as well as a "goddamn devil" and a "bastard bird."[102]

Just as the Jews of Woodenton were willing to expel their unwanted Jews, so is Cohen ready to expel Schwartz. "Why us?" they both seem to ask. Why should we be the ones responsible for these unwanted Jews? There is no sense of "he ain't heavy, he's my brother" among assimilated American Jews as far as Roth and Malamud are concerned. Schwartz, recognizing that he might not be able to avert expulsion this time, finally asks, "Mr. Cohen, why do you hate me so much. . . . What did I do to you?"[103] Cohen is just as frank with Schwartz as he has been since their first meeting and tells Schwartz he is an "A number 1 troublemaker, that's why. Now scat or it's open war."[104] The threat of violence, always in the background of the interactions between Cohen and Schwartz, has finally been articulated.

Finally, as had to happen, the situation comes to a head. Cohen's mother dies and Maurie comes home from school the next day with a zero in arithmetic. Cohen flies into a rage, and as soon as his wife and son are out of the house he "openly attacked the bird."[105] He chases Schwartz with a broom, and when the bird tries to hide in his birdhouse, "Cohen triumphantly reached in, and grabbing both skinny legs, dragged the bird out, cawing loudly. . . . He whirled the bird around and around his head." Schwartz managed to grab hold of Cohen's face and "hung on for dear life." Cohen rips the bird from his face, swings him around again, and then, "with a furious heave flung him into the night."[106] This is actually the only time we see Cohen perform a Jewish ritual; he is mimicking the Yom Kippur practice of *kapparot* in which Eastern European Jews swing a chicken around their heads to transfer their sins onto the bird. Schwartz has literally become a ritual object in this moment, so his humanity, animality, and Jewishness are all stripped away as he becomes a Thing of the Thing; lower even than the Thing itself are the items associated with the Thing. If we dehumanize those who may embarrass us or cause us to feel exposed and uncomfortably visible in society, what can we expect but that we treat them like animals onto whom we may place our communal sins and then sacrifice them for the good of the whole?

Cohen tosses the birdhouse and feeder after him and guards the balcony, broom in hand, for an hour waiting for Schwartz to return, "but the brokenhearted bird didn't."[107] Neither Mrs. Cohen nor Maurie question the situation, but both express quiet signs of grief for the loss of the bird. They were not strong enough to stand up for Schwartz, but they know enough to miss him now that he is gone. The end of the story is comparatively brief:

> In the spring when the winter's snow had melted, the boy, moved by a memory, wandered in the neighborhood, looking for

68   Chapter 2

> Schwartz. He found a dead black bird in a small lot near the river,
> his two wings broken, neck twisted, and both eyes plucked clean.
> "Who did it to you, Mr. Schwartz?" Maurie wept.
> "Anti-Semeets," Edie said later.[108]

Whether Mrs. Cohen suspects her husband's role in Schwartz's demise is unclear. Certainly Maurie does not recognize the violence his own father's attitude toward the bird had caused. The brevity of the story's final chapter keeps a sad event from becoming saccharine or maudlin. As Philip Hanson put it, "Even given the comic terms of 'The Jewbird', Malamud is unwilling to sentimentalize Schwartz."[109] Many Jewish authors have attacked the way in which the Jewish community responded to Displaced Persons, perhaps none more scathingly than Roth in "Eli, the Fanatic," but Malamud's way of approaching the subject is both more oblique in the use of an animal analog, and more hopeless in the death of Schwartz at the end.[110]

It is unclear whether or not Cohen killed Schwartz. The twisted neck and broken wings certainly seem like results of Cohen's attack, but Schwartz obviously managed to crawl away to the lot in which Maurie eventually found him. There is culpability enough to share as Malamud seems to, "underscore the moral and existential responsibility for the suffering of others" that all members of a community share.[111] Even if Cohen did not kill Schwartz he did attack him, leave him defenseless, turn his back on him, and throw him out to the antisemites, apparently not caring whether or not they killed Schwartz, which, in Malamud's view, means Cohen might as well have done the deed. "Here," according to Eileen Watts, "the worst anti-Semites are the Jewish ones, who evidently don't even know who they are."[112] Another way of putting it is that "the fundamental absurdity of the fable's story-line precisely parallels the absurd position of the Jewish anti-Semite."[113] And Malamud seems as though he is cautioning that this is the inevitable result of not only making Judaism and traditional Jews into Things, but then treating those Things not as harmless heirlooms but as something dangerous.

Malamud's second point about Jewish self-abuse has to do with the role of language. Dan Ben-Amos has already described for us the relationship between Jewish humor and language, but there is also a relationship between Jewish identity and language. Sander Gillman writes about the role of language in antisemitism in his seminal *Jewish Self-Hatred* and explains the ways in which Jews in Europe, particularly in Germany, were not credited with full use of the language. They may have been speaking German, but they were always thinking "Jewish," and therefore anything they said or wrote in German was necessarily a lie. This played out again in America, where the broken and Yiddish-inflected English of the refugee was contrasted, repeatedly, to the proper American English of the assimilated Jew. As Gillman writes, "it is the 'bad' Jew, the Jew as different, whose language is damaged, who is mute, who is the antithesis of the 'good' Jew, the Jew [who speaks] in the cultured language of the West."[114]

Gillman even goes so far as to say "the Eastern Jews, the Yiddish-speaking Jews, are inarticulate. They are essentially different. They are animal-like."[115] This seems to be a large part of Malamud's point about the American Jewish community's treatment of their Eastern European counterparts. Their lack of facility with English has rendered them less than human, and if on a communal level they are being treated that way, why not represent them as a filthy, freeloading animal in the eyes of people like the Cohens? The greenie in "Eli" was also rendered mute by his inability to communicate in English. As with Roth, the bleak picture is of the human condition and the indictment, if there is one, is against a community as a whole. Is Yiddish a separate Thing, or is it a feature of the Judaism-Thing? It could be seen either way in these two stories, but regardless, it is clearly a part of the ossified problem. Both Malamud and Roth ultimately agree that Jewish culture and Jewish uniqueness must be preserved, and the way to do that is to preserve refugee Jews, even when their traditions make us uncomfortable. This is not a defense of Judaism per se, but it is a staunch defense of the Jewish people against all enemies, both foreign and domestic.[116]

Roth and Malamud demonstrate a clear vision of how Jews should be treating other Jews. They also demonstrate the ways in which Thingification is case-specific. For modern American Jews they seem to say (and Allen and Heller say even more clearly), religion qua religion is holding you back, and keeping you subjugated. But for *other* Jews, Jews from other places or other cultures, Judaism is very live and vital and not at all a Thing. Bourgeois American Jews need to throw off the shackles of

70   Chapter 2

organized religion, sure, but not at the expense of a wider sense of Jewish community that can accept and support those Jews for whom Judaism matters. Different versions of Judaism can coexist in the Jewish community, and only by realizing the ways in which Judaism is a Thing for them can assimilated American Jews properly recognize the Jewishness of someone like the greenie or Schwartz.

3
The Baby Boom, Copycat Generation

R. Eleazar said: When the Israelites gave precedence to "we will do" over "we will hearken," a Heavenly Voice went forth and exclaimed to them, Who revealed to My children this secret, which is employed by the Ministering Angels, as it is written, Bless the Lord, ye angels of his. Ye mighty in strength that fulfil his word that hearken unto the voice of his word: first they fulfil and then they hearken?

—Talmud Shabbat 88a

Two Rabbis were discussing their problems with squirrels in their synagogue attic. One Rabbi said, "We simply called an exterminator and we never saw the squirrels again." The other Rabbi said, "We just gave them all a bar mitzvah, and we never saw the squirrels again."

—Anonymous joke

Wade Clark Roof famously called the Baby Boom generation "A Generation of Seekers."[1] For Roof, this commonality is why a generation that so clearly "constitutes a 'generation' in the broader social sense," meaning they "have a common, unifying social experience and develop a collective sense of identity" also seems to exhibit so much more individuality and less social cohesion than previous generations.[2] The Baby Boom generation is one of the easiest to define because unlike other generations that are delineated in hindsight based mainly on major events that would have shaped and influenced the worldviews of those who were young at the time, the Baby Boom was an observable demographic trend. The birth rate in the United States had declined steadily during the twentieth century but took a precipitous drop during the Great Depression. It

72   Chapter 3

had fallen to under twenty births per one thousand people for the first time in 1932 and remained low into the 1940s. It began to climb back up incrementally during World War II but underwent a massive spike immediately after the war ended. The sudden growth in prosperity and security for the middle class helped the rate move from 20.4 in 1945 to 24.1 in 1946 and 26.6 in 1947. It did not drop back down to prewar levels until 1965.[3] So while the Baby Boom generation also had galvanizing events—the Cold War, the Kennedy assassination, Vietnam and Woodstock, among others—it was also easy to define this generation based on objective demographic trends.

This overdetermination could be why Roof also says that "virtually all aspects of the lives of Baby Boomers—their family styles, moral values, work habits, political views—defy simple generalization."[4] This precise tension, easy to define yet impossible to pin down, is what the humor produced by Baby Boomers exemplifies as well. Their humor, for the most part, reflects the approach of whatever neighboring generation is exerting the most cultural pressure. Throughout the 1970s, 1980s, and into the 1990s Baby Boom comedians continued the trends begun by the Silent Generation, while in the twentieth century Baby Boomers seem to be imitating the attitudes of Generation X, which we will see in the next chapter. The Thingification of Judaism we identified in the previous chapters, that feeling that organized religion was a joke at best and an actual danger at worst, remains present in the humor of Baby Boomers in the late twentieth century. Boomers do not, perhaps, do nearly as much as Roth or Malamud to critique disunity or inauthenticity in the Jewish community, but they still tend to shy away from jokes that are simply ridicules of Jewish people and their behaviors. The things that are ridiculous remain the vestiges of religious practice, with particular attention paid to how absurd religious rituals (and those who perform them) are in the modern world. As they have aged and as Generation X comedians have become the driving forces in twenty-first century humor, the Baby Boomers have started to soften in their critique of ritual and become more like their Gen X children in depicting ritual as the thing that might actually hold families together.

This greater focus on ritual is particularly noteworthy because it is one of the things Baby Boom comedians do bring to the table that they do not seem to be borrowing from the Silent Generation. Judaism has

The Baby Boom, Copycat Generation   73

long been described as a religion of action, a religion that, according to Menachem Kellner, "expresses itself in terms of behavior, rather than in terms of systematic theology."[5] Moses Mendelssohn argued in *Jerusalem* that ritual performers, such as mohels, for example, who are the functionaries trained to perform ritual circumcisions, could still fulfill their ritual obligations even if they had lost their faith in God.[6] Arnold Eisen pointed out in *Rethinking Modern Judaism* that understanding the relationship between belief and action in Judaism is further complicated by the fact that, "modern Jewish thinkers, like their predecessors, have generally been loath to speak systematically about the God who is addressed in prayer or invoked in ritual practices."[7] Debating the merits of this view of Judaism is not important in order to acknowledge that the role of practice in Judaism is privileged.[8] Consider how one describes members of a religious community. Jews are called "observant," while Catholics, for example, are "devout."

Ritual is a bit more ephemeral than one might expect from the textual parodies or the indictments of communal inauthenticity we saw in the previous chapters, in part because it is quite difficult to decide what, precisely, constitutes a ritual in religious terms. Ronald Grimes, for example, one of the major figures in ritual theory, says "ritual does not 'exist' . . . ritual is an idea scholars formulate,"[9] while Catherine Bell says that "ritual, like action, will act out, express, or perform . . . conceptual orientations."[10] Jan Snoek said it perhaps most clearly when he wrote that "the number of definitions proposed is endless, and no one seems to like the definitions proposed by anyone else."[11] For the purposes of this book ritual means the formalized activities around life cycle events, especially birth, coming of age, and death. This is not because I am making a claim about what ritual is but because circumcisions, bar mitzvahs, and sitting shiva are among the most visible and well-known Jewish ritual practices, so those become the tropes that comedians exploit. This is why the second epigraph for this chapter is funny: it's funny because it's true, as they say.[12] The joke is lampooning the fact that for many American Jews it is *only* around important life cycle events that they participate in Jewish congregational life. Circumcision, bar/bat mitzvah, and funerals represent three of the four major life moments (marriage being the fourth), and those rituals hold social or psychological meaning even in families where they lost any theological meaning generations ago.

74   Chapter 3

Circumcision is by far the most commonly satirized ritual. There is a case to be made for circumcision being *the* ritual act that defines Judaism.[13] The covenantal relationship between God and Abraham begins in Genesis 12 when God tells Abraham to leave his home and everything he knows so that God can make him into "a great nation." Although this lays the groundwork for the covenant, it is not until five chapters later, Genesis 17:23, when the covenant is actually sealed. Abraham circumcises himself, his son Ishmael (who is thirteen at the time), and all of his male slaves as God had commanded. The traditional Hebrew term for the ritual is *brit milah* (Yiddishized as "bris"), which translates as "covenant of circumcision," so the covenantal nature of the ritual is explicit in the name. Every day, all over the world, eight-day-old Jewish boys and their families are reentering this covenant and reenacting the biblical relationship between God, Abraham, and his (male) descendants.

It is easy to see why the circumcision remains the most defining ritual of a Jewish life. In 2007 the World Health Organization estimated that 98 percent of Jewish boys were circumcised (compared to 80 percent of American boys in general and significantly lower numbers elsewhere in the world).[14] The second most prominent life cycle ritual (which will be discussed at greater length shortly) is the bar or bat mitzvah, and while it is more difficult to estimate its prevalence, a 2013 Pew study found as many as 30 percent of American Jews have no synagogue affiliation, which would make observing a bar or bat mitzvah difficult.[15] So a generous estimate would be that 70 percent of boys and a lower percentage of girls celebrate their bar or bat mitzvah, although many families keep a synagogue affiliation until their children get through bar or bat mitzvah and then leave, making any assumption based on affiliation data tenuous at best.[16] Both cultural cachet and statistical data would seem to support the notion that the circumcision remains the most definitive ritual of a Jewish life, or it is as far as most satires are concerned, because satire deals with perceptions and assumptions. Satire must be anchored in the real world in order to work, but a perceived real world is often much easier to satirize than a *real* world that involves nuance and gray area.

It is not a coincidence that all or most of the satirists dealing with circumcision are men. First of all, as a ritual with no female equivalent it is something with which men are more concerned. But women have sons, so it is not as though they are unaware of or unaffected by circumcision.

The Baby Boom, Copycat Generation   75

Freud said of sexual or obscene jokes that "a chance exposure has a comic effect on us because we compare the ease with which we enjoyed the sight with the great expenditure which would otherwise be required for reaching this end."[17] In short, accidental genital exposure is funny and enjoyable because normally you have to work so hard to see someone's genitals. This is a *very* gendered assumption. Few women would think that accidental exposure to a strange man's genitals is an opportunity for laughter. Even fewer would see the accidental exposure of their own genitals as a fun time. So if Freud is correct, it stands to reason that most of the people joking about circumcision are men.

It is perhaps self-evident why there are more circumcision jokes than jokes about other rituals, and more secular comedians and writers use a circumcision as a canvas for humor than other life-cycle events. Sophomoric as it may be, to many people (especially men, for whom most twentieth-century comedy was written) penises are funny. There is a combination of benign violation humor and superiority humor at play in joking about a minor violence being perpetuated against such a sensitive part of someone's body.[18] Circumcision jokes have existed for centuries and, as long as both humor and certain elements of Jewishness remain normatively male, they are likely to persist.[19]

The bar mitzvah is the second major lifecycle ritual of a Jewish boy's life. The bar mitzvah we know today has developed over centuries, dating back to the Middle Ages. Although statistics and tradition indicate that the bris is the ritual par excellence, for those who undergo a bar mitzvah it is much more central to their personal religious perception since they neither remember nor played any sort of active role in their own bris. References to and jokes about the bar or bat mitzvah are, therefore, almost as common as those about circumcisions. The phrase "today you are a man" has been uttered as a joking reference to someone's achievements innumerable times.[20] So the bar (or bat) mitzvah occupies a different space than does the bris. It is more public, more widely known, and more memorable.

The bar mitzvah, therefore, plays a much larger role in autobiographical or semiautobiographical works, because memory and nostalgia place it in a different category. M. Gail Hamner writes of the relationship between nostalgia and ritual, "ritual, like the nostalgia that feeds it, is a double edged-sword, potentially either desiccating life or nourishing it."[21] There is an indivisible relationship between ritual and nostalgia, because ritual is always, on some level, the physical enactment of tradition, and tradition is just another aspect of nostalgia. So Hamner's point is pertinent here, in particular, because the bar mitzvah's disproportional representation in satire makes more sense when viewed as not only a function of nostalgia but also something that nourishes life. Living things crave nourishment, and if ritual can actually nourish, then perhaps that is why, after a generation of ritual starvation, the contemporary satirists seem so desperate to find a new place for ritual.

The nostalgia element of humor around bar and bat mitzvahs takes on an additional layer of meaning when viewed through Rachel Gross's argument that nostalgia has a religious function for American Jews. She claims, in part, that "American Jews of all types of religious affiliation, including no affiliation, engage in ostensibly non-religious activities that provide personally meaningful engagements with American Jewish pasts. Attention to American Jewish nostalgia identifies robust forms of religious meaning in works of public and personal histories, emphasizing the centrality of emotional and commemorative norms in American and Jewish religious practices and consumer habits."[22] If (as recent surveys have shown) American Jews see a sense of humor as a specifically Jewish quality, and if American Jewish nostalgia adds religious dimensions to personal histories, then Jewish humor that touches nostalgia for childhood moments like a bar or bat mitzvah is doubly enmeshed in the reframing of American Jewish engagement with ritual.

As Ronald Grimes tells us, "because social density is so typical of ritual, ritual actions are usually *inter*actions."[23] Whether or not a child has much true choice in undergoing the bat or bar mitzvah, it is nonetheless quite interactive and it is she or he alone who is in front of the congregation, reading and speaking, regardless of how much her or his parents and tutors may have pushed and coached her or him. The child undergoing the bris has no agency at all (which of course is one of the major reasons there is an anticircumcision movement growing worldwide) and he is in no way interactive with either the mohel or *sandek* (the person who holds the baby, as depicted in the *Seinfeld* episode detailed below). The baby moves, but the bat or bar mitzvah girl or boy acts, because, as Grimes says, "human intention is what distinguishes action from movement."[24]

There could therefore be a potential psychological difference between what is being satirized when one uses the bris as one's canvas as opposed to using the bar mitzvah. Because a person does not remember his own bris, humor surrounding it more likely satirizes an entire religious system through the use of the bris in a synecdoche for the whole of Judaism. A man cannot have a memory of the bris being enacted upon his own body, so he is drawing not on personal memory but on cultural memory when he describes the scene. Even more so if a woman were to be the one describing the scene; she not only has no physical memory but also has no bodily stake in the conversation. On the other hand, when Jewish satirists use a bat or bar mitzvah they are more likely making a more personal or familial statement. They may bring stereotypes of the whole of American Judaism into the scene (as the ballooning cost and materialism of contemporary bar or bat mitzvahs is a popular focus of satiric barbs), but the template upon which they are building their satire is more likely to be their own personal and family history.

This chapter is going to look at twentieth-century Baby Boomer comedy, especially focusing on the rise of ritual as the focus of its satires. Examples will come from a much broader range of media and humor forms. This chapter will include a few well-known (and in some cases controversial) sketches from the long-running television series *Saturday Night Live*, as well as episodes from *Seinfeld* and a cameo by one of our Silent Generation exemplars to further illustrate the move from textual critique to visual and material. In the next chapter we will examine twenty-first century Generation X and Baby Boomer humor, which will illustrate the ways in which the Baby Boom generation has largely taken their cues from the generations that surround them.

Saturday Night Live

Saturday Night Live (*SNL*) premiered in 1975, and for all its many years has tried to be an equal opportunity offender. With its diverse cast and a large writing staff it reflects a melting pot more than any one cultural milieu.[25] Nevertheless, during its early years the writing staff was more than 50 percent Jewish and an occasional Jewish joke or reference would get thrown in, often as an "inside joke" for the writers more than for the audience. As Marilyn Susanne Miller, a writer on the show from its

78   Chapter 3

inception in 1975 until she left the show in 1978 said, "*Saturday Night Live* waved the wand and said 'Let there be Jews,' and there were Jews, on the network, on the show, openly discussing their lives in sketches, as writers and actors."[26]

In the early years of the show these references generally occupied the liminal space of the "fauxmercial," the fake commercials for which *SNL* became famous. One of the first fauxmercials was Jewish-themed, and became one of the most well-known sketches from *SNL*'s first few seasons. Unlike other, more controversial fauxmercials it was not defying stereotypes but was instead living up (down?) to them. In the first episode of the third season, airing on September 24, 1977, there was a fauxmercial for the fictional car "Royal Deluxe II." From Ricardo Montalban's famous 1975 Chrysler commercial with its "soft Corinthian leather" to the 1973 Pontiac Grand Am commercial featuring "scientists" beating the car with tire irons and bouncing it off of walls, the 1970s were known for car commercials that built brand loyalty on the backs of ridiculous claims and bizarre descriptions. The Royal Deluxe ad is a perfect parody of the larger body of 1970s car commercials, and as such that is the primary satiric motivation of the sketch. But there is a secondary satire taking place as well, one that both makes a Thing out of Jewish tradition and satirizes late twentieth-century Jewish upward mobility.

The sketch is only about ninety seconds long, so the specific content is not the most important feature. In brief, Dan Ackroyd narrates the ad and introduces the car: "A luxury name and a luxury ride at a middle-range price? Impossible? We've come to Temple Beth Shalom in Little Neck, New York, and asked Rabbi Mayer Taklas to circumcise eight-day-old Benjamin Cantor while riding in the back seat of the elegant Royal Deluxe II." They then drive the car over an especially pothole-filled road while the rabbi performs the circumcision. "Poifect," he exclaims when the job is done. Dan Ackroyd closes by telling the audience, "You may never have to perform a circumcision in the Royal Deluxe II, but if you do, we're sure you'll agree with Rabbi Taklas" and the rabbi responds, "That's a beautiful baby . . . and a beautiful car!"[27]

There are two primary issues for our purposes here: one has to do with the commercialization of the rabbi, and the second, larger issue has to do with what the sketch tells us about how ritual is being thought of and used. The first is related to the use of the rabbi as a spokesman and

The Baby Boom, Copycat Generation   79

expresses a sense of "selling out." The critique of Jewish materialism will come up in greater length later in this chapter, but whereas that satire is clearly meant as a critique, the writers of *SNL* are more concerned with tapping into the zeitgeist in order to generate laughs. They were banking on the non-Jewish percentage of their audience—their audience, mind you, not the American population as a whole—to know enough about Jewish stereotypes to recognize the humor. They kept the language purposely broad; they say "circumcision" twice, but never "bris"; they refer to Rabbi Taklas, but never call him a mohel. *SNL* draws about seven million viewers weekly, and has held steady with those numbers for about the last decade. That would put it, for comparison, just outside the top twenty-five prime time shows and with the all-important demographic of males aged 18–49 they score much higher: in the top ten of all TV shows.[28] So their audience is young, male, and largely urban and suburban. In the 1970s when the show premiered and when this ad ran, the total viewers may have been slightly lower, but their ratings share and demographic draw was the same if not higher. For that audience, "circumcision" rather than "bris" and "rabbi" rather than "mohel" were the correct choices.

But they also included code words for their Jewish viewers as well, inside jokes meant to speak to their knowledge base. We are told we are visiting "Temple Beth Shalom in Little Neck, New York." Beth Shalom is one of the most generic synagogue names you could invent, which many Jews would recognize. In fact, a quick scan of the Union for Reform Judaism's directory shows thirty-one Beth Shaloms in seventeen different states. *SNL* is aired to a live audience, and you can hear the laughter build halfway through that line. Up to that point there has been nothing about the commercial that was unlike any other car commercial, but when Dan Ackroyd says "Temple Beth Shalom in Little Neck" the audience has already begun laughing, because a significant portion of them now see where the joke is going. Thomas Hobbes called laughter "a kind of sudden glory," which D. H. Monro explains is used "in the sense of 'vainglory', or self-esteem."[29] The audience laughs because they recognize a reference that in and of itself may not be funny, but by laughing they show themselves to be superior, or a part of the in-crowd. It is an instinctual response and a way to make sure everyone knows you "get it."

80   Chapter 3

The sketch speaks to two audiences simultaneously, and the payoff of the joke also functions on multiple levels. The slapstick middle portion, in which the rabbi works on the baby while the car goes over potholes and even slams on the brakes to avoid a ball in the road, is meant to appeal to everyone. It is broad humor that you do not need to be Jewish to appreciate; all you have to do is know what circumcision is. The end of the joke is similar to the beginning in creating an insider/outsider dynamic. The rabbi's name, "Taklas," is probably a play on the Yiddish and Hebrew word *tachlis*, meaning the point, the heart of the matter. Also, the rabbi's strong Yiddish accent in his line ("Poifect!") brings to mind an image of Old World, traditional Judaism, despite this being most likely a Reform rabbi.[30] It is yet another example of Dan Ben-Amos's point that a particular relationship to and use of language is what makes Jewish humor distinctive. Furthermore, his final line, "That's a beautiful baby . . . and a beautiful car!" is the bow that wraps up the entire sketch. His loyalties are divided. His priority should be the baby, but he is equally enamored of the car.

In theory this sketch should be seen as offensive. Other Jewish-themed *SNL* sketches certainly were. Just three years later another fauxmercial lampooned not Jewish ritual but Jewish women. Gilda Radner (who was the mother in the "Royal Deluxe II" ad, and often served as *SNL*'s primary Jewish character actor) brought the character of Rhonda Weiss to *SNL* in a 1980 fauxmercial for "Jewess Jeans." The sketch plays on the growing trend of ham-fistedly multicultural clothing ads, perhaps best exemplified by early '80s ad campaigns of the United Colors of Benetton. In this ad Rhonda is front and center, in skintight, purple jeans and a black tube top. She has huge hair and even bigger sunglasses. As with the Royal Deluxe ad, the entire sketch is only about ninety seconds. The lyrics for the jingle are as follows:

> *Jewess Jeans*
> *They're skin-tight, they're out of sight*
> *Jewess Jeans*
> *She's got a lifestyle uniquely hers*
> *Europe, Nassau, wholesale furs.*
> *She's read every best-selling book*
> *She's a gourmet blender cook.*

The Baby Boom, Copycat Generation   81

She's got that Jewess look.
Jewess Jeans
they're uptight, alright
Jewess Jeans.
She shops the sales for designer clothes
She's got designer nails and a designer nose.
She's an American princess and a disco queen.
She's the Jewess in Jewess Jeans.
She's the Jewess in Jewess Jeans.

ANNOUNCER: You don't have to be Jewish.
RHONDA WEISS: But it wouldn't hurt.
ANNOUNCER: Jewess Jeans. Guaranteed to ride up.

There is almost no part of the Jewish American princess stereotype (JAP) upon which this doesn't hit.[31] The JAP, traditionally, is spoiled, and Rhonda traveling the world in furs evokes that image. Furthermore, while JAPs have the best education money can buy, they are uninterested in a sophisticated life of the mind, instead preferring populist escapism in the form of bestsellers. JAPs may have husbands and children, but they are not domestic and neither cook nor clean, hence Rhonda being a "gourmet blender cook." What could all be seen as, potentially, just good-natured fun, especially as Radner herself was Jewish, ends on an unexpectedly mean-spirited note with the admission that the jeans are "guaranteed to ride up." Most of the critiques of the JAP highlighted in the sketch are statements of fact (whether true or not), perhaps reframed in a negative light. The JAP travels. She likes nice things. She reads popular books. She doesn't cook much. "Guaranteed to ride up" has a different tone, as it hearkens to the imputation that the JAP has a proverbial stick up her ass. That is not a negative restatement of what is otherwise fact; that is an unquantifiable critique of her personality and who she is as a person. Without the last line the ad is mostly playful. With the last line it is biting.

Although there were those who enjoyed the sketch's send-up of the JAP stereotype, others found the portrayal of Jewish materialism and vanity offensive. In particular, people reacted poorly to the line "She shops the sales for designer clothes / She's got designer nails and a designer

Chapter 3

nose." The conflation, again, of liking nice things, which on its own is not a bad thing, with the kind of vanity that leads to unnecessary plastic surgery such as rhinoplasty struck some people as a bridge too far. Ann Beatts, another Jewish woman who wrote for *SNL* from its inception until 1980 described Radner as someone who drew comedy from her own experiences and her own pain, but who "refused to apologize for being beautiful at the same time."[32] There was a degree of defiance in the "Jewess Jeans" sketch that involved contravening the conventions of what female comics should say and do, which could have something to do with why the sketch was controversial. Rhonda Weiss, the character in question, danced in the middle of the screen while her multiethnic backup dancers performed behind, looking longingly at the fabulous-looking Weiss. The ad presents the Jewess as aspirational, but does it through the repetition of several longstanding antisemitic tropes. Radner may have seen the ad as reclaiming a space for a Jewish woman to be desirable and for a comedian to be beautiful, but the audience reacted poorly to what they saw as just another stereotypical JAP being played for laughs. The sketch was, perhaps, ahead of its time. It was not a critique of Jewish upward mobility à la Roth or Malamud, and as such it transgressed the Silent Generation's unspoken rule. It ridiculed not the evils of institutional religion, or the danger inherent in Jews turning their back on those Jews who make them uncomfortable. "Jewess Jeans" was really just ridiculing a particular type of contemporary Jewish personhood, and that did not sit as well with the audience as the safer mockery of rabbis and circumcisions had three years earlier.

This line in the sand became even clearer with the sketch "Jew, Not a Jew." This sketch pushed so close to the edge of acceptability that when it was first written the network vetoed it. It was written, originally, for Tom Hanks's first episode as host in 1985. But as Hanks recounts, "Standards and Practices wouldn't let it on the first time but, like, when I did the show, I don't know, either the fourth, fifth, sixth time, by that time there was no Standards and Practices, and so we were trying to figure out something to do. Then Al Franken said, 'well how about "Jew, Not a Jew?"' I said, 'you guys haven't done that yet?' And so we pulled out 'Jew, Not a Jew' and it killed."[33] Standards and Practice were the first line of defense against the FCC and external censorship and sanctions. Each network had their own, and they could veto any content for the shows on that network. In this case, in 1985, they thought "Jew, Not a Jew" was too offensive. But by Hanks's third time hosting (his memory was good, but slightly off) in 1988 NBC had retired their Standards and Practices department and the sketch was allowed to run.[34]

The sketch was a fictional game show in which two couples compete for points by correctly identifying which celebrities are Jewish. Hanks played the host, and the two couples were played by some of *SNL*'s non-Jewish cast members, Kevin Nealon, Victoria Jackson, Jan Hooks, and Phil Hartman. Al Franken, who wrote the sketch, was the only Jewish performer in the sketch and that as only the unseen narrator. When Franken introduces the show he calls it, "The game all Americans love to play: 'Jew, Not a Jew.'" Although it is a running joke in Jewish circles that Jews have always played this game (think of one version of Adam Sandler's "Chanukah Song," which claims, "Bruce Springsteen isn't Jewish / But my mother thinks he is"), the idea that it is actually a generic American pastime to sit around discussing which celebrities are Jews is funny, and then slightly unsettling. The contestants all identify themselves by religion, telling the host they are "hardcore Protestant" descendants of French Huguenots, or half Irish Catholic, half Swedish Lutheran. The simultaneous "wink" element of the sketch, signaling to Jewish viewers that Franken and the other writers know about the Jewish tendency to catalog famous Jews, is mitigated by the sense that it is rarely a good thing when non-Jews are also keeping track of who is and is not Jewish.

The results of the game are mostly in the contestants' favor. They, like so many others, incorrectly guess Penny Marshall is Jewish, but they are correct that both Michael Landon and Ed Koch are. The announcer offers a bonus round to the viewing audience where "You Make the Call," and introduces Sandy Koufax as the final query. Hanks believed the sketch "killed," but the reception was much more mixed. Brandon Tartikoff was president of NBC when the sketch aired and called it "the sketch that gave him the most grief."[35] Apparently the phones rang off the hook on Sunday with complaints about it, including one call Tartikoff fielded from his mother, who called it "the most anti-Semitic thing I've ever seen."[36] Al Franken recalled that the Monday after the sketch aired he got a call from the Anti-Defamation League (ADL). When Franken explained the sketch the agent from the ADL laughed, but the network still received a formal complaint letter a few weeks later, and when

84   Chapter 3

Franken called the man back to ask why he still sent the letter, the man explained that people were offended, and he was doing his job.[37]

As with "Jewess Jeans," "Jew, Not a Jew" sat poorly with a large enough portion of the audience to cause trouble for the network. *SNL*'s target audience might be young people, but it was unlikely that 18-year-olds make calls to the ADL to complain about antisemitism in television sketches. So even as late as 1988, when Gen X was beginning to come into their own, it was still Baby Boom writers and Baby Boom (or even Silent Generation) audience members fighting over which satires of Jewish life were okay ("Royal Deluxe II") and which were not okay ("Jewess Jeans") or *really* not okay ("Jew, Not a Jew"). The fact that "Royal Deluxe" was not considered offensive speaks to an underlying issue at play in all these satires. The second half of the twentieth century saw a shifting sense of what it meant to be Jewish in America. In an earlier time a nationally televised sketch turning a rabbi into a car shill of questionable ethics would have been seen as poor taste at best. But by the late twentieth century, attitudes toward what could safely be satirized changed, and while *Saturday Night Live* has tended to be at the leading edge, pushing the boundaries of what is acceptable, the reaction to this sketch shows it as inbounds.

As we have seen time and again, throughout this period Judaism was increasingly set aside and made into a Thing. So while "Jewess Jeans," with its critique of Jewish social life and moral standards, is threatening, challenging, and upsetting, and "Jew, Not a Jew" is downright antisemitic to large numbers of viewers, an opportunistic and profit-motivated rabbi is largely neither: the rabbi with his Old World accent stands for religious traditions and vestiges of a life that was quickly being abandoned; lampooning him does not hit home. All Jews have culture, after all, but not all attend synagogue or care much about the way the nation as a whole feels about rabbis. Making fun of *Jews*, as "Jewess Jeans" seemed to, or "outing" Jews as sport, is going to ruffle some feathers. But making fun of *Judaism* goes unremarked, at least in 1977. This demonstrates the generational difference in attitudes toward satirizing Judaism. The ways in which Baby Boom comedians (and even more so, audiences) held on to Silent Generation attitudes about what was safe to mock and what was not are also on display in one of the most well known exemplars of Jewish humor, *Seinfeld*.

Seinfeld

Seinfeld is, of course, one of the quintessential TV shows of the 1990s and is to TV what Woody Allen is to movies, namely, the first thing many people think of when you say "Jewish humor." Ironically, however, *Seinfeld* not only rarely makes reference to religion at all, but the writers and performers purposely play fast and loose with our assumptions about Jewish characters. Based on the sheer quantity written about *Seinfeld* and Judaism as compared to other shows, one might assume that it was a show about Jews, at least.[38] In reality, however, of the main characters only Jerry himself is actually Jewish. Despite George being written as a stereotypically Jewish character (and his parents being written and performed as *very* Jewish) and Elaine being often seen as a "Jewish American Princess type," neither character is Jewish. Jason Alexander and Julia Louis-Dreyfus, who play George and Elaine, are Jewish (Alexander) or from historically Jewish families (Louis-Dreyfus).[39] The inspirations for the characters, according to the writers, were Carol Leifer (a comedian and one of the writers for the show) and Jason Alexander himself, both Jews. Jeffrey Shandler describes the characters as, "crypto-Jews who were deliberately, playfully, and transparently disguised as something else," which aligns with the ways the writers of the series have spoken of the fun they had in creating non-Jewish characters and then making them as Jewish as possible.[40] There has been debate over whether, perhaps, George's mother is Jewish, although when Estelle Harris (the actress who plays Mrs. Costanza) asked the show's cocreator and writer Larry David, his response to her was, "What do you care?" Vincent Brook has gone on record asserting that, "diegetically speaking, George is manifestly non-Jewish,"[41] although Jarrod Tanny points out that Mrs. Costanza refuses to ride in German cars, which is much more of a nod to post-Holocaust Jews than to Italians. There is some question as to whether Kramer is Jewish, but if he is, it is never mentioned.[42] And he is never specified as *not* Jewish. So it is with their tongue firmly in their cheeks that the writers set out to make the most Jewish non-Jews on television.

Nathan Abrams, in *The New Jew in Film* discusses the ways that "Jews" were coded on screen, at least through *Seinfeld*'s era. He says representations of Jews were "racialized and anti-Semitic; invisible or nonexistent; idealized, de-Judainized and de-Semitized; often replaced by the Gentile mimicking the Jew; ethnicized, anxious, and neurotic; or victimized and humiliated. Furthermore . . . [there] were certain recurring stereotypical tics . . . including fast-talking intelligence, physical weakness, small stature, and sexual preference for the blonde *shiksa*."[43] The characters on Seinfeld tick almost every box, especially the "Gentile mimicking the Jew," which is what George and Elaine could be seen as doing, though the Jewishness of Alexander and family history of Louis-Dreyfuss make them almost Jews mimicking gentiles mimicking Jews.

This is a phenomenon that Vincent Brook identifies as "perceptually Jewish" characters, which he contrasts with "conceptually Jewish" characters.[44] Conceptually Jewish characters are those who are Jewish by design, but that fact may seldom or even never come up in the show itself. Examples include Monica and Rachel from *Friends* or Fran on *The Nanny*.[45] The opposite of this are characters who are "perceptually Jewish," which means that the audience reads them as Jewish, but they actually are not. George and Elaine are both examples of this, and it is by no means accidental. Jerry Seinfeld, Larry David, and Larry Charles, all of whom are Jewish, were the head writers and producers of *Seinfeld* and knew exactly what they were doing in making the religious identity of their characters so seemingly clear, but in reality quite muddy. This makes those instances in which the show did address religion explicitly somewhat chaotic, which was their goal, because the audience would be faced with settings and situations that are dissonant with their (usually false) understandings of who the characters are.

One episode in which the writers of *Seinfeld* signaled this identity slippage was "The Yada Yada," which revolves around Jerry's dentist, Tim Whatley, converting to Judaism. Within a day Dr. Whatley is telling Jewish jokes because he claims "I am a Jew, I can tell these jokes," and this bothers Jerry, who thinks he only converted for the jokes. Dr. Whatley also continues to tell Catholic jokes, because he used to be a Catholic. When Jerry goes to Dr. Whatley's priest to complain, the priest asks Jerry if this behavior offends him "as a Jewish person," to which Jerry responds, "No, it offends me as a comedian!" At the end of the day, *that* is Jerry's primary identity marker and the thing that, when threatened, causes him to lash out. It is not his Jewishness, but his "comicness" that he needs to defend and protect.

This take on identity was never more clearly on display than in the episode "The Bris." It was the fifth episode of *Seinfeld*'s fifth season, originally airing October 14, 1993. In this episode Jerry and Elaine are made godparents to the newborn son of their friends Stan and Myra. This, they are told, primarily entails taking roles in Stephen's bris in eight days.[46] Elaine is to choose the mohel, while Jerry will be the *sandek*, holding baby Stephen during the ritual. Although the episode never mentions the specifics of this role, it actually portrays a very traditional scenario. The *sandek* who holds the baby is traditionally a respected Jewish male, and Jerry is apparently liked by this couple much more than he likes them in return. And though it is not referred to in the episode, an empty chair has been set next to the one in which Jerry sits for the ritual, which traditional Jews often do to leave a place for the Prophet Elijah, should he return during the ceremony. Just using the words "bris" and "mohel" shows that Larry Charles, the primary writer for this episode, was going for more insider jokes than the *SNL* writing staff had been. *Seinfeld* is a show about New York, and New York is the most Jewish city in the United States. So, is Charles speaking to Jews? To New Yorkers? To New Yorkers now living in Los Angeles, as the cast and crew of the show were?[47] To people who want to be New Yorkers? In truth, it was probably a combination of all of these.

Seinfeld premiered in the late '80s, so the work Seinfeld, Larry David, and Larry Charles did on the show, especially early on, feels more in line with the attitudes and treatment of religion we have seen from the Silent Generation satirists than with those of Gen X. *Seinfeld* never really broke out of that, so by the end there were things about the show and the characters that began to feel dated or anachronistic, such as the much-maligned finale. The characters on the show were often described as narcissistic or unlikeable and the finale demonstrated that there had been no growth for any of them across nine seasons and that the four main characters were just as shallow and unlikeable at the end as they were at the beginning. That may be an indication that the show started with certain themes and never evolved past them, because the writers have definitely evolved in their other projects. Both Larry David and Larry Charles have shifted dramatically away from "Baby Boomers following Silent Generation lead" to "Baby Boomers following Gen X lead." Charles went on to direct Bill Maher's antireligion documentary *Religulous* and to write for Larry David's *Curb Your Enthusiasm*, HBO's *Entourage*, and Sasha Baron-Cohen's film *Borat*, all of which exhibit an attitude toward Jews

88   Chapter 3

and Judaism that is much more aligned with twenty-first century, contemporary sensibilities. In "The Bris," however, we clearly see the conflict at work as traditional details of the ritual are included, even when they are not referenced and do not really need to be there, while at the same time the ritual goes all wrong. "You try to perform antiquated, barbaric rituals, you have to expect to get terrible results," the episode seems to say.

One of the most interesting features of the episode is the role of Kramer. Though character development was never *Seinfeld's* primary goal, Cosmo Kramer is still notably less well rounded than the other characters. He is manic, unpredictable, inappropriate, and strange. He is based on Kenny Kramer, a Jewish comic, but played by Michael Richards, a non-Jewish actor.[48] Like most of the characters on *Seinfeld*, Kramer is (sort of) perceptually Jewish and yet he vocally and vehemently speaks against the ritual circumcision of baby Stephen throughout the episode. He calls it outdated, comparing it to other ancient rituals like human sacrifice. He calls it "a barbaric ritual," claims the argument that circumcision is hygienic is a "myth," argues that the ritual "cuts off a piece of [Stephen's] manhood," and eventually tries to steal and run away with the baby before the mohel can perform the deed.[49] The best the opposition can muster is Jerry's argument that it is an ancient ritual (which prompted the human sacrifice comparison) and the mohel's announcement that everyone has gathered to witness "a sacred, ancient ceremony symbolizing the covenant between God and Abraham. Or something." Kramer speaks passionately against the alleged barbarism of circumcision, while the traditional camp can only come up with "or something." It is the hallmark of a calcified tradition that one cannot defend it with a convincing argument beyond "tradition." Kramer seems to have the moral high ground here.

In fact, there is a throwaway line toward the end of the episode that further indicates that the writers' views are more in line with Kramer's than Jerry's. The circumcision does not go off without a hitch (apparently because Jerry "flinched," though we do not see it happen) and Jerry's finger gets cut badly enough to require stitches. As George and Elaine drive him to the hospital, Jerry whines about his finger from the backseat, complaining about the mohel, the blood, that it is his "phone finger," and at one point saying, "I am going to need stitches; I'll be deformed!" The

The Baby Boom, Copycat Generation   89

line goes by without comment, but when viewed as part of the dispute about circumcision it is difficult not to see it as ironic; Jerry pooh-poohed Kramer's argument against the barbarity of circumcision, but is aghast that his finger might be "deformed" in the process.

The mohel himself is a complete caricature. He is jumpy, nervous, apparently hates crying babies, and delivers all his lines like Rodney Dangerfield, only hysterical and shrill. Elaine claims he came "highly recommended," but it is difficult to see how, since he screams at everyone present, goes into an apoplectic fit over where Elaine placed her wine glass, and ultimately cuts Jerry along with Stephen. He and the rabbi from the *SNL* ad are cut from similar cloth in that both reduce what should be a deeply meaningful ritual into a socially tone-deaf farce. And yet, as with the *SNL* ad, there was really no negative response to the episode. In fact, *Seinfeld* rarely if ever got criticized for its treatment of religion.[50] It is here that the Baby Boom begins to resemble Gen X. Apparently, by this time more American Jews were willing to laugh at themselves in a way they were not even five years earlier when "Jew, Not a Jew" caused such an uproar. This episode makes a strong case for why Bill Maher would have chosen Larry Charles as the director for his anti-religion film. But *Seinfeld* was so embraced by the Jewish community for setting off the renaissance of Jewish characters on prime time TV that during its original run it could almost do no wrong.

In fact, later in the fifth season there is a two-part episode called "The Raincoats." The plotline involves the fallout that comes from Jerry's being caught making out with his girlfriend Rachel during *Schindler's List*. These episodes perfectly illustrate the process of Baby Boomers tipping from their early similarities to the Silent Generation toward their later similarities to Gen X. On the surface everyone's horror that Jerry could be so callous as to become amorous during a movie as somber and serious as *Schindler's List* mimics the precise criticism of assimilated American Jews Roth and Malamud leveled. Jerry, like Roth's Jews of Woodenton or Malamud's Cohen was more concerned with his own needs and wants than the suffering of Jewish victims of antisemitism. Unlike those critiques, however, it really is not the protagonist that is the sole source of scorn here, it is also Jerry and Rachel's parents and their overreactions that are the butt of the joke. In this instance both Malamud's Cohen (Jerry) *and* Schwartz (the parents) are made to seem

90   Chapter 3

ridiculous. The Holocaust is the topic most likely to move the boundary of acceptability back and forth, even well into the twenty-first century. "The Soup Nazi" episode (season 7, episode 6) elicited an angry response from Abraham Foxman at the Anti-Defamation League for making light of Nazis, and more than twenty years later Larry David's *Saturday Night Live* cold open containing jokes about picking up women in concentration camps caused no small uproar.[51] For Baby Boomers Holocaust jokes still fall into a gray area.

The Silent Generation largely protected the Jewish people, and Gen X does not. The Baby Boom generation at times did both and neither. They started their careers in the shadow of the Eichmann trial, so continuing the Silent Generation's approach of skewering organized religion to protect the Jewish people seemed logical. But the more time that went by, the more they seemed to agree with the up-and-coming Gen X comedians who were all for tearing down tribalism in the interest of multicultural harmony. The Baby Boomers continued the depiction of religious ritual as useless while also opening up the door to satirize Jews as people.[52]

4
The Turn of the Century

[A pilot] flew the Newark to Palm Beach route, right? So it's December twenty-third, and as they touch down in Florida, one of the flight attendants takes the microphone and delivers her standard landing speech. "Please remain seated until the FASTEN SEAT BELT sign has been turned off and be careful when opening the overhead bins. We'd like to wish you a merry Christmas and, to those of you already standing, happy Hanukkah."

—David Sedaris

Two old Jewish women sit down at a local restaurant to catch the early bird special. Their waiter takes their orders, brings out the food, and then goes to wait on a different table. Five minutes later, he decides to check in on the two women. He comes up to their table, and with a bright and chipper smile asks: "Good evening ladies, is *anything* alright?"

—Anonymous joke

Although Baby Boom humor started out resembling that of the Silent Generation, by the turn of the millennium they had largely come under the sway of Generation X. Generation X is known for being the Brat Pack generation—angry and edgy while simultaneously nihilistic and disengaged. On the whole they are much more interested in directing their barbs at the social flaws of the Jewish community and less in making organized religion a topic of ridicule. Silent Generation humorists like Woody Allen saved their harshest criticisms for the trappings of religion while, as we noted, showing reticence to ridicule the concept of Jewishness. Even something that would seem like an exception, such as the way Philip Roth and Bernard Malamud cast aspersions on the comfortable, bourgeois lives of assimilated Jews, suggested a desire to see the

92   Chapter 4

Jewish community survive. Authors like Roth and Malamud did turn a very critical eye on the Jewish people, in part for turning their back on other Jewish people, buying into the American Dream at the expense of their European coreligionists. In the twenty-first century, however, that instinctive fear of painting "the Jews" in a bad light has faded, and there is much more specific criticism aimed at both individual people and the Jewish community as a whole.

Following Gen X's lead, Baby Boom comedians switched from the mentality that would "discard Judaism in order to save the Jews," which we've identified as dominating American Jewish humor from the 1950s on, to a mode in which Jews, both individually and as a people, were fair game while religion and tradition were newly deemed valuable. I chose the epigraphs for this chapter in particular because they both highlight that shift. In part this shift stems from time and distance. Somewhere in the late 1990s there was a palpable change in attitudes toward the Holocaust. Holocaust jokes are still controversial, and still considered to be in poor taste by many, but by the '90s there were now enough people driving popular culture who had no real, personal connection to the Holocaust that, for example, *Life Is Beautiful* could win an Oscar in 1997. Many people found (and still find) that movie's plotline, which reduces the Holocaust to a game, to be both unfunny and distasteful, especially as the filmmaker is not Jewish. However, the time had passed when that negative response was enough to keep the film from being successful. And once the Holocaust was no longer absolutely sacrosanct, it became possible to openly mock Jews *as* Jews without appearing to invite antisemitism and anti-Jewish violence. Suddenly it is okay for even non-Jews, like David Sedaris, to make jokes that are essentially saying, "Jews are ridiculous, right?"

In this chapter we will look at twenty-first century humor from both Generation X comedians and the Baby Boomers working with them. This will include Jennifer Westfeldt's film *Kissing Jessica Stein*, Jonathan Tropper's novel *This Is Where I Leave You*, and a rare literary parody of the type we saw in chapter 1, "Sister Hills," by Nathan Englander. We will use those texts to better understand a side-by-side comparison of two Coen brothers films, *The Big Lebowski* and *A Serious Man*. The chapter will conclude by looking at Larry David's ongoing, absurdist self-portrait, *Curb Your Enthusiasm*, as an example of a Baby Boomer who seems excited to now have permission to make Jews look ridiculous, but is less concerned with the reclamation of the power of ritual that is happening all around him. Arguably, that lacuna is what makes his show feel dated at times, even though it is set in the present day.

Kissing Jessica Stein

Jennifer Westfeldt, born in Connecticut in 1970, is Jewish on her mother's side and from Swedish nobility on her father's, and though she was raised Jewish and identifies as Jewish, she rarely if ever speaks about her feelings toward Judaism or her Jewish identity. She writes herself non-Jewish roles as often as Jewish ones, but in most of her scripts she includes aspects of interfaith relationships, even when she is portraying the non-Jewish half. As a writer she tries to show the struggles and foibles of everyday Jews, which for many (if not most) means involvement in interfaith relationships. Although Westfeldt's films generally take place in New York City, she is more likely to write a token Jewish character into her films and leave the majority of the characters to be, by exclusion, generic American civil religionists. The New York Westfeldt inhabits is centered on places like Greenwich Village or SoHo, areas known for being young, artsy, bohemian, but not necessarily Jewish. Even before we analyze Westfeldt's treatment of Jews and Jewish rituals, the very picture of what New York City looks and sounds like is different in her films than it was for the Silent Generation in the 1970s and 1980s.

Because Westfeldt does not speak publicly about her private life in anything but the most general terms, it is only through her writing that we can gain an understanding of her relationship to Judaism. Judaism for Westfeldt seems to be a useful object, but very differently deployed than for the older comedians. For all her similarities to someone like Allen (to whom she is often compared) as a filmmaker, she is still very clearly of her generation when it comes to imbuing Judaism with use and function, reobjectifying and making it no longer a useless Thing. Westfeldt, as part of Generation X, is responding to the Judaism she inherited, which was already shaped and changed by the Silent and Baby Boom generations, and she is adjusting it to what she believes modern Jews need and want.

Westfeldt is among those who grew up with the sociological and psychological concept of "role conflict," a term rarely encountered before

94   Chapter 4

the 1980s. Role conflict means that you are constantly balancing your multiple identities.[1] At home you may be a wife or a mother. At work you supervise some people and are subordinate to others. You are a child to your parents and a parent to your children. In every different social interaction, in every different group, your behavior changes, from your language and syntax to your body language and mode of dress. The building blocks for the ideas of "intersectionality" or "code switching" are here, but in Westfeldt's work the conflict seems to be less foundational than intersectional identities may be, and more based on interpersonal interactions. To someone like Westfeldt a character who acted the same way at all time with all people would seem two-dimensional and not realistic. The Woody Allen model of Jews who are so Jewy that they cannot ever lead with any other part of their personality doesn't fully work in Westfeldt's New York. So her characters express their Jewishness (and sometimes their Judaism) differently and at different times than those of the satirists who came before her.

Westfeldt first gained major notoriety with the film *Kissing Jessica Stein*, which she cowrote with her costar Heather Jurgensen. It is based on their off-Broadway play *Lipschtick*, which, like the movie, is an updated "sex and the single girl" type of work, following the dating foibles and failures of a couple of hip young Manhattan professionals.[2] Westfeldt's Jessica and Jurgensen's Helen find each other through the personal ads (already a dated model, despite this being a twenty-first-century film), and though neither has previously dated a woman, they hit it off and begin a relationship. It is through Westfeldt's treatment of Jessica and her family that we can glean some information about how she utilizes—and renormalizes—Judaism in her writing.

The Jewish women in this film say a great deal about Westfeldt's stance on the traditional role of Jewish women in comedy. The characters are "interesting and not stereotypical."[3] Traditionally there are two things a Jewish woman can be: "the selfless, self-abnegating, overbearing, neurotic Jewish Mother or the materialistic Jewish American Princess (JAP)." A third option is really just a subset of the JAP, "the Jewess [who] is a *zaftig*, awkward, and neurotic brunette, the female counterpart to the *schlemiel*."[4] Jessica is a new breed of JAP. Westfeldt seems unable to do away with the archetype entirely, but she is willing to explore different dimensions of the JAP. According to Nathan Abrams, Jessica is:

A neurotic, New York Jewish princess who . . . is blind to her own privilege . . . Jessica's *physiognomic* Jewishness is also not immediately apparent. At the same time, she is highly intellectual and defined not just by her ethnicity. The film opens in synagogue, where Jessica is seated between her *kvetching* mother and grandmother during the Yom Kippur service. As the women's voices rise in pitch Jessica exasperatedly shouts "Would you shut up? I'm atoning." As Michele Byers states, "this opening positions Jessica as a new kind of JAP, one who is fluent in a discourse of moral value seen to be absent from, and unknown to, her foremothers."[5]

The character of Jessica's best friend, Joan, comes the closest to simply reinforcing old misogynistic stock characters. Though one review said that the character stayed "just the right side of caricature," Westfeldt walks a very fine line.[6] Joan is the ugly duckling, the awkward, unattractive sidekick to the pretty but vapid JAP. What saves Joan from being the same tired character (in addition to Jackie Hoffman's particularly good performance) is that Joan breaks the mold by being, instead of sexless, an enthusiastically sexual creature. First of all she is pregnant, which immediately sets her apart from Jessica and from the typical JAP. Despite there being a direct, biological connection between the JAP and her Jewish Mother, the JAP cannot ever truly become a Jewish Mother; her upbringing and socioeconomic status are too different.[7] Therefore, the typical JAP (and Jessica) is frigid, while Joan, in addition to reproducing, is actually excited about sex. In one scene, Joan "proclaims herself 'impressed' that Jessica is sleeping with a partner of the same sex," demonstrating that Joan sees sex as a positive thing.[8]

Westfeldt seems to put the most work into rehabilitating the role of the Jewish mother. Westfeldt has some experience with having a Jewish mother herself, so despite the Jewish mother being one of comedy's lowest hanging fruits Westfeldt actually treats that character remarkably well. The Jewish mother may have been one of the first aspects of Jewishness to be Thingified, in that she became very early on something that was undesirable, and she therefore calcified. As one critic put it, however, Westfeldt "avoided the temptation to turn Jessica Stein's Jewish mother into a stereotypical screaming Jewish mother who freaks when her daughter has a lesbian affair with a non-Jew. Rather, the mother was

96   Chapter 4

a multi-dimensional person who sensitively tried to understand what her daughter was going through."[9] Tovah Feldshuh's performance as Judy was universally praised, and described as "achingly poignant" by one reviewer.[10] Westfeldt wrote the role especially for Feldshuh, so she was always the embodiment of what Westfeldt felt she wanted to portray a Jewish mother to be.[11] Judy is a model of what Abrams calls "the New Jewish Mother," one who loves her children unconditionally (and equally) no matter what life choices they make.

One of the most insidious aspects of the JAP and Jewish mother stereotypes has been the difficulty in their relationship. The Jewish mother is seen, traditionally, to favor her sons, and many Jewish mother jokes involve her obsessive pampering and blind worship of her son. Her daughter, on the other hand, was more often a target of her scorn and was seen to be more of a "daddy's girl." Just the fact that the mother-daughter relationship in *Kissing Jessica Stein* is overall positive and Judy does not seem to prefer Jessica's brother is a major step toward dismantling the Jewish mother stigma.

For all the effort Westfeldt made to rehabilitate the images of Jewish best friends and mothers, her own character may have been more problematic and was less well received. She seemed to be trying to make Jessica into the new breed of "gentle JAPs" who are "explicitly identified as smart. . . . [She] is professional, economically comfortable, middle class, well to do, and her parents and family live in suburban affluence."[12] These things are all true of Jessica, but where the character appears to have fallen short is in "reclaiming Woody Allen territory and swapping the roles of the male *schlemiel* and the JAP."[13] This caused the character of Jessica to be referred to as "a highly neurotic single," the "neurotic Jewish heroine," and a "Jewish Ally McBeal."[14] In her attempt to make Jessica something other than the traditional JAP, Westfeldt instead made her so much like her male schlemiel counterpart that she lost some dimensionality. If the JAP is a Thing the way the Jewish mother is, then Westfeldt may have been trying to reverse the Thingification process as she undid the stereotype. If, however, that was her intention it was not terribly successful. As it turned out, it was not in the reobjectifying of JAPs that Westfeldt exceled, but in the reobjectifying of Judaism.[15]

If the remaking of Jewish stereotypes was the film's only aspect of Jewish identity, it would be questionable whether the film would fall under the purview of this study. There is, however, a deeper analysis of what it means to be a Jew in twenty-first century America going on, making it a natural analog to many of the Silent Generation humorists. There is a different sort of irreverence toward Judaism in *Kissing Jessica Stein* than in, for example, Joseph Heller's work. Westfeldt is painting a word picture of what it means to be a single Jewish woman in modern day New York. To Westfeldt, what it means is that you have, first and foremost, a mother and a grandmother breathing down your neck to find a nice Jewish boy and get married. You have to be wise-cracking and neurotic, simultaneously well dressed and awkward. And finally you have a social circle full of both nominal Jews and non-Jews (or perhaps perceptual and conceptual Jews), all of whom express Jewish stereotypes more than they embody Jewish practice. Westfeldt's work, on the surface, is exactly what critics like Allen Guttmann were talking about when they argued that this type of comedy was not actually Jewish at all; it was simply done by Jews.

When one looks a little deeper at the film, however, one finds that this is not strictly true. The film opens with the Stein family at synagogue for Yom Kippur. Though the dialogue is light-hearted, the liturgy is rendered in its traditional form and it is the Steins who are being mocked, not the Judaism. Similarly, when the family gathers for Shabbat dinner at the Stein home in Scarsdale, Jessica sings the *Kiddush*, her coworker Josh sings a lovely *Motzi*, and despite the rapid-fire, almost farcical scene happening around the table at the moment when the blessings are being sung, everything else stops, and all attention is focused on the prayer. This direct inversion of the Silent Generation's patterns, as we will see, is a feature of Generation X humor and satire. Throw Jews under the bus if you please, but save a little respect for Judaism.

In synagogue, at Shabbat dinner, and at Jessica's brother's wedding, tallits and yarmulkes abound. The clothing that was such a problem in Roth's Woodenton and in the Cohen apartment Malamud created is now on display as a part of a normal American Jewish life. It was important to Westfeldt that the Stein family be proudly and observantly Jewish because that orientation guides the development of the characters, but every time there was an easy joke opportunity to use the family's Jewish identity as a punchline, she pulled back. In fact, at the pivotal moment at the rehearsal dinner when Jessica appears to be struggling with how

98   Chapter 4

to finally tell her mother about Helen, rather than falling back on stereotyped reactions her mother simply chokes back her tears and tells Jessica
"I think she's a very nice girl," not making Jessica say the words at all.
This scene is highlighted in many of the discussions of the film, having
been called both "poignant but unsentimental," as well as an especially
"memorable scene."[16] Overcoming stereotypes is, of course, a worthy goal
on its own. However, Westfeldt's desire to overcome stereotypes *through*
religious rituals and liturgical events sets it apart as being concerned
with a religious Jewish identity above and beyond any ethnic or cultural
Jewishness. Here Judaism very much has a use, which makes it the furthest thing from a Thing. This is the renormalization of Jewish identity
that Westfeldt is attempting, and this is what Rachel Adler had in mind
when she said that comedy provides, "a continuous movement towards
the transformation of the audience's moral universe, a practical vision
of how we are going to get from here to there."[17] Westfeldt is remaking
the audience's universe by staking a claim to the idea that the funniest
thing about Jews can actually be something *other* than Judaism. What a
concept.

Kissing Jessica Stein does double duty. Westfeldt wove traditional
Jewish elements into her screenplay not as a joke, but as the humanizing
antidote to the joke. When the stereotypes of young New York become
almost overbearing, she reverts to a moment of quiet prayer or piety to
remind the viewer that these are real people, not just walking joke facto-
ries. In dramatic works we are familiar with the concept of "comic relief."
Writers have known for centuries that an audience cannot feel pathos
for hours on end; they eventually grow numb and the denouement of
the drama loses its punch. So, comic relief: include a comic scene, or
song, or character to break up the dramatic action, allowing the audience to breathe before the final push. Comedy works similarly. It is hard
to maintain laughter for hours on end. Stand-up comedy sets are rarely
more than an hour long. So Westfeldt uses internal, personal moments
of religious ritual as a sort of "dramatic relief," the pause that refreshes.
She gives the audience a chance to catch their breath before the next
farcical scene. Jessica is not displaying her Jewishness at all times with all
people, but at the same time, if you removed all the prayers and liturgical
moments from the film, you would still have something generally identifiable as "Jewish humor" because of Jessica's neuroses, sarcasm, and verbal

wit. This is what Mel Brooks meant when he said Jewish humor was just urban, just New York, and this is the type of humor Guttman had in mind when he said there was no religion in Jewish humor. That humor, however, is not all there is to the film. Westfeldt understood that the film needed the religious aspects to save it from being precisely the kind of caricature Guttmann would have accused it of being.

This Is Where I Leave You

Jonathan Tropper was (like Westfeldt) born in 1970. He grew up in an Orthodox family from Riverside in the Bronx and attended Yeshiva University (which is affiliated with Orthodox Judaism) as an undergraduate. He worked in the jewelry industry for several years, writing in his free time until he landed a publishing contract. He speaks even less about his Jewish upbringing than Westfeldt does, yet he also encodes it much more strongly into his writing. His 2009 novel *This Is Where I Leave You* demonstrates an attitude toward Jewish ritual similar to the one seen in *Kissing Jessica Stein*. It is also an example of the ways in which humor about Jewish rituals is become more universalized. Circumcision jokes are unlikely to disappear entirely, but it is nevertheless true that they traditionally sprang from an androcentric view of Judaism. Women were included in God's covenant with Abraham only insofar as they married men and gave birth to boys. Their inability to undergo circumcision meant they were only covenant-adjacent. Death, on the other hand, comes for us all. Nearly every culture on Earth has ceremonies marking death. Sometimes they are very simple, like sailors saying a few words before dropping a body over the side of a ship. Some are extremely complex, like the funerals of the Toraja people of Indonesia, which can last weeks and are so expensive that it sometimes takes years after a person has died to raise the funds necessary to perform the funeral.[18] Sometimes the funeral is, at least in part, about the journey the deceased is making. Not all cultures believe in an afterlife, however, or believe in an afterlife that can be influenced by the funeral rite itself, in which case the death rites may not be entirely for the deceased and may be primarily for the community.

This is borne out by the fact that a number of cultures include humor in their funeral rites.[19] You can only mourn for so long before it begins to

100   Chapter 4

lose meaning. If too much time passes between death and the funeral, the ritual must reengage the mourner to avoid being what ritual theorist Tom Driver calls "pro forma, something everybody does at times like this, so hold your breath and go through with it. The ceremony is not in the least transforming and [the mourner] knows she will have to deal with her grief some other way."[20] Comic relief exists because of a basic human need to take breaks from long periods of strong emotion. Whether sadness, joy, terror, or excitement, after a point you become numb to that emotion, which is not necessarily the same as "getting over" whatever the impetus for the emotion was. Therefore, these funeral rituals, in deed if not in word, acknowledge that they are for the living, for the mourners, as much if not more than they are for the dead.

This is very much the case for Jewish funeral rites specifically. Jewish funerary practices, unlike those mentioned above, do not include any elements of humor or light-heartedness. They are actually quite somber. Yet funerary and mourning practices can become sources of humor almost as much as circumcisions and *bar/bat/b'nai mitzvot*.

For seven days after the funeral the family of the deceased "sits shiva." Perhaps because this lasts so much longer than the funeral, perhaps because it is so unique to Judaism, or perhaps because it traps a bunch of emotional people together for a long period, sitting shiva is a favorite topic for jokes and humor.[21] *This Is Where I Leave You* is essentially a novel about the Foxman family's shiva.[22] There are satires based around funerals, but there are nevertheless many fewer funerals in Jewish satire than circumcisions or bar and bat mitzvahs. Perhaps this has something to do with Gail Hamner's earlier point that nostalgia feeds ritual. There is little nostalgia to be found with funerals. By definition you cannot remember your own, even in the abstract, whereas one can think back on a circumcision they do not actually remember. Neither is there in most people a desire to think back on other funerals they have attended. If there is less nostalgia available to feed the funeral ritual, then that could make it less tangible, more ephemeral, and therefore more difficult to work with as a satiric canvas.

This Is Where I Leave You was Tropper's fifth novel. It takes place, as most of his writing does, in a fictionalized version of Westchester County, New York. Tropper uses the towns and experiences of his childhood as a backdrop to his writing, but his books (and especially his young, male protagonists) are not author analogs. According to Tropper, "Fiction is making things up. I'm a fiction writer and my whole gift is being able to create something that sounds honest and authentic. The fact that I'd only be able to pick from my own life is ignorant."[23] So the Foxmans are not the Troppers, but the fictional Westchester County nevertheless rings true to many readers because it is based on the real Westchester County. In *This Is Where I Leave You*, Tropper's approach to Jews and Judaism is very similar to that of other Gen X humorists.

"Dad's dead." This is the first sentence of the novel, like a modern-day "Jacob Marley was dead to begin with." The plot is thin: Mort Foxman has died, and his dying wish (to the shock of everyone) was that his family sit shiva for him. So, in typical family farce style, in troop a series of Foxmans, each more dysfunctional than the last. The reader then spends the better part of four hundred pages being uncomfortable as people say terrible things to each other. It is part rom-com, part family saga, part midlife coming-of-age, but what is important here is that the presence of the shiva in the story is more than a simple plot device.

Wallace Markfield's *To an Early Grave* is a good example of the way the Silent Generation dealt with death and funeral rituals. The actual funeral—in a book about a funeral—is an afterthought; Jewish funerals are described in that book as, "One-two-three. In and out, no big deals."[24] For Tropper, however, the funeral and shiva of Mort Foxman remain a constant presence throughout the book; the ritual itself drives the action, not just the lead-up to the ritual as in *To an Early Grave*. Markfield made ritual into a Thing; it was a throwaway. Tropper breathes new life into it by casting it as the central character. Mort Foxman, we learn throughout the book, had no more need for religion than the other members of his generation. When first-person narrator Judd is told that Mort requested the shiva his immediate response is, "but Dad's an atheist."[25] The rabbi at the funeral even admits that, "Mort was never a big fan of ritual."[26] Yet, while this return to ritual is completely befuddling to Mort's family, they honor his wishes and come in from near and far to sit together for a week.

The first hint that Tropper is giving ritual more purpose than his predecessors comes during the traditional tossing of dirt onto the grave by family and friends. This is a key moment of a traditional Jewish funeral, mourners taking turns tossing a shovelful of dirt into the

102   Chapter 4

open grave, coming together as a community to bury the deceased. Judd expresses emotion over the death of his father for the first time, seemingly as a direct result of this tradition. "When the dirt hits the coffin I can feel something in me start to shake," Judd Foxman narrates.[27] This is a theme throughout the novel, and it is also seen throughout Gen X satire: the redemption of religion and religious traditions from ossified Thing status is not, per se, about determining that they have any supernatural basis or purpose. When the twenty-first-century satirists reclaim religion it is almost always because they show it serving real, emotional, or psychological purpose for the practitioners. If a funeral tradition can help a son mourn, that gives it purpose, and that moves it from Thing to not-Thing.

Nevertheless, there is nothing easy or one-dimensional about Tropper's treatment of ritual. On the Sabbath during shiva, the family goes to the Temple to say *Kaddish* (something they only know to do because the rabbi showed up at their house and told them). The family does not take this very seriously, and the Foxman brothers end up smoking a joint in the bathroom of the Hebrew school wing of the building. There is nothing treacly or overly pious about the arrival of the family at the Temple. But Judd says of the *Kaddish*,

> for reasons I can't begin to articulate, it feels like something is actually happening. It's got nothing to do with God or souls, just the palpable sense of goodwill and support emanating in waves from the pews around us, and I can't help but be moved by it. When we reach the end of the page, and the last "amen" has been said, I'm sorry that it's over. I could stay up here a while longer . . . I don't feel any closer to my father than I did before, but for a moment there I was comforted, and that's more than I expected.[28]

What clearer expression is there of the transformation of ritual from something outdated and archaic into something useful and meaningful? The fact that the responsive nature of the prayer and the "waves of goodwill" are important parts of Judd's feeling of comfort reiterates David Cole's idea about the performative nature of ritual as theater and the transformative power of the audience's experience. The *Kaddish* in a vacuum may have had no impact on Judd, but as part of a congregation,

The Turn of the Century   103

it moves him. The shiva becomes, eventually, the only thing holding some of the Foxmans together. As Judd reflects on the impending end of the shiva he says that the rabbi will come "lead us in a small closing ceremony, snuff out the shiva candle, and then we'll part ways, back to the flaming wrecks of our individual lives."[29] The shiva has given the family a focus, but now that it is about to end they will go back to being near-strangers.

This is another aspect of what both differentiates Tropper's satire from that of the earlier generations and also saves his treatment of the shiva from being precious or saccharine. He is brutal in his treatments of people, both as individuals and as groups. In addition to the scathing depictions of most of the family members, old Jews as a group do not fare well here. Old Jewish men are lascivious, smelly, and indecorous, while old Jewish women are pushy, nosy, and inappropriate. He falls back on many traditional antisemitic stereotypes—the lecherous Jewish man, the overbearing Jewish woman, the snobby Jewish princess, the coddled Jewish prince—in ways that are often much harsher than the things that got Philip Roth branded an enemy of the people in the 1960s. Yet those sorts of personal attacks are commonplace today. Judd Foxman says of his family that, "some families, like some couples, become toxic to each other after prolonged exposure."[30] The Foxmans have done and said all manner of unspeakable and awful things to each other in the week that they spent together (including lying, manipulating, ruining romantic relationships and getting into physical fights) and yet the shiva somehow united them and gave them purpose. *They* may be toxic, but the ritual was not. It makes sense, then, in the closing pages of the book, when we find out that Mort actually had no dying wish at all, and it was the Foxman matriarch who concocted the dying request story in order to force her family to spend time together and mourn their father. She, it seems, already sensed how cleansing and oddly satisfying the rituals could prove to be for her children, so she manipulated them into spending an otherwise miserable week together.

Tropper seems to be saying something about the power and importance of traditions for keeping a family afloat. These would have been impossible attitudes for a mainstream satirist of the 1960s or 1970s to express because to them organized religion, and especially the outmoded rituals thereof, were the enemies of a free, liberated, and thinking society.

104   Chapter 4

In Tropper's novel we find the shiva emerging as the one real interaction these people have had with each other in decades, or maybe ever. The family is combative, cold, distant, grudge-holding, and unhappy, but by actually fulfilling the Jewish funereal and mourning requirements, from burial to shiva to *Kaddish*, it came together at least to a degree. Tropper makes it unambiguous that it is the power of ritual and ritual performance that allows for that.

"Sister Hills"

Nathan Englander (like Westfeldt and Tropper) was born in 1970 on Long Island to an Orthodox Jewish family. He grew up with the same New York cultural Jewish experience comedians like Allen, Heller, and Seinfeld had, but with the addition of a deeply religious family and community whose influence stuck better with Englander than such influences did with some others. He went to parochial school growing up and stayed in New York for college, graduating from SUNY-Binghamton. While he may not have remained as Orthodox as he was raised, his connection to Judaism has remained very strong. He is both a good example of a Gen X satirist and an outlier. His willingness to engage difficult topics with frankness and candor makes him in some ways a modern-day Philip Roth. Of all the Gen X satirists I am profiling he is the most willing to dig deeply into traditional Judaism. That is also what makes him an outlier, because he was both raised religious, and has continued to be religiously affiliated as an adult. He moved to Israel in the 1990s and lived there for about five years, an experience that has influenced much of his writing, but especially the short story "Sister Hills."

Nathan Englander shares very little with Tropper, but the theme of traditions, even outdated ones, holding families together does link them. Englander's work is almost entirely about Jews and Jewish themes and is very often set within Orthodox communities. He is best known for short stories, and his first collection, *For the Relief of Unbearable Urges*, won him immediate acclaim and attention. "Sister Hills" appeared in his second collection, *What We Talk about When We Talk about Anne Frank*. Just the fact of his constant and unambiguous use of Jews, Judaism, and Jewishness in all his works speaks to the generational difference between his writing and that of the Silent Generation. Those earlier writers often

The Turn of the Century 105

included inside jokes for Jews, but their satire rarely presented an image of Jews or Judaism drawn from ordinary life, because their social commentary was preoccupied with presenting Judaism as a Thing. Englander's Jews and Judaism are real, living, and very much vital. Conflicted and troubled, but by no means obsolete or useless, Englander's Judaism may be an object, but it is not a Thing.

A close comparison to what Englander does in "Sister Hills" can be made with the fiction of Allen and Heller we looked at in chapter 1, because "Sister Hills" is a scriptural parody in addition to being a satire or critique of certain Jewish attitudes. What, therefore, does Englander's story tell us about how satiric parody of Jewish scriptural texts has changed in recent years? How do we identify the generational difference between the way Allen and Heller use biblical parody and the way a Gen X author does? The most obvious answer is that formal parody— i.e., a parody that replicates the form or structure of the original—has declined as a serious art form in recent years. Today it is thought of as the domain of humor magazines and comic performers such as Weird Al Yankovic. The most popular forms today parody a genre rather than a specific work, which is what we find in television shows like *The Daily Show* and *The Colbert Report*. Looking, therefore, for a contemporary example of the same style Allen and Heller utilized yields practically no results. Formal parody has become a fixture of broad comedy, and is considered ill suited to biting satire today.

The example before us uses a model of intertextual referencing that is not formal enough to be parody, not serious enough to be pastiche, and not respectful enough to be homage. Linda Hutcheon, the woman who wrote the classic study of parody, tries to differentiate pastiche from parody and ultimately finds it difficult.[31] As she reports, though, the commonly cited differences between them are that pastiche is "more serious and respectful than parody," and that "parody is transformational . . . pastiche is imitative." We are left, therefore, without a good term for what we find here. Allusion comes closest, but can an entire work be one long allusion? Regardless of what we call it, this text-linking practice can describe both the Coen brothers' film *A Serious Man* and Englander's "Sister Hills."

In "Sister Hills" Englander uses the biblical story of Solomon and the two mothers as the emotional frame for his story.[32] If this can even be

106   Chapter 4

considered a parody, it is most assuredly not the same sort employed by Allen and Heller. Reviews of the story make it clear that the Solomonic undertones are not even noticed by all readers. While one calls it a "reimagining" of "the old Bible story of the child claimed by two rival mothers,"[33] another sees in it not Solomon but "biblical overtones of lost birth rights and rash vows and terrible covenants."[34] A third sees Englander wrestling not with scripture, but with "the complexly obligatory strictures of Jewish culture,"[35] and yet a fourth sees the story as "a parable, with echoes of Tolstoy's late fables."[36] The variety of interpretations do not surprise Englander, who was quoted as saying that "'Sister Hills,' more than anything else he has ever written, functions as a 'Rorschach test' for many of his readers."[37] So while some readers may pick up on the resemblances to Solomon's story, the reference is oblique enough to give others a sense that the story is building on a different basis.

The actual story is quite simple: it chronicles the life of a Jewish settlement in the West Bank from 1973, when the settlement is just two families, to 2011, when it is a thriving metropolis. One night in 1973, Yehudit's baby daughter becomes very ill, and as a last-ditch effort to save the girl Yehudit falls back on an old, rarely used custom where, by selling her daughter to someone else, she can hide her from the Angel of Death and keep the girl alive. In the middle of a stormy night she sells her daughter to the matriarch of the other settler family, Rena. Yehudit says she will take the "burden" of raising the child "as if I were her mother—though I am not," and Rena agrees to loan her new daughter back to Yehudit until she is grown.[38] As time moves forward Rena's husband and all of her sons are killed, all but one in the fighting over the West Bank. Yehudit's family, on the other hand, thrives. When Rena therefore shows up on Yehudit's doorstep twenty-seven years later to claim Aheret, no one can quite believe she is trying to make Yehudit's desperate bargain stick. Least of all Aheret, who was completely unaware of the story of her sale.

Yehudit forces the issue to a religious court (*beit din*) to try to get the contract declared invalid, but Rena is ultimately successful. If this is meant to be an allegory for the Jewish settlements of the Occupied Territories, it is an extremely opaque one. Englander says, "Right-wing people come up to me and say, 'You see, this is why we need the settlements. This is why they're important,' And then left-wing people say,

'This is why the settlements are amoral. This is why they're corrupting the soul of Israel.'"[39] With whom is the reader meant to side? Is it Rena, who argues so eloquently that if any contracts in Judaism are valid then they all are, and that includes both the three-thousand-year-old contract with God for the land that now makes up the West Bank, and the twenty-seven-year-old contract over Aheret. Or is it Yehudit, who argues for relationships over technicality and love over legalism? Perhaps surprisingly (or maybe not), the *beit din* sides with Rena. Rena loses everything over the ideal of the settlements and eventually forces a young woman to live with and take care of her through her old age and into her death. Nevertheless, if Englander means for that to impart a moral conclusion about the settlements, it is anyone's guess as to what that conclusion is. Englander's story stretches satire to its limits, showing the reasons why satire and humor are not always one and the same, even though the majority of time they are. "Sister Hills" is deathly serious, especially for the families involved. Englander's critique is just as satiric as Allen's or Heller's, and is covered by a patina of irony, despite not being what would generally be thought of as funny.

His moral vagueness, however, speaks to the larger issue of how his use of Judaism and Jewish themes sets him apart as different from Silent Generation satirists like Allen and Heller. Traditionally the assumption would be that the ethical message of a midrash would be readily apparent. Midrash does a poor job of acting as scriptural spackle—filling the gaps in our understanding—if it is too inscrutable or the meaning is too obscure. Englander's story, however, appears to support one's views no matter which side of the settlement issue one is on, which makes it different from his predecessors. Englander is satirizing, through the seemingly illogical outcome of the story, the very concept of "sides" more than he is satirizing one side or the other, because to his sensibility the connection between Judaism and land has significant flaws. This functions as satire because it is aimed at society's complacencies. Returning for a moment to Linda Hutcheon's definition of satire, it consists of "critical distancing and . . . value judgments" and "generally uses that distance to make a negative statement about that which is satirized—'to distort, to belittle, to wound.'"[40] That which is satirized in this case is not the Bible itself (where we first see the covenant for land explained) and is not Judaism itself; the problem is people and the way people have used

108   Chapter 4

and possibly twisted the traditions and texts to suit their own purposes. Because Englander stays rather coy about whether or not he supports one side of the settlement issue or the other, the story opens itself up to myriad understandings. But on both sides there is a belief that the relationship between Jews and the land has gone awry.[41]

Is the worshiping of land a problem? Maybe, maybe not. Tony Kushner and Englander had that very conversation in 2011 and Kushner argued that, "You don't worship a graven image—including a graven image on a map. The heart of Judaism is being supplanted by a map."[42] In response to that, Englander asked the question: "If a map isn't what we're supposed to hold in that metaphysical space that is the ideological heart, what is it that should go there?"[43] One possibility Englander presents, even unwittingly, in "Sister Hills" is that there is not much room for a map in that metaphysical space because it is already occupied by the fetishized Thing-images of scripture. Englander's use of the story from scripture in such a slight way shows that he likely does not care if every reader "gets it" (and as we see from the reviews, they did not). Nevertheless, those who do get it have seen this story translated into shorthand because the *presence* of the story matters more than the *content* of the story. The use of the text, slight though it is, is enough. It does not have to have a clear moral message because the text has been invoked and that is sufficient. And Englander's much more subtle reliance on specific textual forms and clues shows the way that the text, once it has been made into a Thing, has been internalized and normalized over the course of a generation or two from Allen and Heller to now, and is being reinvigorated and given new life and new purpose.

The most obvious counterexample may be the work of Shalom Auslander. Auslander and Englander were born the same year, in the same general part of the country, into similarly Orthodox communities, and both went on to become writers known for their short stories. Even their phonetically similar last names contribute to the conflation of the two. On the surface, however, Auslander bucks all the trends of his fellow Gen X artists. His 2005 short story collection *Beware of God* is a particularly good example in that it is made up of fourteen stories, almost all of which show God to be a murderous sociopath and Jewish ritual or theological observance to be the thing that is ruining the lives of Jews. In that, his stories read like a throwback to a previous generation. The

The Turn of the Century   109

penultimate story in the collection is a small but important reminder that things are rarely that simple. At first glance, "God Is a Big Happy Chicken" is like the rest of the book in that it shows the folly of belief in a deity that is not what you have been led to believe. In this case God is, as the name suggests, actually a giant chicken. When Yankel Morgenstern dies and discovers this, he begs to return to Earth so he can disabuse his family, and the world, of their understanding of God. When the moment comes, however, Morgenstern maintains the lie because he realizes the happiness it brings. "The light from the Shabbos candles flickered in the eyes of his children. Little Meyer was wearing a brand new yarmulke, and couldn't stop fidgeting with it. Shmuel held a handful of Torah notes from his rabbi he would read after the meal, and the girls would be looking forward to singing their favorite Shabbos songs."[44] The God his family believes in doesn't exist, but Morgenstern realizes that the value of the belief is not in its rightness; it is in what it gives to those who believe. Auslander's overall attitude may be unbelieving, but just as with *Kissing Jessica Stein*, and *This Is Where I Leave You*, and even, as we will see, *A Serious Man*, there is still something about religion that adds value to a life and brings families together.

Generation X's move to a rapprochement with rituals and religious practices is bold. It reflected the conservative swing America was undergoing in the early twenty-first century and pushed their contemporaries to think of Jewish practice in new ways. Adam Sandler's "Chanukah Song," for example, works in both directions. It is both a rallying cry to young Jews who want to reclaim their Jewish identity, and a mockery of the insularity of the Jewish community and the practice of painstakingly tracking who is and is not Jewish. Those Baby Boomers still producing significant work watched and learned from what Gen X was doing, as we will see in the remainder of this chapter. But the generation of Birthright Israel and the internet were also raised on these Generation X ideas. So as the concluding chapter suggests, the ongoing story of Millennial comedians comes back to this early twenty-first century moment as well.

The Coen Brothers

Joel and Ethan Coen were raised in a Jewish suburb of Minneapolis, Minnesota, which differentiates them from the creators of *Saturday Night*

Live and *Seinfeld*, who represented the coastal experience of the majority of American Jews. Current estimates show about forty thousand Jews in Minneapolis within a total population of four hundred thousand, so while it is a city with a longstanding and robust Jewish community, the Coens did not grow up surrounded and saturated by Judaism the way many Jews in New York and Los Angeles did.[45] This explains why their humor is more focused on small towns and Middle America than most of their contemporaries.

Those Baby Boomers, like Larry David, who grew up in heavily Jewish surroundings seemed to suffer the same religious fatigue as their parents and leaned heavily toward making Judaism into a Thing. Those who grew up more isolated, like the Coens, have leaned toward revivifying it. Even the presence (or absence) of Judaism conforms to this model. As discussed, *Seinfeld* played fast and loose with audience assumptions about the Jewishness of the characters, and Judaism was always both there and not there, just as it has been for Silent Generation satirists like Allen and Roth. The majority of the Coen brothers' films in the 1980s and 1990s were not at all Jewish; one or two had nominally Jewish characters (such as Barton Fink), but there was no aura of Jewishness in their films. It was only with *The Big Lebowski* in 1998 that they began to engage with Judaism in any real way, so although they are Baby Boomers, their real engagement with Jewish rituals and traditions on film are more twenty-first century than twentieth.

The Coen brothers have always chosen films that interest them and have always been involved in as many aspects of the filmmaking process as possible. They have not, therefore, produced at the rate of someone like Woody Allen, who makes a film per year, but they have averaged a film every two years over their forty-year career to date. The majority of their films have been dark—dark comedies almost all involving crime or criminals. In Joel's mind, their Judaism is there in their films even when not explicit because, "there's no doubt that our Jewish heritage affects how we see things."[46] From an audience standpoint, especially in the Jewish or Judaism-adjacent portion of the audience, the perceptual Jewishness of the Coens may also influence how audiences view their films. "Coen" is a very common Jewish surname, even if more commonly with an "h", so an assumption that the filmmakers are Jewish could lead to seeing more Judaism in the films than might otherwise be apparent.

To the Coen brothers Judaism was a piece of their background, one they acknowledged as important but did not feel the need to exploit or explore until 2009, when they cowrote and codirected *A Serious Man*.[47]

But let us return first to 1998, and to *The Big Lebowski*. *The Big Lebowski*, like most Coen brothers films, revolves around criminals, hijinks, and impossible situations. Set in Los Angeles in 1991, it follows a group of hapless bowlers led by The Dude, a stoner with a flair for badly bastardized Eastern philosophy. The Dude is mistaken for another, wealthier man who, improbably, is also named Jeffrey Lebowski. A pornographer is trying to kidnap the wealthy Lebowski, but gets The Dude instead. What follows is a barely controlled riot of misdirection and mayhem involving the placement and removal of many rugs, more kidnapping, a severed toe, and German nihilists.

The Coen brothers acknowledged that the film is sort of an homage to film noir, especially Raymond Chandler films like *The Big Sleep*. It is not, in any appreciable way, a Jewish film. But there is one notable Jewish character: Walter Sobchak, a foul-mouthed, aggressive, violence-prone Vietnam vet played by John Goodman. The Coen brothers have certainly written Jewish characters throughout their career. Their 1991 film *Barton Fink* is about a Jewish playwright trying to get into Hollywood and the Jewish studio heads who are making that impossible for him. But though almost all of the characters in that film were Jewish, that arguably only aimed at verisimilitude. Walter Sobchak is Jewish, but that actually matters to the character and the film. Ethan Coen said, "we've created Jewish characters before, but we didn't make their Jewishness into a comic element" the way they did with Sobchak.[48]

Sobchak is an embodiment of the stereotype of the Vietnam vet who returned angry and paranoid and armed to the teeth. His use of curse words is virtuosic, and he is also prone to using ethnic slurs and other objectionable language. In one memorable scene Donny (Steve Buscemi) approaches Walter and The Dude to tell them the schedule for the next round of their bowling tournament has been posted. Walter asks when they play, and Donny responds "Saturday." Walter then goes on a rant that has become a pop-culture phenomenon:

> Saturday, well we'll have to reschedule. I told that fuck down at the
> league office, who's in charge of scheduling? (Burkhalter) I told that

Kraut a fucking thousand times I DON'T ROLL ON SHABBOS. (Well they already posted it) WELL THEY CAN FUCKING UNPOST IT. (How come you don't roll on Saturday, Walter?) I'm shomer Shabbos. (What's that?) Saturday, Donny, is Shabbos. The Jewish day of rest. That means I don't work, I don't drive a car, I don't fucking ride in a car, I don't handle money, I don't turn on the oven, and I sure as shit DON'T FUCKING ROLL. (Sheesh.) SHOMER SHABBOS. Shomer fucking Shabbos.[49]

This is one of those scenes that is obviously meant to appeal to a Jewishly literate audience. While they do use Donny's clueless questions as a way of explaining to those in the audience who don't know what "shomer Shabbos" means, Walter is halfway through his rant before we get to that explanation. This is superiority humor in its purest form, because the people who are laughing from the first time Walter yells "I DON'T ROLL ON SHABBOS" can immediately tell who else in the audience possesses the insider knowledge. As with any joke the hope is that everyone is laughing by the end. But this scene is designed to build the laughter, starting with those who know right away why it's funny, then adding those who recognize the description of a Sabbath-observant Jew but had not known the phrase "shomer Shabbos," and finally ending with those who don't really get the joke, but are responding primarily to John Goodman's fantastic timing and delivery.

Although the Coen brothers rarely dealt with Judaism in their early films, this scene is a good example of the ways that, when they did, they mimicked Silent Generation and fellow early Baby Boom comedians. Walter's screaming about being "shomer fucking Shabbos" is straight out of the "Royal Deluxe II" playbook. This is a complete rejection of the idea that religious observance aligns with good moral standing, or even that religious observance has any value at all. The idea of vulgar, angry, gun-loving Walter as an observant Jew creates cognitive dissonance. It is such an absurd juxtaposition that it draws attention to the emptiness of religious ritual. It clearly isn't making Walter happy. He isn't fulfilled, or satisfied, or at peace. His Sabbath observances become just one more thing for him to scream about, and one more reason to hate and distrust others. If Walter Sobchek and his shomer Shabbos rant remained the Coen brothers' most noteworthy exploration of Jewish

The Turn of the Century   113

ritual and practice then they would clearly belong in the previous chapter with *Seinfeld* and friends. But it isn't, because in 2009 they released *A Serious Man*.

A Serious Man is semiautobiographical. Although the characters and situations are predominantly fictional, the directors set the film in the same suburb of Minneapolis in which they grew up, in the 1960s, so the world of the film and much of the mise-en-scène is drawn from their experience. They even searched for a location with homes and yards that still looked the way their neighborhood had looked in the 1960s.[50] In this film they wanted to capture and share something of the Jewish world they remembered from their childhood. They expressed their nostalgia in warm terms, evidence that they saw their Jewish upbringing differently than did the jaded antireligion satirists who came before them.

They opened the film with a short vignette that takes place on a snowy night in a nineteenth-century Polish shtetl. The scene is performed entirely in Yiddish, allowing a twenty-first-century audience their last opportunity to see the inimitable Fyvush Finkel perform in the milieu that launched his career. Jeffrey Shandler, in a special issue of the *AJS Review* devoted to the film, said of the opening vignette, "The prologue presents the shtetl as a lost locus of a thoroughly Jewish way of life, marked as such by the use of Yiddish. This bygone milieu is imagined as including both a traditional engagement with the supernatural in the course of daily life (you open the door, and in walks a dybbuk) and a traditional skepticism about this engagement (a dybbuk? Are you kidding?)."[51] The Coens's desire to present "a lost locus of a thoroughly Jewish life" effects the opposite of Thing-making, because it reinvigorates a lost tradition and reminds one of the vigor of bygone Jewish days. Here they follow the Gen X model of using "traditional" Jewish elements to inject a sense of wonder, humanity, or even authenticity. Yiddish is a marker of *real* Jewishness. The brothers Coen themselves have mostly remained mum on precisely what the audience is supposed to take away from this scene, although Joel has acknowledged that they intended the prologue to "discomfit" the audience.[52]

The remainder of the film is about the Gopnik family, specifically the trials and tribulations of the über-schlemiel Larry Gopnik. His wife is demanding a divorce so she can marry another man, his bid for tenure is going poorly, his brother is under investigation for solicitation

114   Chapter 4

and sodomy, and his wife has taken all their money and the house, leaving him penniless and homeless. When it looks as though things could not get any worse, he and his wife's fiancé, Sy, are in almost simultaneous car accidents, and though he is okay, Sy is killed and his wife insists that Larry must pay for Sy's funeral because there is not anyone else to do it. To this point in the film it is not unlike any other Coen brothers film; it is dark, depressing, and highlights the worst of human behavior. But it is how Larry deals with his trials and tribulations that sets him apart from other Coen antiheroes and what sets the Coens apart from the previous satirists. In his darkest moment, Larry turns to Judaism, a decision that seems to have both positive and negative ramifications throughout the film. Judaism does not solve Larry's problems directly, but his son's bar mitzvah is the first positive step toward a possible brighter future for the Gopniks.[53]

There are two primary commentaries about Jewish ritual in the second half of the film. First, there is the treatment of the three rabbis at the Gopniks's synagogue. They are not unlike the ghosts of Christmas past, present, and future (or possibly Goldilocks and the three bears, or the three stations in the Congo in Joseph Conrad's *Heart of Darkness*), and they represent both the best and the worst about religious functionaries. The second commentary comes through the depiction and aftermath of Danny Gopnik's bar mitzvah. Danny's bar mitzvah is a pivotal moment in the film and the ritual appears to have transformative power, if not on Danny himself then on his parents.

Larry's forays into spiritual guidance present rabbis who are similar to the risible figures from *Saturday Night Live* and *Seinfeld*. The senior rabbi, Rabbi Marshak, is never available. So Larry meets first with the junior rabbi, Rabbi Scott, who seems entirely uncomfortable with trying to counsel an older congregant about issues such as marital infidelity and divorce. He tries to explain losing God by talking about what aliens might think if they saw the Temple parking lot. Then he meets with Rabbi Nachter, the middle rabbi, who tells him a long, vaguely kabbalistic story about Dr. Sussman the dentist and "the goy's teeth." Larry wants straightforward answers about what he should do regarding Sy's funeral and his estranged wife, and he is given incomprehensible anecdotes that make even less sense than the analogy Rabbi Scott used. Neither of these rabbis gives any more of a positive impression than *SNL*'s Rabbi

The Turn of the Century   115

Taklas, even if they are not quite as much sellouts. If Larry's experience of the rabbis were all we had in the film, then it would be safe to say that the Coens present just as negative and Thingish a picture of religious functionaries as those we saw in the previous chapter.

But while Larry never does get to see Rabbi Marshak, his son Danny does. Danny walks through heavy wooden doors into a dark office full of books and old, dark, wooden furniture. There sits wizened but nevertheless imposing Rabbi Marshak. He looks at Danny, and then proceeds to quote two lines from Jefferson Airplane's "Somebody to Love" as he passes Danny back the portable radio that had been taken from him in school early in the film. His admission that he listened to Danny's radio, and found something of value in Danny's music makes him immediately more human. All Rabbi Marshak says to Danny is, "Be a good boy," and yet that advice is clearer and more useful than anything the younger rabbis said to Larry. Like *SNL*'s Rabbi Taklas, Rabbi Marshak has an Old World accent, and in him you see a connection to the vignette at the beginning of the film; there is nostalgia for the old locus of a totalized Jewish life, what Gail Hamner calls "the felt tension between irrevocable loss and hope for a world that is different."[54] That loss-plus-hope, or at least loss-plus-beauty, is what sets this apart from the *SNL* fauxmercial; there was no hope there. There was not even really a sense of loss. There was only satire. The Coens treat the younger rabbis the way Silent Generation satires tended to, as ridiculous and unhelpful. But the *rabbinate* still has value, as the portrayal of Rabbi Marshak shows. They may have a problem with some of the people who hold that office, but they are not writing off the rabbinate as a whole, which means they are not writing off the importance of religious functionaries in the lives of their congregants. They treat the bar mitzvah in much the same complicated way.

Danny Gopnik's bar mitzvah is the central moment of the film's third act. Much of the action and angst of the film has been building toward the moment when Danny ascends the *bimah* to undergo this coming-of-age ritual. The scene is handled with a combination of nostalgic reverence and Coenesque irreverence. Through the use of a wide shot we see a lovely synagogue with an open (and interestingly Sephardic) floor plan and four men standing around the open Torah scroll while one of them chants the blessings before the reading of the Torah in a lovely baritone. But then we switch to a close-up of Danny, and what he

116   Chapter 4

is seeing and experiencing. He stares, slack-jawed, at the *bimah* and the shot takes on a fuzzy-around-the-edges quality because in addition to being nervous, Danny is stoned out of his mind. Throughout the film the audience knows that Danny has a bit of a marijuana habit, and just before Danny's big moment we saw a five-second scene of two sets of shiny dress shoes (that we can only assume belong to Danny and his friend) crammed into a bathroom stall with three or four joint-ends on the floor and the sounds of smoking from within. As in *This Is Where I Leave You*, smoking marijuana on synagogue property becomes a symbolic act of rebellion in the face of religious conformity.

In the bar mitzvah scene the Coens do something that seems to be indicative of a different attitude toward Judaism in twenty-first-century writing and film. The ritual itself is aesthetically pleasing. It is not commercialized, it does not result in mishaps or trips to the hospital, no one is railing against the barbaric, tribal nature of the ritual; what we see of it is simple, traditional, and appreciated by the congregation. It is individual Jews and Jewish families who are being put on satiric display, not the practice of Judaism. As Danny approaches the *bimah* the film switches to a point-of-view shot in which the world tilts crazily and Danny is surrounded by a sea of Kafkaesque faces staring at him, enveloping him, pressing in on him. When he gets to the *bimah* he does not seem aware he is standing on a box he ought not to be. He seems utterly befuddled by the *yad* (pointer) the cantor is handing him to aid in reading his Torah portion. The Hebrew letters seem to swim on the page in front of him, he cannot find the proper starting place, and even once directed to the proper place he stares, blankly, as the cantor twice chants the first few words to Danny to jog his memory. Finally, all the training and practice kick in and he begins to chant the portion on his own.

We see only a second or so of Danny actually chanting, and then the scene cuts to a point at which his work is done, as he sits on the *bimah* listening to someone drone in the background. His posture and body language have not changed and he looks just as stoned as he did before. On the surface at least, becoming a man has not made a significant impression on Danny. It has, however, made an impression on his parents, who are sitting together, beaming, and perhaps reconciling as they stare in rapt adoration at their son. The bar mitzvah is thus similar to circumcision in that the ritual is transformative, but not for the person actually

The Turn of the Century   117

undergoing the life-cycle transition. The circumcised baby experiences nothing but pain and fear; his initiation among the Jewish people is as a passive recipient of the ritual. Danny's passage into Jewish adulthood is similarly passive; he performs more of a role than does the circumcised baby, but he seems outwardly—or inwardly—to change just as little as the baby did. His family, however, has benefited greatly. His father's tenure case seems to have been helped by the fact that his department chair is feeling warm and generous in the afterglow of a successful addition of another link to the chain of Jewish tradition, and his estranged parents seem as though they may be coming back together as a couple. Far from being a pointless Thing, this ritual unites a family and a congregation and is therefore still a very vital and effective occasion.

This also reinforces the idea that the ritual is, perhaps, more for the audience than it is for the ritual actor. David Cole points this out in discussing the relationship between ritual and theater. As Roland Grimes puts it, "actors and shamans do not teach us to journey; rather they journey on our behalf."[55] Theater, and ritual, "render imaginative truth physical," and the intention of the ritual actor matters less than the reception by the willing and engaged audience.[56] Just as Danny's parents get more out of his becoming a bar mitzvah than does Danny himself, a television show or film may take on ritual meaning for an audience regardless of what its creator intended.

As in *Kissing Jessica Stein* and *This Is Where I Leave You*, the ritual in *A Serious Man* is the most sensitively handled element of a story otherwise awash with indignities and insults. The ritual is the heart, the core, the really real. In the case of *A Serious Man*, reviewers and audiences alike derived deeper meaning from the film than the Coens themselves may have anticipated. It was, of course, based on their childhood, so those who wish to see it as an image of what it meant to be a Jew in America in the 1960s are not stretching the meaning significantly. But there emerged in the wake of the film's premiere a consistent reading of the film as an allegorical retelling of the biblical account of Job, which actually surprised the filmmakers. A review in the *New York Times* from the day before the film premiered began, "Did you hear the one about the guy who lived in the land of Uz, who was perfect and upright and feared God? His name was Job. In the new movie version, 'A Serious Man', some details have been changed."[57] This takes it for granted that the film *is* a

118   Chapter 4

retelling of Job, not that it could be viewed that way. The perceptual Jewishness of the Coens could certainly lead viewers to derive Jewish meaning from the film. The Coens themselves, when asked point-blank if Job was their inspiration, responded:

> ETHAN: That's funny, we hadn't thought of it in that way. That does have the tornado, like we do, but we weren't thinking of that.
> JOEL: [. . .] we weren't thinking this was like The Book of Job. We were just making our movie. We understand the reference, but it wasn't in our minds.[58]

But nevertheless, review after review and viewer comment after viewer comment insist on scriptural meaning behind the film, which just shows the energy with which a work takes on a life (and meaning) of its own once it is released into the world. There is, perhaps, a relationship between the satires we looked at in the second chapter and this one. If films like *A Serious Man* provide scriptural allegories, then in addition to making Judaism no longer a Thing it may make scripture no longer a Thing as well. This is a subtle use of scripture, whose meaning may depends more on the reader than what is actually on the page. Perhaps this subtler allusiveness is the way to make scripture no longer a Thing in the twenty-first century.

There must be a middle ground between Roland Barthes's "death of the author" method of textual criticism and one that is slavishly devoted to one author-driven set of meanings. Because while it is true that what ultimately matters about a text or film is the way society reads it, when discussing satire—and especially the way satire reflects and changes religious attitudes, as I am discussing here—authorial intent matters insofar as it is the jumping-off point for the analysis. David Tollerton, in his essay "Job of Suburbia?," seems to walk both sides of this issue. He points out that the Coens deny the link between their film and Job, and that there are serious discontinuities between Job and Larry Gopnik. But he nevertheless claims that "there is good reason" not to believe what the Coens have said, and that "their public statements should not necessarily be taken at face value."[59] The alleged discontinuities, he says, are only discontinuities to the viewers who perceive them as such because,

The Turn of the Century   119

"as Margaret Miles reflects, 'film does not contain and determine its own meaning; meaning is negotiated between the spectator and the film.' We might thus conclude that if a viewer comes to understand *A Serious Man* as a retelling of Job, then that is their rightful prerogative quite regardless of the intentions of its creators."[60]

The film is simultaneously an expression of the Coens's attitudes toward Jewish ritual and religious functionaries and whatever it may mean to the individual audience member. So it does not matter if Danny cares about his bar mitzvah; it is transformative to his parents. And it does not matter if the Coen brothers intended their film to ruminate on scripture. The film has meaning to the audience that is out of their control.[61] Ritual cannot be a Thing if it still performs the Durkheimian function of uniting people, and Danny's bar mitzvah certainly does that. Rabbis (or at least Rabbi Marshak) and rituals are given the power to change people's lives in this film, which makes them very different from the rabbis and rituals of *SNL* and *Seinfeld*. And even more than the effect the ritual has on the characters, the response to the film shows that a portion of the audience is reading it as a modern midrash, and through it understanding scripture as no longer a Thing. Ritual requires a community, perhaps because ritual is largely *for* the community.

Curb Your Enthusiasm

No discussion of twenty-first-century Baby Boomer Jewish humor would be complete without a visit with Larry David. David, as mentioned in the previous chapter, was one of the creators of *Seinfeld*, which ended in 1998. He almost immediately went to work on a mockumentary about himself, which evolved into a new series. The new series would be similar to *Seinfeld* in the sense that it was centered on a main character who bore striking similarities to the actor behind the role, only in this case David himself would be the central character. Moreover, because this series would be on HBO and not a broadcast network, David had significantly fewer restrictions in writing his new show than he had had with *Seinfeld*. Thus, in 2000, *Curb Your Enthusiasm* premiered.

Curb Your Enthusiasm exists in a liminal space between fiction and reality. Jerry Seinfeld, the main character on *Seinfeld*, was a comedian, but most of the other details about the character were fictional.

120   Chapter 4

Larry David, the main character of *Curb*, is the creator of *Seinfeld* and is now rattling around in his huge Los Angeles home, paid for with the millions of dollars he earned during the nine years *Seinfeld* was on the air. As Josh Toth put it, "*Curb* is different because it is more inclined to privilege the (possibility of the) real. The show constantly risks effacing the line that separates the fictional Larry and the real David."[62] *Seinfeld* was "the show about nothing," but *Curb* is about something. It is, "a show about one man's struggle to find post-success success."[63] Writer David sees the space between himself and the character Larry, even if the audience sometimes has trouble separating them. Larry, David says is, "pretty happy. He's a lot happier than I am, I could tell you that. He doesn't work as much as I do."[64] So in Larry, David had a character who could in all ways be *more* than the characters on *Seinfeld*. He had more money, was more unpleasant, could be more vulgar, and was more Jewish. As Jason Zinoman once put it, "the Jewishness . . . that is the subtext of much of 'Seinfeld' becomes the text of 'Curb.'"[65] Something like the ridicule of Holocaust sacralization *Seinfeld* enacted when Jerry and his girlfriend were caught making out during *Schindler's List* (an episode that David wrote) is amplified to an extraordinary extent on *Curb* when Colby Donaldson argues with a Holocaust survivor that his experience on the TV show *Survivor* was the more difficult ordeal.[66]

David was born in 1947 and grew up in Brooklyn. His Jewish upbringing seems to have been similar to what Joseph Heller described—something that was both totalizing and nonexistent. Compared to other Baby Boom comedians still working in the twenty-first century, such as the Coen brothers, David has made the least rapprochement with elements of traditional Jewish practice. He has enthusiastically grabbed onto the paradigm shift that now allows him to present Jews, as a people and as a community, as ridiculous, but he is doing it without the corresponding acknowledgement of ritual as a humanizing and valuable experience. In some ways that makes *Curb* feel dated. The humor, especially around Judaism, can be funny, but also seems like a throwback to an earlier, less nuanced era. *Curb* is not interested in exploring the religious lives of Jews, only setting Larry lose to wreak havoc on the lives of everyone around him with his awkwardness, ineptitude, and misanthropy.

The Turn of the Century   121

Two episodes in particular illustrate the sledgehammer approach David takes toward Judaism on *Curb*. The first is "Palestinian Chicken," the third episode of season 8. As with every episode of *Curb*, there are several vaguely related subplots in the episode, but the two of relevance here are his friend Marty Funkhouser's refusal to play in their golf tournament on Shabbat, and the quality of the chicken at Al-Abbas, a new restaurant owned by a Palestinian family. The Funkhouser plotline is a clear throwback to the attitudes of "Royal Deluxe II," and even further to Silent Generation comedy that saw Judaism as something that was keeping Jews down. But unlike the Silent Generation, who thought that it was worth trying to save the Jewish people from the clutches of organized religion, *Curb* seems willing to throw both out. Funkhouser has recently "found religion"; he has been attending a (probably Conservative) synagogue and has begun wearing a yarmulke. He never before had a problem golfing on Saturday, but suddenly, like Walter Sobchek before him, he is shomer Shabbos and can't roll (or putt) on the Sabbath. When Larry and the other members of his foursome complain that they will forfeit the whole tournament if Funkhouser doesn't play, he simply says that his rabbi told him not to play on the Sabbath, but if she told him he could play, he would.

This is intertwined with the plotline about Larry and Jeff secretly eating at the new Palestinian chicken restaurant. They wax rhapsodic about the food, talking at some length about how it is the best chicken they have ever had—chicken that could solve the Israel-Palestine conflict. Larry jokes that it would be a great place for a Jew to take his mistress, because no other Jews were willing to be seen there, so the assignation would remain secret. The negative response of the Jews around Larry to this restaurant is so out of proportion, so absurdly negative, that they all seem to be weirdly narrow-minded and bigoted. Moreover, *Curb* tells us, they are all liars and hypocrites.

Larry goes to see Funkhouser's rabbi. He has with him takeout from Al-Abbas, and the rabbi makes a comment that he should keep the chicken away from her, "no matter what." Of course that means that we will immediately cut to a scene of Larry and the rabbi grappling over her desk as she attempts to rip the chicken out of his hands while he tries to force her away. Her politics, and her resolve, crumble under the temptation of delicious chicken. The rabbi here is an utter fraud, simultaneously

122   Chapter 4

barring Funkhouser from playing in the golf tournament on religious grounds and turning into a madwoman with a ravenous appetite. Not surprising, after their chicken fight the rabbi allows Funkhouser to play after all, and when Funkhouser asks Larry how he managed it he replies, "let's just say I had something she really wanted." The rabbi is a modern-day Esau, trading away her moral high ground for a morsel of chicken.

The rest of the Los Angeles Jewish community does not fare much better. Not only are other Jews secretly eating at Al-Abbas (some of whom are, in fact, using it for extramarital rendezvous), but they are protesting the very existence of the restaurant on the ridiculous grounds that it is wrong for a Palestinian restaurant to open too close to a deli. The episode ends with a protest in front of the restaurant, where Jews are carrying signs saying things like "Not on This Block," "The Cluck Stops Here," "No Terrorist Chicken," and most absurdly, "The New Shoah." These are people with absolutely no sense of context, decency, or proportion. For David, yes, rabbis continue to be hucksters peddling a dangerous product, but Jews are also absurd, especially in groups, and more often than not they make their own problems.

One of the few places where David's humor shows a glimmer of what I am identifying as the twenty-first-century comic consciousness was the season 6 finale, "The Bat Mitzvah." As with *A Serious Man*, the bat mitzvah here is the culmination of the episode and is the thing that brings people together and sets people up for a better future. Larry had spent the sixth season trying to win back his ex-wife Cheryl and fighting off persistent rumors that he had done unspeakable things with a gerbil. Larry doesn't win Cheryl back, and he embarrasses both himself and his friends Jeff and Susie when he gives a speech after their daughter's bat mitzvah that is just a denial of the gerbil rumor and not a celebration of Sammi and her accomplishments. But Larry does end up dancing with Loretta Black (played by Vivica A. Fox), and the end of the episode moves through a montage of Larry and Loretta in bed with her kids, Larry as a soccer dad, Larry in the car pulling out the "don't make me come back there" line, Loretta defending Larry against a tirade from Susie, and Larry posing for family photos with the Blacks. Larry and Loretta don't last, and they break up early in season 7, but that brief montage coming after a bat mitzvah is perhaps the most normal, happy, and well-adjusted that Larry is at any point across the eleven seasons and twenty-one years (and counting) that the show has been on the air. Most of the time David hews closest to the older, outmoded, Thingish way of handling Judaism and Jewishness on *Curb*. But once in a while there is nod to the revivification of Judaism that was such an innovation of Generation X.

5
What Will Millennials Kill Next?

Two women were complaining about the brunch they just had.
"That may have been the worst brunch I ever tasted," said the first.
"I know!" said the second, "And such small portions!"

—Anonymous Joke

The story of Jewish humor in America will continue as long as Jews and America go on together, but the story of this book must end. Much has been written about Millennials in the media and the popular press, but there is little scholarship yet on this young, innovative, tech savvy, often angry generation. Millennials are generally defined as those born between 1980 and 1995, so the oldest Millennials are currently in their forties, while the youngest are in their mid-twenties. It is, therefore, the generation that is beginning to assert itself in business, politics, education, and popular culture. Because we are still very much in the middle of the rise of the Millennials, we lack the critical distance needed to fully contextualize their creative work. Even if we could, there are still at least two decades to come in which Millennials will be the driving force in comedy, so today we're working with only the leading edge of their work. Nevertheless, there are some examples of Millennial humor that can offer insights to this study, and which can serve us as a sort of coda.

The first and perhaps most important thing to recognize is that we may have reached the point at which Millennials are simply too far removed from their Silent Generation great-grandparents for there to be meaningful comparison of the two. Yes, Woody Allen still produced films at the same time that *Broad City* aired, but that does not really make them contemporaries. One of the things I argue for, in contrast to much existing scholarship on Jewish humor, is the contention that humor is intensely localized both geographically and temporally. Laughter may be universal, but trying to flatten the differences between Jewish communities across time and space ignores dramatic changes in what we laugh at. The mere fact that "too soon" is a typical response to morbid or ghoulish humor relies on an assumption that there will be a point at which such jokes are on time.

In this case the most salient issue may be, as it has been throughout this book, distance from the Holocaust. Part of what I have been arguing is that the palpable shift between Silent Generation attitudes and Gen X attitudes had to do with the former's direct memories and experiences of World War II and the Holocaust. That generation may have found organized religion to be a dangerous force, but they nevertheless wanted to protect and preserve the Jewish people. Gen X, on the other hand, lacked that immediate, personal experience of the war, so they had lost the existential fear that kept humorists from targeting Jewishness itself too directly. If that is true, then those restrictions bind Millennials even less tightly than they did Generation X. A recent study found that knowledge of and attention to the Holocaust has dropped significantly among Millennials, and nearly half of them cannot name a single concentration camp or ghetto.[1] While that study was of all Americans, not specifically Jews, it stands to reason that Jewish Millennials would display less knowledge than their parents, even though they may know more than their non-Jewish counterparts. Additionally, with each passing year we come closer to the death of the last Holocaust survivor and what a recent study termed "the Post-Witness Era."[2] Most Millennial Jews have never met and will never meet a survivor. That could explain why Holocaust humor, while still controversial, is nevertheless becoming mainstream.[3] The Thing theory construct also falls apart with an analysis of Millennial humor. Either everything is a Thing, or perhaps nothing is a Thing, or maybe everything and nothing is a Thing. Millennials do not seem to fear organized religion, nor do they crave the stability it offers. They seem largely ambivalent: if you enjoy that sort of thing, it's fine; if you don't, that's also fine. They do not seem to have the same intentionality in their depiction of Jewish things, so while they can be compared to the earlier generations, they also defy efforts to fit them into the same superstructure.

By way of conclusion, therefore, I also want to create a space to begin looking at Millennial Jewish humor on its own, and in relation to events that may have had more of an impact on their generation, rather than continuing to see distance from the Holocaust as a primary distinguishing feature. Millennial Jewish comedians still mine many of the same veins we have already discussed. *Broad City* did a shiva episode. *Crazy Ex-Girlfriend* had a bar mitzvah episode. The @CrazyJewishMom Instagram account revisits the relationship between Jewish mothers and daughters. They do these things, however, with a sense of abandon that feels new. Every new generation, of course, evokes "those kids today!" responses from the generations that came before. So while it may be easy to say that for Millennials nothing is sacred and they don't take anything religious or traditional seriously enough, much of that attitude is simply a function of time. In twenty years the Millennials will be saying the same thing about Gen Z (generally dubbed Zoomers).

What does seem clear about Millennials is that they are the generation that fully broke with the traditional process of building a career in comedy. The salt mines of comedy clubs and nightclubs were still the primary jumping-off point to wider recognition well into the twenty-first century. The hope was to be discovered by a big star or a talent agent who would thrust you into the limelight. It was the way comedians had broken into film and TV from their earliest days. It is the process we see nostalgically recreated in the television show *The Marvelous Mrs. Maisel*. The Marx Brothers' early films were essentially filmed versions of their vaudeville performances. Milton Berle turned his stand-up career into a job hosting Texaco Star Theatre and the distinction of being arguably the biggest star of TV's first wave. Woody Allen was an unknown stand-up when Mort Sahl caught his act and helped him achieve his dreams as a filmmaker. Into the 2000s the myth of the path to stardom persisted. It became, in part, a self-fulfilling prophecy because the networks saw that taking a comedian and building a sitcom around them was a cheap, easy, and often (enough) successful recipe for success; for decades they kept doing it. From *Sanford and Son* and *Mork and Mindy* in the 1970s, this model grew and bloomed so that in the eighties and nineties it seemed as though almost every sitcom, from *The Cosby Show* to *Full House* to *Roseanne* to *Home Improvement* to *Seinfeld*, was built around a stand-up comedian.

One of the things sociologists have used to think about the line between Gen X and Millennials in general is their relationship to technology.[4] So it stands to reason that one of the things that distinguishes Millennial comedians is that they have harnessed new and emerging technologies to reach different audiences, and to build a career differently. Gen X, even the greats like Adam Sandler and Sarah Silverman, followed the "stand-up to TV to film" formula for honing their craft, getting discovered, and becoming a star. Millennials go in different directions. *Broad City* started as a web series created by Abbi Jacobson and Ilana Glazer. They developed a devoted internet following, which eventually caused Comedy Central to pick the series up and develop it into a cable show. Similarly Rachel Bloom, creator of *Crazy Ex-Girlfriend*, built her career writing and producing satiric, often obscene YouTube videos, which is how Aline Brosh McKenna first came across her work and decided to reach out about making a TV show. Kate Siegel might be the best example of this phenomenon; she became famous not for videos but for her Instagram feed, @CrazyJewishMom. She posted screenshots of her conversations with her mother, which went viral and resulted in a book called *Mother, Can You Not?* as well as TV appearances for both Siegel and her mother Kim. Even the people who came up through stand-up harnessed the changing landscape of American entertainment. Amy Schumer started out doing stand-up, but instead of waiting to be discovered in the comedy clubs she auditioned to be on a reality competition series called *Last Comic Standing*. She did not win, but she was on the show long enough to get the exposure she needed (and her career has far outstripped those of the comedians who beat her). To see how far we have come I am going to analyze two episodes of *Broad City*, two songs from *Crazy Ex-Girlfriend*, and some examples from the @CrazyJewishMom feed. I am focusing entirely on women here, in short, because I can. Women are, perhaps for the first time, driving at least as much (if not more) of the production of Jewish humor in the twenty-first century as men and that is worth celebrating.

Broad City

Abbi Jacobson and Ilana Glazer were twenty-five and twenty-two, respectively, when they began to write, produce, and star in their web series, *Broad City*. The production values and size of the staff may have changed dramatically from when Comedy Central picked up the show

128   Chapter 5

for their 2014 season, but the heart of it stayed true to the original vision of Jacobson and Glazer, to dramatize the lives of young Jewish women trying to make it on their own in New York City with very little in the way of money, education, skill, or experience. Although Jacobson and Glazer were quite young when they created it, their characters are explicitly even younger still. Jacobson was born in 1984, but her character, Abbi Abrams, was born in 1988, and Glazer was born in 1987 while her alter ego Ilana Wexler was born in 1992. Jacobson and Glazer are solid, mid-generation Millennials, but they wrote their characters to be much closer to the Generation Z cusp. The show ran for five seasons, ending in 2019.

The Jewishness of the characters, and therefore the show, is often unspoken, yet implied. At times it isn't an important part of the characters' lives while at other points it becomes more of a focus. In fact, a running theme throughout the show is that Abbi is not Jewish enough. We know significantly less about Abbi's family than Ilana's. Ilana's parents are played by notable Jewish character actors Susie Essman (the same Susie from the "Palestinian Chicken" episode of *Curb Your Enthusiasm* discussed in the previous chapter) and Bob Balaban, who has made a career out of playing nebbish characters.[5] Abbi's parents, on the other hand, are rarely mentioned and not seen until the later seasons. She is from Philadelphia's Main Line, a suburban region so associated with WASP culture that it gave us the term "mainline Protestant." Her father, when we finally meet him, is played by Tony Danza, while her mother, who we meet even later, is played by Peri Gilpin. Neither actor is Jewish. Ilana is thus depicted as a more typical New York (specifically Long Island) Jew, while Abbi is used as a foil whose frequent Jewish illiteracy can highlight Ilana's sometimes warped view of Jewishness.

Although there are references to Jewish things throughout the show, the episode "Knockoffs" from season 2 and "Jews on a Plane" from season 3 highlight the ways in which we can begin to speculate about Millennial attitudes toward Judaism and Jewishness. The secondary plot in "The Knockoffs" involves the death of Ilana's grandmother and her subsequent shiva.[6] Unlike the shiva as a hollow farce of the Baby Boomers or the shiva as a chance to learn something about yourself of Gen X, this Millennial shiva is an opportunity to highlight how strange, but ultimately loving and functional, Ilana's family is. Where the Foxman family spent *This Is Where I Leave You* at each other's throats and doing terrible things to each

What Will Millennials Kill Next?   129

other, the Wexlers bicker but love and support each other. Ilana encourages Abbi to seize the opportunity to "peg" her new romantic interest, in part by pointing out, "we are going to my grandmother's shiva, okay, and the only reason I'm not sitting and crying is because that bad ass bitch did everything she ever wanted to." Abbi heeds Ilana's advice, resulting in a comedy of errors around the care and cleaning of sex toys, such that when Abbi finally arrives at the shiva and Ilana's mother insists on examining her purse (the acquisition of illegal, knockoff handbags was an additional subplot of a very busy twenty-two-minute episode) she pulls out a large dildo. But because the Wexler family is ultimately accepting and highly functional, no one shames or judges Abbi, and the episode even ends with straight-laced Mr. Wexler agreeing to allow Mrs. Wexler to peg him. Funerals, they say, are for the living, but in particular in this case the shiva is not a catalyst for learning lessons as much as it is a celebration of life for both the living and the dead.

"Jews on a Plane" is arguably *Broad City*'s most Jewish episode.[7] In this season 3 finale Abbi and Ilana decide to go on a "Birthmark" trip to Israel, obviously modeled on the popular Birthright Israel program. The episode is essentially a long series of jokes aimed at certain stereotypes of Jews, sexual Zionism, and the creation of Jewish identity in young people. This is also one of the places where Abbi's "less than" model of Jewish identity is highlighted and mocked. During a discussion of circumcision, and the controversial practice of *metzitza b'peh* (oral suction) as part of the ritual, Abbi seems to know nothing about a bris and Ilana asks her "Honestly, are you Jewish? You're not supposed to be on this trip if you're not." Further, when Abbi needed to cause a distraction for Ilana, Ilana tells her to stand up and sing. The only song she can come up with is the Christmas carol "Angels We Have Heard on High," causing Ilana to ask her again if she's even really Jewish. The enthusiastic tour leader tries to pair couples up based on where they went to school, their occupations, even their names or hair color, all in the service of inspiring Jewish marriages. One couple does manage to get engaged before the plane even lands, about which Ilana points out the absurdity of the fact that at least one member of the couple was confident (or hopeful) enough to have brought an engagement ring along just in case.

What this episode highlights well is the way in which Millennial ideas of Jewishness were influenced by the Gen X humor with which

130   Chapter 5

they grew up. Adam Sandler's "Chanukah Song" premiered on *Saturday Night Live* in December of 1994. Jacobson and Glazer were ten and seven years old, so the attitude Sandler was peddling to young Jews, that it was hip and cool to be Jewish à la Lenny Bruce's "Jewish and Goyish" from nearly a half-century before, was aimed at kids like them. In the character of Ilana especially, we see the final fruition of that attitude. She is a young Jew who sees being Jewish as cool and fun, and mocks or pities Abbi when it is clear that Abbi's sense of Jewish identity is much less well defined than Ilana's. *Broad City* speaks to a certain Millennial Jewish experience that is changing the narrative of American Jewishness. Mrs. Wexler is loud and pushy, but she and her daughter love spending time together, and she treats Abbi like an adopted daughter. Gone is the stereotypically toxic relationship between Jewish daughters and their mothers, replaced instead by a relationship in which both parties can have certain stereotypical tendencies while simultaneously being fiercely attached and lovingly defensive of each other. They may fight, but they do not hate. And they may lean a bit too hard on Jewish stereotypes, but that is couched in an overall positive idea of being Jewish.

Crazy Ex-Girlfriend

Rachel Bloom and Aline Brosh McKenna's musical fantasy TV series *Crazy Ex-Girlfriend* shares some of those elements with *Broad City*, but is not nearly as willing or able to dispense completely with a few of the more damaging Jewish stereotypes. Like Jacobson and Glazer, Rachel Bloom began her career making web videos. Her oeuvre was funny, usually obscene music videos for songs she wrote, such as "Fuck Me, Ray Bradbury," which was her breakthrough video, and "You Can Touch My Boobies," for which she won the 2013 LA Weekly Web Award for Best YouTube Song (and which, it should be noted, takes place in the mind of a teenage boy in Hebrew School). Brosh McKenna, who was best known for writing romantic comedies like *27 Dresses* and the fashion comedy *The Devil Wears Prada*, saw Bloom's videos and reached out to her about collaborating. Eventually, *Crazy Ex-Girlfriend* was born, combining Bloom's skill with satire and music with Brosh McKenna's aptitude for romantic comedy. Bloom is the same age as Ilana Glazer, but Brosh McKenna is one of the oldest members of Gen X, born only two years after the end of the Baby Boom. This may account for some of the reasons why *Broad City* and *Crazy Ex-Girlfriend* had similar geneses but ended up with remarkably different tones.

Crazy Ex-Girlfriend's protagonist, Rebecca Bunch (played by Bloom), shares with other members of Generation "Chanukah Song" (if I may call it that) the sense of Jewishness as something that is cool and hip, as opposed to tragic and burdensome. From the pilot episode we see Rebecca experiencing casual antisemitism from her new boss, and rather than just letting it go she says things like "let's circle back about the 'Jew' thing, because that's a conversation we need to have." She doesn't wear her Jewishness on her sleeve like Jessica Stein, or even Ilana Wexler, but neither is she willing, when it matters, to sublimate it. As the show progressed (it ended in 2019 after its fourth season) the tone got darker and more serious, and Rebecca's references to her Jewishness got more frequent and more thoughtful. Two songs, both from the first half of the show's run, demonstrate elements of this. "JAP Battle" both plays on and problematizes stereotypes of Jewish women, and "Remember That We Suffered" is a sharp satire of the perceived Jewish obsession with the Holocaust and retaining a victimized identity. The reprise of "JAP Battle" in one of the show's final episodes, while not as clever as the original, does show the evolution of the show's treatment of Jewish themes.

"JAP Battle" pits Rebecca against her longtime frenemy Audra Levine. Audra stayed the course and has made partner at Rebecca's old law firm, while Rebecca gave that all up to move to California and chase her dream of true love. In this number the two self-identified Jewish American Princesses square off in a rap-battle format grudge match, dredging up their long history together. There is a great deal that can be and has been said about this song and the implications for the concept of the JAP as she exists in contemporary culture.[8] For the purposes of this study it is enough to say that although Audra and Rebecca both self-identify as JAPs, it is not at all clear that their association with the stereotype reaches beyond the name. Neither of them exhibit many (if any) of the standard characteristics. Both of them fit better into the category I have dubbed the MAAW, the Modern Ashkenazi-American Woman. The MAAW may share some qualities with the JAP, but she is overall a much more confident and less reviled figure. Regardless of whether the song adequately establishes Rebecca as a JAP, it does speak to how Rebecca

132   Chapter 5

sees her Jewishness in the first season. Essentially, according to the song, to be a young Jewish adult is to be well educated and success-driven, to be socially liberal but supportive of the State of Israel, and to maintain "Jewish" as only one of many identifiers of an intersectional identity.

By season 4, however, there have been some slight but significant changes. When "JAP Battle" is reprised in one of the show's final episodes, Rebecca has gone to Las Vegas to try to convince Audra to return home to her family. Audra has had a mini-breakdown and abandoned her husband and infant triplets because "it got hard." Despite Audra's lifelong antagonism of Rebecca, Rebecca is willing to go try to help Audra in her moment of need. The lyrics of the reprise reflect this, and instead of trying to outshine each other as they did in season one, they competitively complement each other, trying to outdo each other in support. Notably, in the first iteration of the song, when the term JAP was used, lyrics interjected, "Find that term offensive? Well too bad, yo." This time around Rebecca breaks in with a spoken note that JAP, "Which does stand for Jewish-American Princess, a term that, on one hand, does reinforce negative, negative stereotypes about both Jews and women but, on the other hand, is a term that we want to reclaim and own. Also, should acknowledge that me saying 'dap to this JAP' is appropriative and a little problematic, if we're being honest." Rebecca seems less sure that her reclaiming of the term JAP is actually a good thing and is much more open to the problems inherent in the language she used so freely and carelessly in the earlier season. As her Jewishness became more prominent in the show, her thoughtfulness about what that means increased as well.

"Remember That We Suffered" is a different and much more critical evaluation of American Jewish identity. This song takes place at Rebecca's cousin's bar mitzvah, and is performed primarily by Naomi, Rebecca's mother (played once again by the go-to Jewish mother Tovah Feldshuh), and the rabbi (played by Patti Lupone). Here the lyrics explain that even at a happy event, Jews can never be happy, because they have to remember the Holocaust. The song includes lyrics such as "being happy is selfish, remember that we suffered!" and "I don't want to bring up the Holocaust, I know, I know, the Holocaust. But the Holocaust was a really big deal!" The show is very clearly targeting Jewish narratives of victimhood and the imagined sense that Jews cannot let go of the tragedies of nearly a century ago. This is a fine line for a popular show to walk, especially as *Crazy Ex-Girlfriend* aired on one of the basic broadcast networks (albeit the smallest one, The CW). There may be internal Jewish discussions about whether the Holocaust should continue to define and color contemporary Jewish experiences, but to satirize that publicly is to wade into more dangerous waters. In 2019 a judge in Tennessee, Jim Lammey, posted racist and antisemitic content on his social media pages, including a statement that "Jews should get the fuck over the Holocaust." In 2015 Shaul Magid had published a book review in *Tablet* magazine titled "American Jews Must Stop Obsessing over the Holocaust."[9] That was a safe stance to take, in a Jewish publication, at that moment. But in the wake of Judge Lammey's comments we instead saw the publication of essays in less narrowly focused media with headlines such as "Jews Can't, and Shouldn't, Just 'Get Over' the Holocaust."[10]

Sixty years ago Philip Roth was branded a traitor for depicting Jewish characters who were morally flawed and unpleasant. The Yiddish phrase *a shonde fur di goyim* exists for just this purpose—it means, roughly, a scandal in front of the non-Jews. The idea that those conversations need to be private was important to the Greatest and Silent Generations in the wake of WWII, and Roth was seen as "bad for the Jews" because he opened Jews up to criticism and ridicule at a time when they were still feeling vulnerable. *Crazy Ex-Girlfriend* is doing the same thing, but without fear of reprisal or being labeled the new Philip Roth–style "self-loathing Jew." As with *Broad City*, this implies that one hallmark of Millennial Jewish humor may be a prominent, even fierce attachment to a Jewish identity with much less interest in having that be defined by affiliation with a synagogue, ritual performance, or attitudes about the Holocaust or Israel. It is important to these women that they identify as Jewish, and they seem not to be bothered by criticism that their Jewishness is hollow, superficial, or even dangerous to the survival of the Jewish people. The members of Generation "Chanukah Song" know they are part of an exclusive club, and they are proud of it.

@CrazyJewishMom

I want to end with what is arguably the most Millennial, but also the most difficult to analyze example, and that is Kate Siegel's Instagram feed,

134   Chapter 5

@CrazyJewishMom. If Millennial humor is defined, in part, by creativity around the form and medium that constitute it, then a career that began as an Insta feed is archetypical Millennial humor. What started as Kate Siegel's chronicle of text conversations with her mother Kim, primarily by screenshots, has now spawned a lifestyle and advice website that the two run together (Mother & Spawn, as they call themselves), a book by Kate (*Mother, Can You Not?*), numerous media appearances, and a loyal fan base—the original Instagram account has almost three-quarters of a million followers. What makes @CrazyJewishMom so interesting is that it is simultaneously progressive in form and regressive in content. The Jewish mother-daughter relationship remains a major theme in Jewish humor, but the depiction of Jewish mothers and Jewish daughters has changed significantly. Characters like Rebecca and Audra may call themselves JAPs, but they are a world away from the original JAPs like Philip Roth's Brenda Patimkin or Herman Wouk's Marjorie Morningstar. This is why I find the MAAW a more useful descriptor, which avoids stretching an old term further and further from what it initially meant. But the depiction of Jewish mothers has evolved more slowly.

Joyce Antler's comprehensive study of the Jewish mother in popular culture, *You Never Call, You Never Write: A History of the Jewish Mother*, discusses the fact that, "it is the most unflattering aspects of the Jewish mother that have endured and are most familiar."[11] She speculates that the reason for this is that, "comedy is in large part responsible for making the negative Jewish mother stereotype so pervasive and disproportionately popular."[12] The longevity of the Jewish mother stereotype in comedy is therefore a bit of a self-fulfilling prophecy—comedy promulgates the myth, so then comedians continue to exploit it because audiences recognize it because comedy promulgates it. Despite the stereotype's persistence, both *Broad City* and *Crazy Ex-Girlfriend* did undermine it. Ilana's relationship with her mother is volatile, but by no means toxic. The two love to shop together, get their nails done together, fight with the police together, and share other elements of a healthy mother-daughter relationship. In *Crazy Ex-Girlfriend*, Rebecca's relationship with her mother is the definition of toxic, but that is in part because Naomi *isn't* a typical Jewish mother. Naomi is a classic 1960s JAP who has aged into being the mother of a Millennial daughter. She is vain, narcissistic, hectors her daughter about her weight and food choices, is unable to take joy in her daughter's successes, and subordinates her daughter's well-being and happiness to her own. Those are all qualities of a JAP, not a traditional overbearing, overfeeding, guilt-wielding Jewish mother.

That is part of what makes Kim Friedman seem so out of place. Much like the character of Shelly Pfefferman, the mother on *Transparent*, Kim seems almost anachronistic. Her embodiment of a type of Jewish mother who appears to have died out lends nostalgic charm to a stereotype that had become very nasty by the end of the twentieth century. Antler points out that the problem of the Jewish mother "is not only in how the stereotype presents Jewish women to society, but also in how Jewish women themselves are affected. Real Jewish mothers internalize the negative attributes of the stereotype, judging themselves and others by these traits. For fear of being labeled as 'Jewish mother,' they may stifle their own 'creativity, warmth, caring, and expressiveness.'"[13] Kim's version of the Jewish mother combines the negative qualities of being overinvolved in her children's lives and constantly nagging them about grandchildren with twenty-first century sensibilities of sexuality and expression in order to create a sort of foulmouthed Yenta figure. For example, Siegel tells a story of her mother calling a radio station during a hurricane to complain that the barricades were keeping her from rescuing her animals. "Chris Christie wants to murder my animals?" Kim texted, "Not so fast, motherfucker!"[14] A kind firefighter named Lenny heard Kim on the radio and offered to get her past the barricades to her pets. This results in the following exchange between Kim and her daughter:

> Holy Fireman, Kate. Couldn't say it on the phone, this man is gorgeous.
>
> I was expecting a balding guy with a potbelly. He is GORGEOUS & he loves animals? SPERMINATOR ALERT. I'm giving him ur number.
>
> Mother, can you just focus?
>
> Oh, calm urself. I showed him ur pcture and he thinks ur cute. His butt is like a perfect bubble bottom. I'm going to try and sneak pix for u after this.
>
> Omg btw, he threw this huge blue plastic tarp over me for hiding. Like the kind they wrap dead bodies in in movies. My god, this

136   Chapter 5

material, it's scratching up my skin! U would think they would make these things nicer.

You just said, "like the kind they wrap dead bodies in"

OMG do u think they used THIS one for that?!

Not actually, Mother!

I'm taking it off!!

MOM! DO NOT DO THAT!

Mom?

Mom?!

Mother, answer me! Did you get arrested?

STOP TEXTING, SPAWN. LENNY YELLED AT ME. IT DINGS EVERY TIME U WRITE SOMETHING AND WE'RE AT THE BARRICADE![15]

Kim is some amalgamation of stereotypes that have come together to form a new type of Jewish mother who could only exist in the twenty-first century. Like *Crazy Ex-Girlfriend*'s Naomi Bunch, Kim is obviously someone who had JAP tendencies in her youth, but she does not continue to express them with nearly the vehemence that Naomi does. She nags her daughter to get married, but not to marry a nice Jewish doctor or lawyer, just to marry the next firefighter with a nice butt she encounters. She is at times obsessively worried about her daughter and at other times dismissive. She (apparently) communicates with her daughter primarily through text messages, so unlike Antler's Jewish mother, who uses the age-old guilt trip "You don't call . . . you don't write . . . ," Kim is proactive about contacting her Spawn (perhaps more often than her daughter would like) and does not sit around waiting for her to call. The screenshots on the @CrazyJewishMom feed and in Siegel's book seem authentic, but it has never been entirely clear if they are truly candid or if Kim or Siegel or both are cultivating these personae. Certainly at this point it seems like Kim is a character the real Kim Friedman plays up and embellishes, and Spawn is probably an overdramatized simulacrum of the real Kate Siegel. An Instagram feed consisting largely of screenshots cannot have the depth of content that a television show can, even if the texts are purposeful fabrications by now. Nevertheless, @CrazyJewish-Mom does give us more information about the direction of Millennial humor and the shape it may take in the years to come.

Conclusion

Millennial Jewish humor does not look like the humor of the generations that came before it, but it is just as dependent on that foundation as we have seen each generation to be. The Silent Generation, indelibly marked by a war they did not fight and taking up the banner of the 1960s counterculture, fought against organized religion and all the hypocrisy they thought it stood for. Religion, it seemed, had nearly been the death of the Jewish people, and its continuation was a danger to Jewish survival. The Baby Boomers were the teenagers of the counterculture, absorbing and consuming the narrative their idols set down about the danger of empty religion. They set out to tell the same story, but toward the end of the twentieth century that changed. Generation X grew up in a different time. The 1980s was a darker, scarier, more corporate age; the years of "Meism" and "greed is good" and AIDS and crack and heroin and myriad other social ills led the members of Generation X to see a society without religion as a society without cohesion. They came back, if not to belief, to the power of community, the value of family tradition, and the way that religion can serve as a port in an emotional storm.

Millennials seem to want to check the none-of-the-above box. They were raised on the pop culture of the 1990s and 2000s, when things like *Seinfeld* were already becoming passé, but "The Chanukah Song" and *Friends'* Holiday Armadillo and the films of Ben Stiller made them think being Jewish was fun. They are less worried about remembering that Jews suffered and more concerned with climate change. They are less worried about the existential threats to the State of Israel and more concerned with whether they will pay off their student loans before they retire. Their humor reflects a change in the depictions of Jewish mothers, daughters, families, and communities. They are by no means relying less on stereotype; if anything, their humor is more based in stereotypes. The stereotypes they are using, however, show an evolving sense of what it means to be Jewish and why it matters. They are not remaining Jewish to avoid (in Emil Fackenheim's words) "handing Hitler posthumous victories"; they are doing it because they like it. It remains to be seen what the "it" they like actually is, because there are questions about whether they will enroll their children in religious school, or have them celebrate *b'nai mitzvot*, or join a JCC, or any of the other things that have traditionally denoted engagement in Jewish life. We already know they are moving away from Israel and the Holocaust as the touchstones of what it means to be a Jew. Any description of this generation (and Generation Z, as far as we can tell so far) that depict them as devoid of Jewish identity simply because their generation is associated with the rise of the "religious nones" is taking a shortsighted view of what Jewishness is and can be. The kids are alright, so to speak. They are still satirizing Jewish life the same way their parents and grandparents did. They just do not seem as worried that Judaism itself is in danger.

Notes

Introduction: Funny, You Don't Look Funny

1 I will be using "humorist" and "comedian" interchangeably. Traditionally "humorist" referred to writers while "comedian" referred to performers. But many of the people I will be surveying are both, and it seems pedantic to refer to the same person by different titles depending on whether I am discussing a written piece or a performance, which may have been based on a written piece itself. I will also avoid "comedienne" as I find it to be outdated, and I will use "comedian" the same way we now use "actor."

2 Ben-Porat, "Method in Madness," 247.

3 Freud, *Jokes and Their Relation to the Unconscious*, 107.

4 Berrin, "Mel Brooks and Philip Roth on Jewishness and Love," http://www.jewishjournal.com/hollywoodjew/item/mel_brooks_and_philip _roth_on_jewishness_work_and_love.

5 Guttmann, "Jewish Humor," 329.

6 Ibid.

7 Koltun-Fromm, *Material Culture and Jewish Thought in America*, 270.

8 Magid, *American Post-Judaism*, 1.

9 This is where my approach to the topic differs significantly from other works, particularly Ruth Weiss's *No Joke* and Jeremy Dauber's *Jewish Comedy*. Both of these works move through time and space, comparing and contrasting Jewish humor from extremely divergent cultural, linguistic, and social contexts. I think humor is too ephemeral to stand up to that sort of rugged approach and that it needs to be situated, as far as possible, in its own time and place to be fully understood.

140 Notes to Chapter 1

10 Isaac, "In Defense of Philip Roth," 96.
11 Moore, *G.I. Jews*, 21.
12 Braiterman, *(God) after Auschwitz*, 162.
13 Herberg, *Protestant, Catholic, Jew*, 194.
14 Ibid.
15 Kaplan, *Judaism as a Civilization*, 4.
16 Glazer, *American Judaism*, 84–85.
17 I do not wish to downplay or ignore all of the immensely difficult emotions many people have surrounding Woody Allen. By virtue of his influence on both American Jews and Jewish humorists he is a vital part of this story, and he does remain a "hero" to many Jews. I have come to neither praise nor bury him, but merely to analyze his relationship to Judaism and chart his comedic influence on those who followed him.
18 Lipkin, "Long Live American Heroes," 13.
19 Glazer, *American Judaism*, 107.
20 Magid, *American Post-Judaism*, 111.

Chapter 1: Midrash for Atheists

1 Lax, *Woody Allen*, 12.
2 Allen's parodic stories were written very early in his career, before he had any cinematic success to speak of and certainly before what most people consider to be his "golden age" from the later 1970s to the late 1980s. Heller was actually fairly late in his career but was at the beginning of his literary relationship to Judaism.
3 Gross, *Beyond the Synagogue*, 6.
4 Lax, *Woody Allen*, 330.
5 Cf. Brenner, ed., *Are We Amused?*; Jackson, *Comedy and Feminist Interpretation of the Hebrew Bible*.
6 Guttmann, "Jewish Humor," 329.
7 Kaplan, *Judaism as a Civilization*, 330.
8 There are also, of course, less savory associations that many people have with his name, but his place in this story is primarily as a writer and his legacy as a foundational figure in the development of late twentieth century American Jewish humor. I will leave other writers with the unenviable task of adjudicating his legacy as a human being.

Notes to Chapter 1   141

9 Or, at least, his American filmmaking. Many people see his move to Europe in the past decades as ushering in a renaissance of his work, though the tone and subjects are quite different now.

10 Arthur Cooper, "Allen the Author," 87.

11 Berkey-Gerard, "Woody Allen and the Sacred Conversation," 60.

12 Commins, "Woody Allen's Theological Imagination," 242.

13 Ibid.

14 Dart, "Woody Allen, Theologian," 587.

15 Speidell, "God, Woody Allen, and Job," 560.

16 Dart, "Woody Allen, Theologian," 585.

17 Dauber, *Jewish Comedy*, 124.

18 Cooper, "Allen the Author," 87.

19 Rubenstein, *After Auschwitz*, xii.

20 There are several different transliterations of this word including "Hasidic," "Chasidic," "Hassidic," and "Chassidic." Because Allen uses "Hassidic" in the title of his story, that is the spelling I will use when referring to the story; however, when other sources are cited, I have retained their individual transliterations; and when not referring to the story I will use the more standard "Hasidic."

21 His quip in *Annie Hall* that "*Commentary* and *Dissent* had merged, forming *Dysentery*" is an excellent example of the short stabs he liked to take at the intellectual community.

22 Nilsen, "Humorous Contemporary Jewish-American Authors," 74.

23 Dan, Preface, xiii.

24 Nachman of Bratslav is a good example of this. Most Hasidic groups are dynastic, with one rebbe being succeeded by a son, grandson, son-in-law, or favored disciple. The Bratslaver group, however, was so attached to Nachman and his tales that they never followed another rebbe, and it is still his stories that guide the group to this day.

25 Allen actually started his career as a writer for Sid Caesar, who was notoriously hard to work for and rarely credited any of his writers specifically, so it is possible that Allen even wrote some of those sketches for Caesar; but unless Allen himself were to claim credit for them there is no way to know that for sure.

26 Dart, "Woody Allen, Theologian," 586.

27 Ibid.

28 Simon, *The Wise Men of Helm*, 4.

142 Notes to Chapter 1

29 Allen, *The Insanity Defense*, 42.

30 Ibid.

31 Ben-Amos, "The 'Myth' of Jewish Humor," 124.

32 Ibid., 43.

33 Ibid.

34 Ibid.

35 Ibid.

36 Geist, "The Rolling Stone Interview—Woody Allen," 40.

37 Ibid., 87.

38 Ibid., 45. It is unclear whether this is the same ninth-century "medieval" rebbe, but if he is it is a further poke at the credibility of the scholar who does not know that the ninth century is not generally considered medieval or that neither of them are the Renaissance. As before, it is just wrong enough to be funny.

39 "Jewish Population in the United States, 1974," 229–38.

40 Jewish population from "World Jewish Population," in *American Jewish Year Book*, 273–79 (New York: American Jewish Committee, 1983). "World population from 1975," *Wikipedia*, http://en.wikipedia.org/wiki/1975#World_population, accessed March 11, 2015.

41 See, for example, Glaser, "The Politics of Difference and the Future(s) of Jewish American Literary Studies," who argues that Jewish-American literature should be studied amongst the other "ethnic studies."

42 Allen, *Insanity Defense*, 47.

43 Ibid.

44 Particularly the varying interpretations as to how a verse about a "strong hand, outstretched arm, great manifestation, signs and wonders" equate the Ten Plagues of the Exodus story.

45 Allen, *Insanity Defense*, 135.

46 Brudnoy, "Without Feathers," 86.

47 Allen, *Insanity Defense*, 135.

48 It is common for Silent Generation satirists, such as Sid Caesar and Mel Brooks, to make Germans look silly.

49 Allen, *Insanity Defense*, 135–36.

50 An additional targum of Job was recovered at Qumran, however this does not seem to be anything Allen is using in his parody.

51 Jason Kalman has written an entire essay on Allen's use of Job and its relationship to Holocaust theology. See Kalman, "Heckling the

Notes to Chapter 1   143

Divine," where he argues, similarly to my argument, that Allen's "comedy offers a serious theological discourse intended to confront the problem of maintaining the belief that God is just and compassionate in the face of the Holocaust."

52   Boston, "Woody, Bill, and Spike," *Punch*, 593.

53   Allen, *Insanity Defense*, 136.

54   Although "the patience of Job" is a Christian theological concept (James 5:11)—in reality, Job is not especially patient—the phrase has entered the common lexicon in a way similar to "turn the other cheek" or "the meek shall inherit the Earth" such that many Jews know the idea, without necessarily knowing its precise origins.

55   Allen, *Insanity Defense*, 137

56   Ibid.

57   *Love and Death*, 1975.

58   Lax, *Conversations with Woody Allen*, 358.

59   Ibid., 125.

60   Although this may be reading too much into Allen's critique, he is dancing around some of the same serious discussions that were happening in post-Holocaust theology in the early 1970s. Eliezar Berkovits, for example, used the figure of Job in *Faith after the Holocaust* (Jersey City: KTAV, 1973), describing contemporary Jews as being like Job's brother; they are close to the victim without being the victim. "The Scrolls" came out the following year, and even if Allen had not read Berkovits's book, he could have come across discussions of it in the *New York Times* or in *Commentary*.

61   Allen, *Insanity Defense*, 137.

62   Ibid., 138.

63   Ibid.

64   Ibid.

65   Dart, "Woody Allen, Theologian," 589.

66   Berkey-Gerard, "Woody Allen and the Sacred Conversation," 63.

67   Friedman and Ruderman, "Joseph Heller and the 'Real' King David," 296–97

68   Pinsker, "How 'Jewish' Is Joseph Heller?" 50.

69   Ibid.

70   Ibid.

71   Ibid.

144   Notes to Chapter 1

72 Friedman and Ruderman, "Joseph Heller and the 'Real' King David," 297.

73 Goodman, "Heller Talks of Illness and King David Book," 13.

74 Heller, *God Knows*, 5.

75 Cooper, "Catching Up with Joseph Heller," 231.

76 Kirsch, "Joseph Heller's Daughter Gets the Final Word," https://jewishjournal.com/culture/arts/96336/.

77 Ibid.

78 Goodman, "Heller Talks of Illness and King David Book," 13.

79 Ibid.

80 Ibid.

81 Clemons, "Turning Scripture into Shtik," 80.

82 "God Knows" September 15, 1984, https://www.kirkusreviews.com/book-reviews/joseph-heller/god-knows/.

83 There is an interesting resonance between Heller's David and Sholem Aleichem's Tevye. Sholem Aleichem had a total mastery over biblical and liturgical literature that allowed him to coin Tevye's constant misappropriations of the Bible. Sholem Aleichem knows the Bible, and the audience knows the Bible, which is why when Tevye gets the Bible wrong it is funny. Heller's audience would not be as biblically literate as Sholem Aleichem's, but they do not need to be because David is not getting the Bible wrong as much as claiming that the Bible got *him* wrong. Heller never mentions Sholem Aleichem in his memoirs, so we do not know if he was an actual influence, but the continuation of Sholem Aleichem's form makes Heller's novel all the more interesting.

84 Friedman and Ruderman, "Joseph Heller and the 'Real' King David," 297.

85 Ibid.

86 Ibid., 297–98.

87 It would certainly not be out of line to read *God Knows* as deeply misogynistic to a twenty-first-century eye. The women in the story are flat, at best, and horribly clichéd at worst. Michal's neuroses, Bathsheba's manipulations and vanity, and Abishag's silence plus the fact that she exists only to serve men all speak to the problem Heller had throughout his career with writing women.

88 Ibid., 298.

Notes to Chapter 2   145

89 Ibid.
90 Heller, *God Knows*, 4–5.
91 Ibid., 21.
92 Ibid., 188.

Chapter 2: Silent No Longer

1   Roth, "Pictures of Malamud," 5–6
2   Thurman, "Philip Roth Is Good for the Jews," http://www.newyorker
    .com/books/page-turner/philip-roth-is-good-for-the-jews.
3   Gross, *Beyond the Synagogue*, 5
4   Mintz, "Devil and Angel," 159.
5   Statlander, *Philip Roth's Postmodern American Romance*, 1.
6   Rockland, "The Jewish Side of Philip Roth," 30.
7   Uris, interview by Wershba.
8   Solotaroff, "Philip Roth and the Jewish Moralists," 89.
9   Isaac, "In Defense of Philip Roth," 85.
10 Ibid., 84.
11 Leer, "Escape and Confrontation in the Short Stories of Philip Roth,"
    133.
12 Ibid., 134, 142.
13 Rockland, "The Jewish Side of Philip Roth," 36.
14 Fishman, "Success in Circuit Lies," 137–39.
15 Ibid., 147.
16 Ibid.
17 Guttmann, *The Jewish Writer in America*, 118.
18 Abramson, "Bernard Malamud and the Jews," 155
19 Leer, "Escape and Confrontation in the Short Stories of Philip Roth,"
    145.
20 Solotaroff, "Philip Roth and the Jewish Moralists," 90.
21 Ibid.
22 Abramson, "Bernard Malamud and the Jews," 150.
23 Chyet, "Three Generations," 37.
24 David Brauner, "Fiction as Self-Accusation," 10.
25 Gittleman, "The Pecks of Woodenton, Long Island," 141.
26 Kranson, *Ambivalent Embrace*, 47
27 Ibid.

146 Notes to Chapter 2

28 Zurawik, *The Jews of Prime Time*, 6.
29 Gittleman, "The Pecks of Woodenton, Long Island," 140.
30 Isaac, "In Defense of Philip Roth," 94.
31 Roth, "Eli, the Fanatic," 255–56.
32 The biggest exception would be Allen, who does see organized religion, including Judaism, as dangerous and malicious.
33 Roth, "Eli, the Fanatic," 262.
34 Cf. Cahan's *The Rise of David Levinsky* and Henry Roth's *Call It Sleep*, both of which also use clothing as a way of showing the transition from European ways to American ways among Jewish immigrants.
35 Roth, "Eli, the Fanatic," 263.
36 Ibid., 264.
37 Ibid., 274.
38 Ibid., 285.
39 Ibid., 286.
40 Cooper, *Philip Roth and the Jews*, 39.
41 Roth, "Eli, the Fanatic," 287.
42 Ibid.
43 Gittleman, "The Pecks of Woodenton, Long Island," 142.
44 Pinsker, *The Comedy That "Hoits,"* 23.
45 Landis, "The Sadness of Philip Roth," 265.
46 Roth, "Eli, the Fanatic," 293.
47 Gittleman, "The Pecks of Woodenton, Long Island," 141.
48 Ibid., 297.
49 Ibid.
50 Ibid., 262.
51 Watts, "Jewish Self-Hatred in Malamud's 'The Jewbird,'" 163.
52 Herberg, Protestant, Catholic, Jew, 238.
53 Isaac, "In Defense of Philip Roth," 96.
54 Furman, "The Ineluctable Holocaust in the Fiction of Philip Roth," 110.
55 Rockland, "The Jewish Side of Philip Roth," 33.
56 Gittleman, "The Pecks of Woodenton, Long Island," 142.
57 Isaac, "In Defense of Philip Roth," 94.
58 Brauner, "Fiction as Self-Accusation," 9.
59 Parrish, "A Comic Crisis of Faith," 31.
60 Roth, "Some New Jewish Stereotypes," 10.
61 Rockland, "The Jewish Side of Philip Roth," 36.

Notes to Chapter 2   147

62 Salzberg, *Bernard Malamud*, 25, no. 17.

63 Ibid., 27, no. 31.

64 Ibid., 35, no. 19.

65 Data is, of course, always in the interpretation. Though it is very true that almost all of the negative responses to "The Jewbird" were published in the first eighteen months after the publication of *Idiots First*, it is difficult to imagine why someone writing many years later would refer to a story they did not like. Only scholars who are using "The Jewbird" for some reason would have cause to discuss it, and because they are using it, they obviously feel it has some utility. So a lack of negative response cannot actually be seen as indicative of a shift in the treatment of the story. However, the sheer number of positive applications of the story as compared to the sheer number of negative mentions of it in the initial flurry of reviews, I think, can be said to indicate a shift in the appreciation and application of the story to larger ideas.

66 Bellman, "Women, Children, and Idiots First," 20.

67 Abramson, "Bernard Malamud and the Jews," 155.

68 Watts, "Jewish Self-Hatred in Malamud's 'The Jewbird,'" 159. Watts calls Cohen an immigrant, but I believe she misspoke here. Cohen seems to be very clearly to be a second if not third generation American.

69 Kennedy, "Parody as Exorcism," 164.

70 It should be noted that there is a school of thought which treats "The Jewbird" as a parody of Edgar Allen Poe's "The Raven." While I do see some of the similarities between the two, I do not hold with the idea that one is directly related to the other, particularly since Malamud himself claimed the story was inspired by Howard Nemerov's "Digressions Around a Crow." "I said to myself, thinking of a jewfish, suppose the bird had been Jewish. At that point the story came to life." It would be difficult to argue that there is such a thing as "accidental parody," so if Malamud is not crediting Poe for the genesis of the story it seems unwise to ascribe an inspiration to it after the fact. Cf. Kennedy's "Parody as Exorcism" or Hanson's "Horror and Ethnic Identity in 'The Jewbird'" for a more complete description of the perceived parodic nature of "The Jewbird."

71 Ratner, "Style and Humanity in Malamud's Fiction," 679.

72 Ibid.

148 Notes to Chapter 2

73 Solotaroff, *Bernard Malamud*, 78.
74 Malamud, "The Jewbird," 136.
75 Ibid.
76 I am calling words like "oy vey," "schmutz," "schlep," "klutz," "glitch," or "maven" first-order Yiddish words in that they are words that many if not most Americans use in conversation, some of which, like "klutz" or "glitch" are no longer even recognized as being originally foreign words at all. Second-order, then, includes words like "gevalt," "bupkis," "goniff," "boychik," "meeskeit," "meshuggeneh," etc. These are still sometimes used by non-Jews, but primarily in areas with an historically large Jewish community. Third-order would involve some level of basic literacy or competency with Yiddish, including being able to formulate or understand whole sentences.
77 Wisse, "Requiem for the Schlemiel," 161.
78 Malamud, "The Jewbird," 137.
79 Ibid.
80 Ibid.
81 Ibid.
82 Hanson, "Horror and Ethnic Identity in 'The Jewbird,'" 363.
83 Malamud, "The Jewbird," 137.
84 Ibid., 138.
85 Ibid.
86 Rudin, "Malamud's Jewbird and Kafka's Gracchus," 11.
87 Malamud, "The Jewbird," 34.
88 Ibid.
89 Richman, *Bernard Malamud*, 126.
90 Rudin, "Malamud's Jewbird and Kafka's Gracchus," 10.
91 Malamud, "The Jewbird," 139.
92 Ibid.
93 Ibid.
94 "Chutzpah" is, of course, a noun, but it is an abstract noun best translated as "guts," or "nerve," it does not, therefore, get an indefinite article before it. "The chutzpah" could work, but "a chutzpah" could not.
95 Malamud, "The Jewbird," 139.
96 Watts, "Jewish Self-Hatred in Malamud's 'The Jewbird,'" 160.
97 Malamud, "The Jewbird," 140.

98 Ibid., 141.

99 Ibid.

100 Ibid.

101 Ibid.

102 Ibid., 141–42.

103 Ibid., 143.

104 Ibid.

105 Ibid., 144.

106 Ibid.

107 Ibid., 144.

108 Hanson, "Horror and Ethnic Identity in 'The Jewbird,'" 362.

109 Ibid., 362.

110 Steven Kellman has a fascinating theory about the use of an animal protagonist in this story. He claims that although animals and humans are often equated in the Bible, in the present day there is a "marked discomfort of American Jews in the presence of living animals" ("Jews, Beasts, and Americans," 5). American Jews have become so urbanized that they no longer even want to be around animals, much less consider themselves in any way equivalent to them. His claim is that an analysis of American Jewish literature shows that "well into the third generation, Jews have scant occasion or taste for the companionship of other species" (ibid., 5). So what is unsettling about Schwartz is not just his traditional, Old World mien but also the fact that he is forcing Cohen to be in close contact with another species.

111 Rudin, "Malamud's Jewbird and Kafka's Gracchus," 12.

112 Watts, "Jewish Self-Hatred in Malamud's 'The Jewbird,'" 162.

113 McCarron, "Inhabiting What Remains of Judaism," 288.

114 Gilman, *Jewish Self-Hatred*, 5.

115 Ibid., 328.

116 Roth's later works reinforce that he sees empty Jewish ritual as one of (if not the) biggest failings of the American Jewish community. This difference is not a contradiction, it is an indictment of assimilated American Jews who use Jewish ritual as a way of establishing hollow Jewish authenticity. That is very different from the place ritual holds in the lives of Tzuref and the Greenie.

Notes to Chapter 3

Chapter 3: The Baby Boom, Copycat Generation

Epigraph: The anonymous joke is also sometime a multifaith joke. Here, for example, is the way it was published in the Rockland, New Jersey *Jewish Standard* in 2009: "A small town had a synagogue and two churches, Presbyterian and Methodist. All three had a serious problem with squirrels in their buildings. So, each group had a meeting to deal with the problem. The Presbyterians decided that it was predestined that squirrels be in the church, and that they would just have to live with them. The Methodists decided they should deal with the squirrels lovingly. They trapped them humanely and released them in a park at the edge of town. (Within three days, all the squirrels had returned to the church.) The Jews simply voted the squirrels in as members and gave them all a bar mitzvah. Now they see them only at Rosh Hashanah and Yom Kippur." (Warren Boroson. "Boroson's Anecdotage," http://jstandard.com/index.php/content/item/11188/)

1 Roof, *A Generation of Seekers.*

2 Ibid., 3

3 Statistics compiled from the CDC and the National Center for Health Statistics. See https://www.cdc.gov/nchs/data/statab/natfinal2003 .annvol1_01.pdf.

4 Roof, *A Generation of Seekers*, 1

5 Kellner, *Must a Jew Believe Anything?* 43.

6 Mendelssohn, *Jerusalem*, 82.

7 Eisen, *Rethinking Modern Judaism*, 101.

8 Louis Jacobs called this view "the caricature of Judaism as a religion with its stress above all on the physical body in its relationship to the divine" in false dichotomy to Christianity, which is focused on the soul. Both understandings are really straw men, according to Jacobs, and we need to move away from this binary understanding of Judaism as pro-body ("carnal Israel") and Protestant Christianity in particular as anti-body ("The Body in Jewish Worship," 71).

9 Grimes, *Ritual Criticism*, 10.

10 Bell, *Ritual Theory, Ritual Practice*, 19.

11 Snoek, "Defining Rituals," 3.

12 Also because there are animals doing human stuff, as discussed in chapter 1.

Notes to Chapter 3   151

13 And while true, this is an ongoing and very obvious problem for women in Judaism.

14 World Health Organization and United Nations Program on HIV/AIDS, "Male Circumcision: Global trends and determinants of prevalence, safety, and acceptability," accessed March 5, 2015, http://whqlibdoc.who.int/publications/2007/9789241596169_eng.pdf.

15 Pew Research Center, "Infographic: Survey of Jewish Americans," http://www.pewforum.org/2013/12/03/infographic-survey-of-jewish-americans.

16 So the true numbers could be higher because of families who have short-term affiliations, or lower since not all children, even of synagogue affiliated families, have a *bar* or *bat mitzvah*.

17 Freud, *Jokes*, 275.

18 Ferro, "FYI: Why Is It Funny When a Guy Gets Hit in the Groin?" https://www.popsci.com/science/article/2013-07/fyi-why-funny-guy-hit-groin/.

19 Interestingly Elliot Oring's recent collection, *The First Book of Jewish Jokes* contains no circumcision jokes, although there are jokes about other Jewish rituals. That could indicate that circumcision is a more recent topic for humor, as the jokes in Oring's collection were published in the early nineteenth century.

20 As mentioned above, the male-ness of these rituals is problematic. Though the more liberal branches of Judaism do now perform bat mitzvahs as well, they do not carry the same weight of tradition because they are more recent and have less historical baggage. Historically, becoming an adult male from a Jewish perspective was important because it allowed you to count toward a *minyan*, be called to the Torah, obligated you to observe the 613 mitzvoth, and allowed you to testify in a court of law. None of these are things women in traditional Judaism were allowed to do, so there was no need to recognize a young woman's passage to adulthood.

21 Hamner, *Imagining Religion in Film*, 20.

22 Gross, *Beyond the Synagogue*, 28

23 Grimes, *The Craft of Ritual Studies*, 243.

24 Ibid.

25 It is well known and well documented that *SNL* has a spotty track record for hiring minorities as performers, especially women of color.

152 Notes to Chapter 3

It was national news when they hired a black, female performer in 2014 because in all their years they had never featured one (see Bill Carter, "'S.N.L.' Hires Black Female Cast Member," http://www.nytimes.com/2014/01/07/business/media/snl-hires-black-female-cast-member.html?_r=1). I am not implying that *SNL* is a perfect model of racial and ethnic inclusion, but I am saying that it does not embody one particular, identifiable religious or cultural point of view.

26 Rom-Rymer, "Live from New York, It's *Saturday Night's* Jews!" http://www.momentmag.com/jewish-enterprise-9/.

27 See this transcript at https://aish.com/jtube-saturday-night-live-a-bris-in-the-royal-deluxe-ii/. The entire commercial can be found at https://aish.com/jtube-saturday-night-live-a-bris-in-the-royal-deluxe-ii/.

28 Blake, "'Saturday Night Live' Has Experienced Significant Loss of Talent," http://www.post-gazette.com/ae/tv-radio/2012/07/20/Saturday-Night-Live-has-experienced-significant-loss-of-talent-but-its-creator-has-a-knack-for-developing-stars/stories/201207200124.

29 Monro, *Argument of Laughter*, 83.

30 In general, only Reform congregations call themselves "Temple."

31 For a more in-depth analysis of the JAP stereotype, see Caplan, "Rachel Bloom's Gaping MAAW."

32 PBS, *Make 'Em Laugh*, 2009

33 Shales and Miller, *Live from New York*, 429.

34 The sketch aired October 8, 1988.

35 Zurawik, *The Jews of Prime Time*, 3.

36 Ibid., 3–4.

37 Ibid., 4.

38 See, for example, Zurawik, *The Jews of Prime Time* and Brook, *Something Ain't Kosher Here*, both of which use *Seinfeld* as their case study and primary stand-in for all the sitcoms with Jewish characters that appeared in the 1990s, despite something like *Friends* running for longer and having more Jewish characters.

39 Julia Louis-Dreyfus does not identify as Jewish, but her father's family is the wealthy French Jewish Louis-Dreyfus family, which includes Alfred Dreyfus of the Dreyfus Affair.

40 Shandler. "At Home on the Small Screen," 251

41 Brook, ed. *Something Ain't Kosher Here*, 106.

42 Tanny, "Decoding *Seinfeld*'s Jewishness," 57.

Notes to Chapter 3   153

43 Abrams, *The New Jew in Film*, 19.

44 Brook, "Bring in the Klowns," 248–49.

45 These characters are also part of a larger problem which Brook calls the "tendency to erase female, as opposed to male, markers of Jewishness." Ross on *Friends* is much more clearly Jewish; he dressed up as the Holiday Armadillo to tell his son Ben the story of the Maccabees for Hanukkah for example. He becomes more Jewish as his son grows up because he has a desire to transmit his Jewishness to Ben. When he has a daughter, Emma, with Rachel we see none of the same things, despite Emma having two Jewish parents. Monica is clearly Jewish because she is Ross' sister, but the way the show treats their religious identities is quite different, and we see the same gender disparity being played out again in Ross' two differently gendered children. Very few Jewish women on television ever *do* Judaism, while men are more often given some relationship to their faith (see the character of Howard on *The Big Bang Theory* for another example).

46 I think it is intentional that the baby was given an extremely non-Jewish name because it establishes the level of religiosity for the family, but I think it is probably a coincidence that they chose the name of someone considered to be one of the most anti-Jewish saints of the early Christian period. It may not be an accident; Larry Charles is very well-read and interested in religion as an intellectual pursuit, but if it was intentional it was a joke they had to have expected *very* few watchers to really get.

47 Despite being considered a quintessentially New York show, *Seinfeld* filmed on various sound stages in LA. They reused the same New York exterior shots, such as the outside of Tom's Diner, throughout the run of the show.

48 In fact, after Michael Richards' infamous racist rant in 2006 many sources, including at least one other comedian (Paul Rodriguez) criticized Richards, saying he should know better than to be so bigoted because of the way Jews have been historically treated (see "Michael Richards: Still Not a Jew," https://jewishjournal.com/community/14043/). Other people claimed that Richards was not born Jewish, but had converted (https://www.ynetnews.com/articles/0,7340,L-3334319,00.html). He did not, but his affiliation with *Seinfeld*, even playing a character who is not necessarily Jewish, continues to cause confusion over his religious orientation.

154   Notes to Chapter 4

49 Ritual theorist Arnold van Genep also believed that the role of circum-cision in modern Judaism was out of place: "It is really regrettable that the Jews should have practiced it, for as a result Bible commenta-tors have given it a place apart which it in no way deserves. If the Jews had linked themselves with Yahweh by perforating the septum, how much fewer would have been the errors in ethnographic literature?" (van Genep, *The Rites of Passage*, 72–73).

50 The biggest controversy was over the episode "Puerto Rican Day," which was blasted for being racist. But the show had already lost the benefit of the doubt about race by that point. It was the last stand-alone episode of the final season, and *Seinfeld* had long been under fire for the lack of racial diversity on the show. It apparently filmed in the same part of New York that Woody Allen and *Friends* used—that is, the part of New York peopled predominantly by white folks.

51 Tanny, "Curb Your Orgasm."

52 It helps that American Jews seemed to feel a sense of ownership of *Seinfeld* that was unparalleled at least on television, matched possibly only by Woody Allen films in the 70s and 80s. Because they felt such pride, they allowed it greater critical room.

Chapter 4: The Turn of the Century

1 Curry, Jiobu, and Schwirian, *Sociology for the Twenty-First Century*, 144–45.

2 Eastburn, "Sentient Smooch," https://www.csindy.com/food_and _culture/culture/sentient-smooch/article_e2a15e13-cee3-54b8-8ae9 -a1385b2bde03.html.

3 Mantilla and Ruby, "Crash Landing for a Promising Lesbian Film," 57.

4 Ibid., 49.

5 Ibid., 54.

6 Loewenstein, "Kissing Jessica Stein," http://variety.com/2001/film/ reviews/kissing-jessica-stein-1200468596.

7 Dundes, "The JAP and the JAM in American Jokelore," 468.

8 Gill, "Reviews: Kissing Jessica Stein," 46.

9 Bloom, "Interfaith Celebrities," http://www.interfaithfamily.com/ arts_and_entertainment/popular_culture/Interfaith_Celebrities_The _Long_Line_of_Interfaith_Indianas.shtml.

Notes to Chapter 4   155

10 Loewenstein, "Kissing Jessica Stein."
11 Neumer, "Tovah Feldshuh Inverview," http://www.stumpedmagazine
    .com/interviews/tovah-feldshuh/.
12 Abrams, *The New Jew in Film*, 52.
13 Johnston, "Joke-Work," 216.
14 Capp, "Single White Female Seeking Same," http://sensesofcinema
    .com/2002/feature-articles/sisterhood/; Lowenstein, "Kissing Jessica
    Stein."
15 There is another critical conversation that has to do with Jessica's sex-
    uality. It is not directly under the purview of this chapter, but it bears
    noting that it has been criticized for the fact that "like nearly all lesbian
    stories written for mainstream consumption, at least one potential
    lesbian must find out that being with a man is really for her, reinforcing
    the stereotypes that lesbian love is only 'practice' for the real thing with
    a man and that only one woman in a lesbian relationship is the 'real'
    lesbian" (Mantilla and Ruby, "Crash Landing for a Promising Lesbian
    Film," 57; see also Lisa Blackman, "The Re-Making of Sexual Kinds,"
    122–35; and Diamond, "'I'm Straight, but I Kissed a Girl").
16 Gill, "Reviews: Kissing Jessica Stein," 46; Eastburn, "Sentient
    Smooch."
17 Adler, *Engendering Judaism*, 2–3.
18 Holloway, "The Toraja People and the Most Complex Funeral Rituals
    in the World," http://www.ancient-origins.net/ancient-places-asia/
    toraja-people-and-most-complex-funeral-rituals-world-001268.
19 In Northern Taiwan, for example, the ritual specialist simultaneously
    performs mudras for the dead, and a sort of stand-up comedy stream
    of jokes for the living. And among the Yoruba of West Africa some
    funerals involve elaborate masked dances that show surrounding or
    enemy groups in ridiculous situations; a Hausa meat vendor stained
    red from nibbling his wares, a Dahomean warrior covered with boils.
20 Driver, *The Magic of Ritual*, 5.
21 The TV show *The League* aired an episode whose tongue-in-cheek
    name was "Sitting Shiva." It was a joke mainly for Jews and those who
    know Jewish ritual, because while there is a funeral in the episode, it
    was actually about winning their fantasy football league's trophy, The
    Shiva (pronounced "she-va," like the Hindu god, not "shih-va," like the
    Jewish practice). Wallace Markfield wrote a novel called *To an Early*

156 Notes to Chapter 4

Grave in 1964 about four friends trying to attend the funeral of a fifth. Larry David has written a play about sitting shiva called *Fish in the Dark* which ran on Broadway in 2015.

22 *This Is Where I Leave You* was made into a film in 2014, but while Tropper wrote the screenplay a great deal was changed, and the book better expresses the Jewish ritual elements.

23 Muchnick, "Author Jonathan Tropper Profile," http://www.westchestermagazine.com/Westchester-Magazine/January-2010/The-Author-Next-Door/.

24 Markfield, *To an Early Grave*, 60.

25 Tropper, *This Is Where I Leave You*, 2.

26 Ibid., 38.

27 Ibid., 41.

28 Ibid., 228.

29 Ibid., 344.

30 Ibid.

31 Hutcheon, *A Theory of Parody*, 25

32 1 Kings 3:16–28.

33 Lasdun, "Review: Short Stories," 10.

34 Marchand, "Perplexed for a Guide," WP.15.

35 Macfarlane, "Love and the Art of Being Anxious," 41.

36 Friedman, "What Is Englander Saying," http://forward.com/articles/151036/what-is-nathan-englander-saying/.

37 Berger, "Nathan Englander Reflects on the Stories Chosen," 4–5.

38 Englander, "Sister Hills," 47.

39 Berger, "Nathan Englander Reflects on the Stories Chosen," 4–5.

40 Hutcheon, *A Theory of Parody*, 43–44.

41 Though he writes occasionally for *Ha'aretz*, so it is a safe bet he at least leans liberal and left of center on such things.

42 Englander, "Angels Perceived as Devils," http://www.haaretz.com/life/culture/angels-perceived-as-devils-1.367780.

43 Ibid.

44 Auslander. *Beware of God*, 174.

45 Sheskin, "2004 Twin Cities Jewish Population Survey," http://www.jewishdatabank.org/studies/details.cfm?StudyID=421.

46 City Mouse Online, Haaretz Service and Amit Kling, "Coen Brothers: Boycotting Israel Is a Mistake," *Ha'aretz*, May 15, 2011.

Notes to Chapter 4   157

47 They have only codirected six of their nineteen films; more often Joel directs alone.

48 Allen, *The Coen Brothers Interviews*, 106

49 Joel and Ethan Coen, *The Big Lebowski*.

50 Campbell, "Coen Brothers to Get 'Serious' in Minnesota," online, site no longer available.

51 Shandler, "'Serious' Talk," 349.

52 Calhoun, "The Coen Brothers Discuss 'A Serious Man,'" online, site no longer available.

53 It is worth noting that in addition to the slightly inscrutable opening, the film's ending is open to interpretation. It is possible to read it as everyone living happily ever after or dying in a violent natural disaster; regardless, Larry probably has terminal cancer.

54 Hamner, *Imagining Religion in Film*, 25.

55 Grimes, *The Craft of Ritual Studies*, 225.

56 Ibid., 224.

57 Scott, "Calls to God," http://www.nytimes.com/2009/10/02/movies/02serious.html.

58 "Q&A with Joel and Ethan Coen," online, site no longer available.

59 Tollerton, "Job of Suburbia?" https://digitalcommons.unomaha.edu/jrf/vol15/iss2/7/.

60 Ibid.

61 There was a panel at the 2010 annual meeting of the Association for Jewish Studies that covered Job, Rashi, and Yiddish in the film in a "lively" discussion "both among panelists and with the audience" ("Symposium: A Serious Man").

62 Toth, *Stranger America*, 205.

63 Kensky, "How Larry David Creates a Jewish Universe All His Own," https://forward.com/schmooze/139667/how-larry-david-creates-a-jewish-universe-all-his/.

64 Maslon and Kantor, *Make 'Em Laugh*, 189.

65 Zinoman. "On Stage, a Comic's Still at Home," 2.

66 Tanny, "Decoding *Seinfeld*'s Jewishness," 70.

158   Notes to Chapter 5

Chapter 5: What Will Millennials Kill Next?

1 "New Survey by Claims Conference Finds Significant Lack of Holocaust Knowledge in the United States," http://www.claimscon.org/study/.

2 See *After the Holocaust: Human Rights and Genocide Education in the Approaching Post-Witness Era*, edited by Charlotte Schallié, Helga Thorson, and Andrea van Noord (Regina, SK: University of Regina Press, 2020).

3 See, for example, the 2016 documentary *The Last Laugh*, or Taiki Watiti's 2019 dramedy *JoJo Rabbit*, as well as scholarship like the 2020 volume *Laughter After: Humor and the Holocaust* (Wayne State University Press, 2020), to which I contributed a chapter.

4 This leads organizations such as the Pew Research Center to conduct surveys trying to quantify this technological division and largely failing. The gap between Gen X and Millennial technology usage is so small as to be barely statistically significant. See, for example, https://www.pewresearch.org/fact-tank/2019/09/09/us-generations-technology-use/. This is why some have tried to carve out a microgeneration of late Gen Xers and early Millennials that they have dubbed, among other things, "Xennials" or "Generation Oregon Trail," named for the early educational video game popular in schools in the late 1980s and early 1990s. See Garvey, "Oregon Trail Generation," https://socialmediaweek.org/blog/2015/04/oregon-trail-generation/.

5 Caplan, "The Nebbish in Popular Culture," 6

6 "Knockoffs," *Broad City*.

7 "Jews on a Plane," *Broad City*.

8 See, for example, several of the essays in the January 2020 issue of the *Journal of Modern Jewish Studies*, which was dedicated to essays about the show.

9 Magid, "American Jews Must Stop Obsessing over the Holocaust," online, *Tablet*.

10 Marks, "Jews Can't, and Shouldn't, Just 'Get Over' the Holocaust."

11 Antler, *You Never Call, You Never Write*, 5

12 Ibid.

13 Ibid., 6.

14 Siegel, *Mother, Can You Not?*, 206

15 Ibid., 208–11

Bibliography

Abrams, Nathan. *The New Jew in Film*. New Brunswick, NJ: Rutgers University Press, 2012.

Abramson, Edward A. "Bernard Malamud and the Jews: An Ambiguous Relationship." *Yearbook of English Studies* 24 (1994): 146–56.

Adler, Rachel. *Engendering Judaism*. Boston: Beacon Press, 1999.

Allen, William Rodney, ed. *The Coen Brothers Interviews*. Jackson: University of Mississippi Press, 2006.

Allen, Woody, dir. *Annie Hall*. 1977. Los Angeles: United Artists, 2005. DVD.

———. "Hassidic Tales, with a Guide to Their Interpretation by the Noted Scholar." In *The Insanity Defense*, 42–47. New York: Random House, 2007.

———, dir. *Love and Death*. Produced by Charles H. Joffee. 1975. Los Angeles: 20th Century Fox, 2000. DVD.

———. "The Scrolls." In *The Insanity Defense*, 135–40. New York: Random House, 2007.

Antler, Joyce. *You Never Call, You Never Write: A History of the Jewish Mother*. New York: Oxford University Press, 2008.

Associated Press. "Michael Richards: Jewish or Not?" *Ynetnews*, November 29, 2006.

Auslander, Shalom. *Beware of God: Stories*. New York: Simon and Schuster, 2005.

Band, Arnold. Introduction to *Nachman of Bratslav: The Tales*, translated by Arnold Band. New York: Paulist Press, 1978.

Barthes, Roland. *Mythologies*. Translated by Annette Lavers. New York: Hill and Wang, 1972.

———. *The Pleasure of the Text*. Translated by Richard Miller. New York: Hill and Wang, 1975.

Baum, Devorah. *The Jewish Joke*. New York: Pegasus Books, 2018.

160 Bibliography

Bell, Catherine. *Ritual Theory, Ritual Practice.* New York: Oxford University Press, 1992.

Bellman, Samuel. "Women, Children, and Idiots First." In *Bernard Malamud and the Critics*, edited by Leslie A. Field and Joyce W. Field, 11–28. New York: New York University Press, 1970.

Ben-Amos, Dan. "The 'Myth' of Jewish Humor." *Western Folklore* 32, no. 2 (1973): 112–31.

Ben-Porat, Ziva. "Method in Madness: Notes on the Structure of Parody, Based on MAD TV Satires." *Poetics Today* 1, nos. 1–2 (1979): 245–72.

Berger, Eric. "Nathan Englander Reflects on the Stories Chosen for 'One Book One Jewish Community.'" *Jewish Exponent*, October 25, 2012.

Berkey-Gerard, Mark. "Woody Allen and the Sacred Conversation." *Other Side*, January–February 1997.

Berkovitz, Eliezar. *Faith after the Holocaust.* Jersey City, NJ: Ktav, 1973.

Berrin, Danielle. "Mel Brooks and Philip Roth on Jewishness and Love." *Jewish Journal*, January 15, 2013. Online.

Blackman, Lisa. "The Re-Making of Sexual Kinds." *Journal of Lesbian Studies* 13, no. 2 (2009): 122–35.

Blake, Meredith. "*Saturday Night Live* Has Experienced Significant Loss of Talent." *Post-Gazette*, July 20, 2012. Online.

Bloom, Nate. "Interfaith Celebrities." *InterfaithFamily*, April 2007.

Boroson, Warren. "Boroson's Anecdotage." *Jewish Standard*, December 11, 2009. Online.

Boston, Richard. "Woody, Bill, and Spike." *Punch*, October 6, 1976.

Braiterman, Zachary. *(God) after Auschwitz.* Princeton, NJ: Princeton University Press, 1998.

Brauner, David. "Fiction as Self-Accusation: Philip Roth and the Jewish Other." *Studies in American Jewish Literature* 17 (1998): 8–16.

Brenner, Athalya. *Are We Amused? Humor about Women in the Biblical World.* London: Continuum, 2004.

Brook, Vincent. "Bring in the Klowns: Jewish Television Comedy Since the 1960s." In *Jews and American Popular Culture, vol. 1*, edited by Paul Buhle, 237–59. Westport, CT: Praeger Press, 2007.

———. *Something Ain't Kosher Here: The Rise of the "Jewish" Sitcom.* New Brunswick, NJ: Rutgers University Press, 2003.

Brown, Bill. "Thing Theory." In *Things*, edited by Bill Brown, 1–16. Chicago: University of Chicago Press, 2004.

Brudnoy, David. "Without Feathers." *Saturday Evening Post*, December 1975.

Cahan, Abraham. *The Rise of David Levinsky*. New York: Harper and Brothers, 1917.

Calhoun, Dave. "The Coen Brothers Discuss 'A Serious Man.'" *TimeOut*. Accessed March 5, 2015. Online. Site no longer available.

Campbell, Tim. "Coen Brothers to Get 'Serious' in Minnesota." *Star Tribune*, September 28, 2007. Online.

Caplan, Jennifer. "The Baal Sham Tov: Woody Allen's Hassidic Tale Telling." *Bulletin for the Study of Religion* 42, no. 3 (2013): 11–19.

——. "Rachel Bloom's Gaping MAAW: Jewish Women, Stereotypes, and the Boundary Bending of *Crazy Ex-Girlfriend*." *Journal of Modern Jewish Studies* 19, no. 1 (2020): 93–109.

Capp, Rose. "Single White Female Seeking Same." *Senses of Cinema*, December 12, 2002.

Carter, Bill. "S.N.L. Hires Black Female Cast Member." *New York Times*, January 6, 2014. Online.

Centers for Disease Control and the National Center for Health Statistics. "Live Births, Birth Rates, and Fertility Rates, by Race: United States, 1909–2003." Online. Accessed December 5, 2019.

Charles, Larry, Larry David, and Jerry Seinfeld. "The Bris." *Seinfeld*. NBC. Aired October 14, 1993.

——. "The Puerto Rican Day." *Seinfeld*. NBC. Aired May 7, 1998.

Chyet, Stanley F. "Three Generations: An Account of American Jewish Fiction." *Jewish Social Studies* 34, no. 1 (1972): 31–41.

City Mouse Online, Ha'aretz Service, and Amit Kling. "Coen Brothers: Boycotting Israel Is a Mistake." *Ha'aretz*, May 15, 2011.

Claims Conference. "New Survey by Claims Conference Finds Significant Lack of Holocaust Knowledge in the United States." Online. Accessed December 5, 2019.

Clemons, Walter. "Turning Scripture into Shtik." *Newsweek*, September 19, 1984.

Coakley, Sarah. *Ritual and the Body*. Cambridge: Cambridge University Press, 1997.

Coen, Joel, and Ethan Coen, dir. *The Big Lebowski*. 2008. Los Angeles: Working Title Films and Polygram Filmed Entertainment, 2009. DVD.

——. *A Serious Man*. 2009. Santa Monica, CA: Focus Features, 2010. DVD.

Cole, David. *The Theatrical Event: A Mythos, An Experience, A Perspective*. Middletown, CT: Wesleyan University Press, 1975.

Commins, Gary. "Woody Allen's Theological Imagination." *Theology Today* 44, no. 2 (1987): 235–49.

Cooper, Alan. *Philip Roth and the Jews*. Albany: SUNY Press, 1996.

Cooper, Arthur. "Allen the Author." *Newsweek*, June 23, 1975.

———. "Catching Up with Joseph Heller." *GQ*, August 1984.

Curry, Tim, Robert Jiobu, and Kent Schwirian. *Sociology for the Twenty-First Century*. Upper Saddle River, NJ: Pearson, 2008.

Dan, Joseph. Preface to *Nachman of Bratslav: The Tales*, translated by Arnold Band, xiii–xix. New York: Paulist Press, 1978.

Dart, John. "Woody Allen, Theologian." *Christian Century*, June 22–29, 1977, 585–89.

Dauber, Jeremy. *Jewish Comedy*. New York: Norton, 2018.

David, Larry. *Fish in the Dark*. New York: Grove Press, 2015.

Diamond, Lisa. "'I'm Straight, but I Kissed a Girl: The Trouble with American Media Representations of Female-Female Sexuality." *Feminism and Psychology* 15, no. 1 (2005): 104–10.

Diner, Hasia. *The Jews of the United States, 1654–2000*. Berkeley: University of California Press, 2004.

Driver, Tom. *The Magic of Ritual*. San Francisco: HarperSanFrancisco, 1991.

Dundes, Alan. "The J.A.P. and the J.A.M. in American Jokelore." *Journal of American Folklore* 98 (1985): 456–75.

Durkheim, Emile. *The Elementary Forms of Religious Life*. New York: Oxford University Press, 2001.

Eastburn, Kathryn. "Sentient Schmooch." *Colorado Springs Independent*, April 17, 2002.

Ehrman, Arnost. *Talmud el Am*. Jerusalem-Tel Aviv, 1965–76.

Eisen, Arnold. *Rethinking Modern Judaism*. Chicago: University of Chicago Press, 1999.

Englander, Nathan. "Angels Perceived as Devils." *Ha'aretz*, June 15, 2011.

———. "Sister Hills." In *What We Talk about When We Talk about Anne Frank*, 31–81. New York: Vintage International, 2012.

Ferro, Shaunacy. "FYI: Why Is It funny When a Guy Gets Hit in the Groin?" *Popular Science*, July 26, 2013. Online. Accessed March 5, 2015.

Field, Leslie A., and Joyce W Field. *Bernard Malamud and the Critics*. New York: New York University Press, 1970.

Fishman, Sylvia Barack. "Success in Circuit Lies: Philip Roth's Recent Explorations of American Jewish Identity." *Jewish Social Studies* 3, no. 3 (1997): 132–55.

Freud, Sigmund. "Humor." In *The Standard Edition of the Complete Psychological Works of Sigmund Freud, Volume 21 (1927–31): The Future of an Illusion, Civilization and Its Discontents, and Other Works*, translated by James Strachey, 160–66. New York: Norton, 1976.

———. *Jokes and Their Relation to the Unconscious*. Translated by James Strachey. New York: Norton, 1960.

Friedman, Dan. "What Is Englander Saying?" *Forward*, February 17, 2012. Online. Accessed March 11, 2015.

Friedman, John, and Judith Ruderman. "Joseph Heller and the 'Real' King David." *Judaism* 36 (1987): 296.

Furman, Andrew. "The Ineluctable Holocaust in the Fiction of Philip Roth." *Studies in American Jewish Literature* 12 (1993): 109–21.

Garvey, Anna. "The Oregon Trail Generation: Life Before and After Mainstream Tech." *Social Media Week*, April 21, 2015.

Geist, William. "The Rolling Stone Interview—Woody Allen." *Rolling Stone*, April 9, 1987.

Gill, Erin. "Reviews: *Kissing Jessica Stein*." *Sight and Sound*, July 2002.

Gilman, Sander. *Jewish Self-Hatred*. Baltimore, MD: Johns Hopkins University Press, 1990.

Gittleman, Sol. "The Pecks of Woodenton, Long Island, Thirty Years Later: Another Look at 'Eli, the Fanatic.'" *Studies in American Jewish Literature* 8, no. 2 (1989): 138–42.

"God Knows." Review of *God Knows*, by Joseph Heller. *Kirkus Reviews*, September 15, 1984.

Glaser, Jennifer. "The Politics of Difference and the Future(s) of Jewish American Literary Studies." *Prooftexts* 29, no. 3 (2010): 474–84.

Glazer, Nathan. *American Judaism*. Chicago: University of Chicago Press, 1988.

Goodman, Walter. "Heller Talks of Illness and King David Book." *New York Times*, September 24, 1984.

Greenspoon, Leonard. *Jews and Humor*. West Lafayette, IN: Purdue University Press, 2011.

Grimes, Ronald. *The Craft of Ritual Studies*. New York: Oxford University Press, 2014.

———. *Ritual Criticism*. Columbia: University of South Carolina Press, 1990.

Gross, Rachel. *Beyond the Synagogue*. New York: New York University Press, 2021.

164   Bibliography

Guttmann, Allen. "Jewish Humor." In *The Comic Imagination in American Literature*, edited by Louis Rubin, 329–38. Piscataway Township, NJ: Rutgers University Press, 1983.

———. *The Jewish Writer in America*. New York: Oxford University Press, 1971.

Hamner, M. Gail. *Imagining Religion in Film*. New York: Palgrave Macmillan, 2011.

Hanson, Philip. "Horror and Ethnic Identity in 'The Jewbird.'" *Studies in Short Fiction* 30, no. 3 (1993): 359.

Heller, Joseph. *God Knows*. New York: Simon and Schuster, 1984.

Herberg, Will. *Protestant, Catholic, Jew*. New York: Anchor Books, 1960.

Herman-Wurmfeld, Charles, dir. *Kissing Jessica Stein*. 2001. Los Angeles: Fox Searchlight Pictures, 2002. DVD.

Himmelfarb, Milton, and David Singer eds. "World Jewish Population." In *American Jewish Year Book*, 273–79. New York: American Jewish Committee, 1983.

Holloway, April. "The Toraja People and the Most Complex Funeral Rituals in the World." *Ancient-Origins*, January 24, 2014. Online.

Hutcheon, Linda. *A Theory of Parody*. Urbana: University of Illinois Press, 1985.

Isaac, Dan. "In Defense of Philip Roth." *Chicago Review* 17, nos. 2/3 (1964): 84–96.

Jackson, Melissa. *Comedy and Feminist Interpretation of the Hebrew Bible*. New York: Oxford University Press. 2012.

Jacobs, Louis. "The Body in Jewish Worship: Three Rituals Examined." In *Religion and the Body*, ed. Sarah Coakley. Cambridge: Cambridge University Press, 1997.

"Jewess Jeans." *Saturday Night Live*. With Gilda Radner. NBC. Aired February 16, 1980.

"Jewish Population in the United States, 1974." In *The American Jewish Year Book*, edited by Morris Fine and Milton Himmelfarb, 295. Philadelphia: Jewish Publication Society of America, 1976.

"Jew or Not a Jew." *Saturday Night Live*. With Tom Hanks, Kevin Nealon, Victoria Jackson, Phil Hartman, Jan Hooks, Al Franken. NBC. Aired October 8, 1988.

"Jews on a Plane." *Broad City*. With Abbi Jacobson, Ilana Glazer. Comedy Central. April 20, 2016.

Johnston, Ruth D. "Joke-Work: The Construction of Jewish Postmodern Identity in Contemporary Theory and American Film." In *You Should See*

Yourself, edited by Vincent Brook, 206–29. New Brunswick, NJ: Rutgers University Press, 2006.

Kalman, Jason. "Heckling the Divine: Woody Allen, the Book of Job, and Jewish Theology after the Holocaust." In *Jews and Humor*, edited by Leonard Greenspoon, 175–94. West Lafayette, IN: Purdue University Press, 2011.

Kant, Immanuel. *Groundwork for the Metaphysics of Morals*. Translated by Thomas Kingsmill Abbott and Lara Denis. Calgary, Alberta: Broadview Press, 2006.

Kaplan, Mordecai. *Judaism as a Civilization*. Philadelphia: Jewish Publication Society, 2010.

Kasher, Menachem. *Gemara Shelema: Massekhet Pesachim min Talmud Bavli*. Jerusalem: Mif'al Gemara Shelema, 1960.

Kellman, Steven. "Jews, Beasts, and Americans." *Studies in Jewish Literature* 5, no. 5 (1986) 61–68.

Kellner, Menachem. *Must a Jew Believe Anything?* Portland, OR: Valentine, Mitchell, 1999.

Kennedy, J. Gerald. "Parody as Exorcism: 'The Raven' and 'The Jewbird.'" *Genre* 13 (1980): 161–69.

Kensky, Eitan. "How Larry David Creates a Jewish Universe All His Own." *Forward*, July 11, 2011.

Kirsch, Jonathan. "Joseph Heller's Daughter Gets the Final Word." *Jewish Journal*, September 21, 2011.

"Knockoffs." *Broad City*. With Lucia Aniello, Paul W. Downs. Comedy Central. February 4, 2015.

Koltun-Fromm, Ken. *Material Culture and Jewish Thought in America*. Bloomington: Indiana University Press, 2010.

Kranson, Rachel. *Ambivalent Embrace*. Durham: University of North Carolina Press, 2017.

Landis, Joseph. "The Sadness of Philip Roth: An Interim Report." *Massachusetts Review* 3, no. 2 (1962): 259–68.

Lasdun, James. "Review: Short Stories." Review of *What We Talk about When We Talk about Anne Frank*, by Nathan Englander. *Guardian*, February 4, 2012.

Lax, Eric. *Conversations with Woody Allen*. New York: Knopf, 2011.

———. *Woody Allen: A Biography*. Cambridge, MA: De Capo Press, 2000.

Leer, Norman. "Escape and Confrontation in the Short Stories of Philip Roth." *Christian Scholar* 49, no. 2 (1966): 132–46.

Bibliography

Levitt, Laura. *Jews and Feminism*. New York: Routledge, 1997.

Lipkin, Lisa. "Long Live American Heroes: God Places Fourth Behind Seinfeld, Sandler and Howard Stern." *Forward*, November 22, 1996.

Loewenstein, Lael. "Kissing Jessica Stein." *Variety*, May 7–13, 2001.

Macfarlane, Robert. "Love and the Art of Being Anxious: Nathan Englander's Short Stories about Jewishness Are Intricately Crafted Gems." *Sunday Times*, January 22, 2012.

Magid, Shaul. "American Jews Must Stop Obsessing over the Holocaust." Online. *Tablet*, January 26, 2015.

———. *American Post-Judaism*. Bloomington: Indiana University Press, 2013.

Malamud, Bernard. "The Jewbird." In *Wandering Stars*, edited by Jack Dann, 135–46. New York: Pocket Books, 1975.

Mantilla, Karla, and Jennie Ruby. "Crash Landing for a Promising Lesbian Film." *Off Our Backs* 32, nos. 7–8 (2002): 57–69.

Marchand, Philip. "Perplexed for a Guide: Nathan Englander's New Short Story Collection of Jews Looking for Meaning in Their Narratives." *National Post*, February 25, 2012.

Markfield, Wallace. *To an Early Grave*. Champaign, IL: Dalkey Archive Press, 2000.

Marks, Laura. "Jews Can't, and Shouldn't, Just 'Get Over' the Holocaust." *Huffington Post UK*, May 16, 2019. Online.

Maslon, Laurence, and Michael Kantor. *Make 'Em Laugh: The Funny Business of America*. New York: Twelve, 2008.

McCarron, Kevin. "'Inhabiting What Remains of Judaism': Jewishness and Alterity in the Fiction of Philip Roth, Saul Bellow, and Bernard Malamud." In *Christian-Jewish Relations through the Centuries*, edited by Stanley Porter and Brook Pearson, 284–97. Sheffield, England: Sheffield Academic Press, 2000.

Mendelssohn, Moses. *Jerusalem*. Waltham, MA: Brandeis University Press. 1983.

"Michael Richards: Still Not a Jew." *Jewish Journal*, November 20, 2006. Online. Accessed March 13, 2015.

Mintz, Lawrence. "Devil and Angel: Philip Roth's Humor." *Studies in American Jewish Literature* 8, no. 2 (1989): 154–67.

Monro. D. H. *Argument of Laughter*. South Bend, IN: University of Notre Dame Press, 1963.

Moore, Deborah Dash. *American Jewish Identity Politics*. Ann Arbor: University of Michigan Press, 2008.

———. *G.I. Jews.* Cambridge, MA: Harvard University Press, 2004.

Muchnik, Jeanne. "Author Jonathan Tropper Profile." *Westchester Magazine*, January 2010. Online.

Nachman of Bratslav. "The Humble King." In *Nachman of Bratslav: The Tales*, translated by Arnold Band, 115–19. New York: Paulist Press, 1978.

Nemerov, Howard. "Digressions around a Crow." In *A Howard Nemerov Reader*. Columbia: University of Missouri Press, 1991.

Neumer, Chris. "Tovah Feldshuh Interview." *Stumped Magazine*. Online. Accessed June 16, 2013.

Nilsen, Don. "Humorous Contemporary Jewish-American Authors." *MELUS* 21, no. 4 (1996): 71–101.

Oring, Elliott. *The First Book of Jewish Jokes: The Collection of L. M. Büschenthal*. Translated by Michaela Lang. Bloomington: Indiana University Press, 2018.

Parrish, Timothy. "A Comic Crisis of Faith." In *Playful and Serious*, edited by Ben Siegel and Jay L. Halio, 25–34. Newark: University of Delaware Press, 2010.

Perlstein, Ferne, dir. *The Last Laugh*. 2016. Warren, NJ: Passion River Productions. Streaming.

Pew Research Center. "Infographic: Survey of Jewish Americans." *Pew Forum*. Accessed December 5, 2015. http://www.pewforum.org/2013/12/03/infographic-survey-of-jewish-americans/.

———. "Millennials Stand Out for Their Technology Use." *Pew Forum*. https://www.pewresearch.org/fact-tank/2019/09/09/us-generations-technology-use/.

———. "A Portrait of American Jews." *Pew Forum*. Accessed March 5, 2015. http://www.pewforum.org/2013/10/01/jewish-american-beliefs-attitudes-culture-survey/.

Pinsker, Sanford. *The Comedy That "Hoits."* Columbia: University of Missouri Press, 1975.

———. "How 'Jewish' Is Joseph Heller?" *Jewish News*, September 10, 1998.

"Q&A with Joel and Ethan Coen." *Working Title Films*. Accessed March 5, 2015. Online. Site no longer available.

Ratner, Marc. "Style and Humanity in Malamud's Fiction." *Massachusetts Review* 5, no. 4 (1964): 663–83.

Richman, Sidney. *Bernard Malamud*. Boston: Twayne, 1986.

Rockland, Michael Aaron. "The Jewish Side of Philip Roth." *Studies in American Jewish Literature* 1, no. 2 (1975): 29–36A.

Rom-Rymer, Symi. "Live from New York, It's *Saturday Night's* Jews!" *Moment* (July–August 2010). Online.

168 Bibliography

Roof, Wade Clark. *A Generation of Seekers: The Spiritual Journeys of the Baby Boom Generation*. New York: HarperCollins, 1993.

Roth, Henry. *Call It Sleep*. New York: Robert O. Ballou, 1934.

Roth, Philip. "Eli, the Fanatic." In *Goodbye, Columbus*, 247–98. New York: Vintage, 1994.

———. "Pictures of Malamud." *London Review of Books*, May 1986, 5–6.

"Royal Deluxe II." *Saturday Night Live*. With Dan Ackroyd, Grant Morris, Gilda Radner. NBC. Aired September 24, 1977.

Rubenstein, Richard. *After Auschwitz: History, Theology, and Contemporary Judaism*. Baltimore, MD: Johns Hopkins University Press, 1992.

Rudin, Neil. "Malamud's Jewbird and Kafka's Gracchus." *Studies in American Jewish Literature* 1, no. 1 (1975): 10–15.

Salzberg, Joel. *Bernard Malamud: A Reference Guide*. Boston: G. K. Hall, 1985.

Sarna, Jonathan. *American Judaism: A History*. New Haven, CT: Yale University Press, 2005.

Schaffer, Jeff, and Jackie Marcus Schaffer. "Sitting Shiva." *The League*. FX. September 3, 2013.

Schottenstein Talmud. New York: Artscroll. 1984.

Scott, A. O. "Calls to God: Always a Busy Signal." *New York Times*, October 1, 2009. Online.

Shales, Tom, and James Andrew Miller. *Live from New York: An Uncensored History of* Saturday Night Live. New York: Little Brown, 2002.

Shandler, Jeffrey. "At Home on the Small Screen: Television's New York Jews." In *Entertaining America*, edited by J. Hoberman, 244–56. Princeton, NJ: Princeton University Press, 2003.

———. "'Serious' Talk." *AJS Review* 35, no. 2 (2011): 249–55.

Sheskin, Ira M. "2004 Twin Cities Jewish Population Survey." *Jewish DataBank*. Online. Accessed March 5, 2015.

Siegel, Kate. *Mother, Can You Not?* New York: Crown Archetype, 2016.

Simon, Solomon. *The Wise Men of Helm*. Translated by Ben Bengal and David Simon. West Orange, NJ: Behrman House, 1973.

Snoek, Jan, A. M. "Defining Rituals." In *Theorizing Rituals*, edited by Jens Kreinath, Jan Snoek, and Michael Stausberg, 1–14. Leiden, Neth.: Brill, 2006.

Solotaroff, Robert. *Bernard Malamud: A Study of the Short Fiction*. Boston: G. K. Hall, 1989.

Solotaroff, Theodore. "Philip Roth and the Jewish Moralists." *Chicago Review* 13, no. 4 (1959): 87–99.

Speidell, Todd H. "God, Woody Allen, and Job." *Christian Scholar's Review* 29, no. 3 (2000): 560.

Statlander, Jane. *Philip Roth's Postmodern American Romance Critical Essays on Selected Works.* New York: Peter Lang, 2011.

The Steinsaltz Talmud. Edited by Adin Steinsaltz. New York: Random House, 1989.

"Symposium: *A Serious Man.*" *AJS Review* 35, no. 2 (2011): 347–48.

Tanakh. Philadelphia: Jewish Publication Society, 1985.

Tanny, Jarrod. "Curb Your Orgasm." *Jewish Film and New Media* 7, no. 2 (2019): 161–86.

———. "Decoding *Seinfeld*'s Jewishness." *Studies in Contemporary Jewry* 29. Ed. Eli Lederhendler and Gabriel Finder. 2016. 53–74.

Telushkin, Joseph. *Jewish Humor.* New York: Quill Press, 1992.

Thurman, Judith. "Philip Roth Is Good for the Jews." *New Yorker,* May 28, 2014.

Tollerton, David. "Job of Suburbia? *A Serious Man* and Viewer Perceptions of the Biblical." *Journal of Religion and Film* 15, no. 2 (2011). Online.

Toth, Josh. *Stranger America: A Narrative Ethics of Exclusion.* Charlottesville: University of Virginia Press, 2018.

Tropper, Jonathan. *This Is Where I Leave You.* New York: Dutton, 2009.

United Nations Program on HIV/AIDS. "Male Circumcision: Global Trends and Determinants of Prevalence, Safety, and Acceptability." *World Health Organization.* Online. Accessed March 5, 2015.

Uris, Leon. Interview by Joseph Wershba. *New York Post.* July 2, 1959.

Van Genep, Arnold. *Rites of Passage.* Chicago: University of Chicago Press, 1961.

Watiti, Taiki, dir. *JoJo Rabbit.* Los Angeles: Fox Searchlight. 2019.

Watts, Eileen H. "Jewish Self-Hatred in Malamud's 'The Jewbird.'" *MELUS* 21, no. 2 (1996): 157–63.

Wershba, Joseph. "Not Horror but 'Sadness.'" *New York Post,* September 14, 1958.

Wertheimer, Jack. *A People Divided: Judaism in Contemporary America.* New York: Basic Books, 1993.

Wisse, Ruth. *No Joke.* Princeton, NJ: Princeton University Press, 2013.

———. "Requiem for the Schlemiel." In *Bernard Malamud: Modern Critical Views,* edited by Harold Bloom, 159–65. New York: Chelsea House, 1986.

Zinoman, Jason. "On Stage, a Comic's Still at Home." *New York Times.* October 14, 2012.

Zurawik, David. *Jews of Prime Time.* Waltham, MA: Brandeis University Press, 2003.

Index

Abraham, 26, 31–32, 74, 88, 99
Ackroyd, Dan, 78–79
Allen, Woody: atheism, 19–21, 30,
 33, 41; and authority, 21–23;
 Christian critics, 20–21; "Hassidic
 Tales," 22–24, 28; and Jewish self-
 importance, 26–27; *New Yorker*
 writer, 19, 23; and organized
 religion, 15–17, 22, 24, 33, 42–43;
 "The Scrolls," 22–24, 27–28, 33;
 social critic, 21; stand-up comic,
 126
Anti-Defamation League (ADL),
 83–84, 90
antisemitism (antisemites), 57, 68–69,
 82, 84, 89, 92, 103, 131, 133
assimilation: and Woody Allen, 21–22,
 42–45; and American Judaism, 6–7;
 and Baby Boomers, 89; bourgeois
 lives of Jews, 19, 91; and Bernard
 Malamud, 42–45, 58–66, 69–70;
 and Philip Roth, 43–45, 50–58,
 69–70
Auslander, Shalom, 108–9

Baby Boom (Baby Boomers): and Larry
 David, 119–20; defined, 2–3, 9–11,
 71–72; and Gen X, 4, 84, 87–93,
 109–12; and humor, 71–72, 77,
 137; and millennials, 128, 131; and

post-halakhic pietism, 11; postwar,
 7–8
bar mitzvah, 33, 71–77, 100, 114–19,
 126, 132, 137
bat mitzvah, 73–77, 100, 122–23, 137
Beatts, Ann, 82
bible: in Baby Boomer humor, 74,
 105–7, 117; and irreverence, 17–18,
 33, 35, 37; and Jewish humor, 5; in
 Philip Roth's work, 46, 56, 64; and
 Silent Generation satires, 16–18,
 21, 26–40, 105. *See also* midrash
Big Lebowski, The, 92, 109–12
Bloom, Rachel, 12, 127, 130–31
Brice, Fanny, 25
Broad City, 124–34; "Jews on a Plane,"
 128–30; "Knockoffs," 128–29
Brooks, Albert, 9
Brooks, Mel, 5, 9, 14, 99
Buber, Martin, 23

Caesar, Sid, 24
Charles, Larry, 86–89
circumcision, 73–74, 82, 88–89,
 99–100, 116–17, 129; bris, 75–79,
 86–88, 129; the mohel, 73, 76, 79,
 87–89; the sandek, 76, 87
Coen brothers, 10, 92, 105, 109–20
Cold War, 13, 72
Comedy Central, 127–28

172 Index

Crazy Ex-Girlfriend, 126–27, 130–36;
   JAP Battle, 131–32
@CrazyJewishMom (Instagram
   account), 126–27, 133–36
Curb Your Enthusiasm, 87, 92, 119–23,
   128; "The Bat Mitzvah," 122–23;
   "Palestinian Chicken," 121–22, 128;
   a show about "something," 120

David, Larry, 85–87, 90, 92, 110,
   119–23
Dayan, Moshe, 5
death: Angel of Death, 106; of the
   author, 118; in *Broad City*, 128; of
   God, 22; in Joseph Heller's work,
   35, 38–40; of Judaism (feared), 137;
   in Bernard Malamud's work, 68; in
   Philip Roth's work, 55; and ritual,
   73, 99–103, 107
dybbuk, 63–65, 113

Englander, Nathan, 12, 92, 104–8;
   "Sister Hills," 92, 104–8

Feldshuh, Tovah, 96, 132
Franken, Al, 82–84
Freud, Sigmund, 1, 4, 6, 38, 75
Friedman, Kim, 135–36
funeral, 73, 99–102, 114, 129

Generation "Chanukah Song," 131, 133,
   137
Generation X: and Baby Boomer
   humor, 11, 77, 84, 87–93, 113; as
   "Brat Pack," 91; and *Curb Your
   Enthusiasm*, 123; defined, 2–4, 14;
   the "Me Era," 11; and Millennials,
   9–10, 125–30; and ritual, 72, 101–
   5, 108–9; and Silent Generation
   humor, 11, 72, 97; and societies
   without cohesion, 137
Generation Z, 126, 128, 138
Glazer, Ilana, 127–30

Hanks, Tom, 82–83
Hasidism (Hasidic), 16, 21–27
Heller, Joseph, 10, 13–19, 59, 69, 97,
   104–8, 120; *Catch-22*, 15–16, 34;
   child of Russian immigrants, 33;
   and David, 35–40; on God and
   rebuilding, 36; on God being
   forced into silence, 39; *God Knows*,
   35–41; midrash, 42
Holocaust: Auschwitz, 7; and *Catch-22*,
   34; concentration camps, 90, 125;
   Hitler, 14, 45, 56, 137; and Jewish
   identity, 133, 138; jokes, 90, 92,
   120; *Life Is Beautiful*, 92; literature,
   30; in Bernard Malamud's work, 62;
   Nazis, 7–8, 34, 53, 62, 90, 131; post-
   Holocaust world, 8; "Post-Witness
   Era," 125; "Remember That We
   Suffered" song, 131–33; in Philip
   Roth's work, 50–51; *Schindler's List*,
   89, 120; theology, 20
humor: benign violation, 18, 75; dark,
   12, 29, 34, 110, 114–15; dialect
   jokes, 25; and Thomas Hobbes,
   18, 79; Jewish as discrete form, 12;
   Jewishness of, 1–2; and language,
   6, 9; New York, 5; "over there"
   versus "over here," 5; sarcasm, 137;
   slapstick, 12, 80; stand-up comedy,
   98, 126–27; superiority, 18, 61, 75,
   79, 112. *See also* parody; satire

identity: and Baby Boomers, 71;
   defining Jewish-American,
   6–8, 18–19; Eastern European
   immigrant, 21; in "Eli, the
   Fanatic," 49–55, 58; generational,
   4, 11, 14; Israeli, 6; in "The
   Jewbird," 59–61; Jewish, 12,
   86–87, 109, 129–33, 138; and
   language, 69; protection of, 42–49;
   and stereotypes, 96–98; Jennifer
   Westfeldt's, 93–94

Index   173

immigrants, 2–3, 6, 13–16, 21, 25, 33, 60, 65–66
Israel, State of, 7, 14, 44, 132, 137

Jacobson, Abbi, 127–30
Jewish: complacency, 9, 19, 24, 47, 58, 107; deli, 122; grandmother, 95, 97, 128–29; moral experience, 48; mother, 34, 44, 47, 83, 85, 94–98, 105–6, 126–37; Old World (thing), 50, 61–62, 65–66, 80, 84, 115; perpetually and conceptually Jewish characters, 86, 88, 97, 110, 118; philosophy, 19–20; self-abuse, 68–69, 94; theology, 7, 18–24, 27, 38, 43, 73, 108; and visibility, 50. *See also* identity; Jews; Judaism; ritual
Jewish American Princess (JAP), 81–82, 85, 94–96, 103, 134–36; JAP Battle, 131–32
Jewish Community Center (JCC), 9, 137
Jews: ability to forget that they are Jews, 49; Eastern Europe, 10, 14, 21, 23, 42, 49–50, 60, 62, 67, 69; generational difference, 3, 84, 104–5; mimicking (mimicry), 86; peoplehood, 3, 8, 11, 44; sacrifice and "defense activities," 56–57; things "good" or "bad" for Jews, 43–47, 59, 133
Job, 28–31, 37, 117–19
Judaism: as civilization, 8–9; Conservative, 8–9, 121; cultural, 21, 98, 104; Orthodox, 9, 16, 99, 104, 108; Reform, 7–8, 79–80; religion of action, 73; "things" of, 55. *See also* Thingification, of Judaism
Jurgensen, Heather, 94

Kaddish, 22, 102–4
Kaplan, Mordecai, 8, 18, 50

Kasher, Moshe, 10
Katz, Mickey, 25
Kiddush, 97
Kissing Jessica Stein, 92–99, 109, 117
Kushner, Tony, 108

Lear, Norman, 6, 9, 46–47

Malamud, Bernard: did not serve in World War II, 42; "The Jewbird," 43, 49, 59–70
Markfield, Wallace, 101
marriage, 36, 73, 97, 99, 129, 136
Marvelous Mrs. Maisel, The, 126
Marx Brothers, 14, 49, 126
May, Elaine, 14
McKenna, Aline Brosh, 127, 130–31
midrash, 15–16, 21, 33, 36–38, 41–42, 107, 119
Millennials: building a career, 126; defined, 2–3, 9–11, 14; and generational religious sensibilities, 9; and Gen X, 109, 129–30; and Gen Z, 128; humor, 4, 11–12, 124–26, 136–37; and Jewish identity, 133; removed from Silent Generation, 124–25; shiva, 128; and social media, 126–27, 133–35
Miller, Marilyn Susanne, 77–78
Moses, 5, 26–27
Motzi, 97

neuroses, 19, 33, 38, 86, 94–99
Nichols, Mike, 14

parody, 10, 15–17, 22–24, 29, 36, 42, 49, 73, 78, 92, 105–6
Passover, 27
Poland, 5, 24–25, 62, 113
practices, religious: and American Protestantism, 7; and Baby Boomer humor, 73, 76, 97, 100, 120; and Gen X humor, 109, 113, 116;

174   Index

practices, religious (*continued*)
Guttman's definition of religion,
5–6, 17–18, 47, 97, 99; in Joseph
Heller's life and work, 33–34; and
Jewish humorists, 2; in Bernard
Malamud's work, 48–49, 65, 67,
72; in Millennial humor, 128–30;
normalization of Jewish, 4; in
Philip Roth's work, 45, 48–49,
56–57, 72; and satire, 11. *See also*
ritual
Protestantism, 7, 20, 57, 66, 83, 128
Purim, 9

Rabbi: in Shalom Auslander's work,
109; Rabbi Ben Kaddish, 25–27;
commercialization of, 78–79;
Rabbi Funkhouser, 121–22; and
Joseph Heller's midrash, 37–38,
41; Rabbi Marshak, 114–15, 119;
in "Remember That We Suffered,"
132; and Philip Roth, 45–46; Rabbi
Scott, 114; Rabbi Taklas, 78–84,
89; Rabbi Telushkin, 1; in *This Is
Where I Leave You*, 101–3
Radner, Gilda, 80–82
refugee, 10, 50, 56, 59, 62, 69; Displaced
Person (DP), 50–52, 56, 59
Reiner, Carl, 14
religion: defined, 5–6; something done
to Jews, 42–43
religion, organized: in Allen's writing,
22–24, 33, 42–43; and Baby
Boomers, 121, 125; in Reform
Judaism, 8; and the Silent
Generation, 15–17, 69–70, 72,
90–91, 103, 137
ritual: for the community, 99, 119;
and "dramatic relief," 98–99; and
nostalgia, 75–76, 100, 113, 115;
and tradition, 17, 36–37, 75–78,
88, 92, 102, 113, 117, 137. *See*

also bar mitzvah; bat mitzvah;
circumcision; funeral; marriage
Roman Catholicism, 73, 83, 86
Roth, Philip: and assimilation, 42–43,
72, 82, 89–92, 97; in conversation
with Malamud, 43–44, 47–49,
59–61; early life, 44–45; "Eli,
the Fanatic," 49–58; identity in
Roth's work, 45–49, 66–69; Jewish
American princesses in work of,
134; among Jewish satirists, 45,
110; and self-loathing, 44, 59, 64,
133; and the Silent Generation,
10–11; as traitor, 103, 133
Rubenstein, Richard L., 22

Sandler, Adam, 9, 83, 109, 127, 130;
"Chanukah Song," 83, 109, 130–33,
137
satire: in Woody Allen's work, 22–26,
29; and critical distance, 107; and
funerals, 100; and Gen X texts,
11–12, 94, 97, 102–7, 113–18;
and Gen Z, 138; in Joseph Heller's
work, 36, 41; Jewish, 5–9; of Jews as
people, 90; in Bernard Malamud's
work, 48, 59; in Millennial texts,
127, 130–33; ritual, 74–79; in Philip
Roth's work, 45–48, 50–52, 58; in
Silent Generation texts, 10–11,
14–19, 42, 48–49, 87, 107, 110; and
SNL, 84; use in volume, 4–5
Saturday Night Live (*SNL*), 77–84, 87,
89, 114–15, 119; fauxmercials,
78–80, 115; "Jew, Not a Jew," 82–84;
Jewess Jeans, 80–84; Royal Deluxe
II ad, 78–80, 84, 112, 121; Rabbi
Taklas, 78–80, 114–15
Schumer, Amy, 11–12, 127
scripture, 10, 15–18, 21, 28–30, 33,
36–38, 41, 105–8, 118–19. *See also*
bible; Torah
Seinfeld, Jerry, 9, 85–89, 104, 119–20

Index 175

Seinfeld: Elaine Benes character, 85–89; "The Bris," 86–88; George Costanza character, 85–88; Cosmo Kramer character, 88; "The Raincoats," 89–90; a show about "nothing," 120; "The Soup Nazi," 90; "The Yada Yada," 86

Serious Man, A: dybbuk, 113; Gen X film, 10, 92; Danny Gopnik's bar mitzvah, 114–17; Larry Gopnik character, 113–14, 118; intertextuality, 105; as Job re-creation, 117–19; ritual as film's heart, 109, 115–17, 122; semiautobiographical, 113

Shabbos, 97, 102, 109, 112, 121

shiva, 37, 50–52, 57–58, 62, 66, 73, 99–104, 126–29

Siegel, Kate, 12, 127, 133–36

Silent Generation: and Baby Boomers, 72–73, 77, 91; defined, 2–4, 8–9; English as first language, 13; generational characteristics, 13–15; and Gen X, 11, 84, 87, 89, 91–93, 97, 101, 104–5; Judaism as something that was keeping Jews down, 121; and Millennials, 124; and parodic midrash, 10–11, 31, 42; as protectors of Judaism, 8, 41, 59, 82, 84; relationship to religion, 35, 42–44, 52, 110, 112, 115; and satire, 16; as second-generation immigrants, 2–3, 8, 14; and *Seinfeld*, 87–90; and World War II, 125, 133, 137

Stern, Howard, 9

Stiller, Ben, 137

Stiller, Jerry, 14

suburbs, 7, 21, 50, 54–58, 79, 96, 109, 113, 128

Tartikoff, Brandon, 83

Telushkin, Joseph, 1

Thingification, of Judaism: and Baby Boomers, 72, 95–96, 115, 123; and the Silent Generation, 3–4, 9, 14, 16, 35, 40, 42, 45–49, 52, 56, 62–65, 69

This Is Where I Leave You, 92, 99–104, 109, 116–17, 128–29

Torah, 7, 16, 25, 50, 53, 109, 115–16

Transparent, 135

Tropper, Jonathan, 92, 99–104, 109, 116–17, 128–29

Uris, Leon, 44–47

Weiss, Rhonda, 80–82

Westfeldt, Jennifer, 92–99, 104

World War II, 2, 7–10, 13–15, 34, 42, 44, 47, 50, 72, 125

Yankovic, "Weird" Al, 105

yeshiva, 37, 50–52, 57–58, 62, 66

Yeshiva University, 99

Yiddish, 5, 13–16, 25, 60–65, 69, 80, 113, 133

Yom Kippur, 67, 95, 97

Zen Buddhism, 23